Hi Reva -
I gifted this book
to you because I kn[e]
what feeding raw diet -
I hope Daisy -
with it!
Hugs, Peg

Raw and Thriving

THE ULTIMATE GUIDE TO GETTING (AND KEEPING!) YOUR DOG HEALTHY

Kristin Clark

Certified Small Animal Naturopath
and Carnivore Nutrition Consultant

Raw and Thriving: The Ultimate Guide to Getting (and Keeping!) Your Dog Healthy / Kristin Clark —1st ed.

ISBN-13: 978-1981437818
ISBN-10: 1981437819

Dedication

This book is dedicated to Adam. You are my rock, my inspiration, my strength. Thank you for your unconditional love and unwavering support, now and forever.

Contents

Chapter 1: We Really Aren't in Kansas Anymore, Are We?

Welcome, my fellow pet parent, to a book that could very well change your dog's life. That's a bold claim, I know, but I think after hearing (well, reading) what I have to say, you'll agree with me. By applying the concepts in this book, you'll be able to help your dog live their optimal life. Exciting, right? You'll no longer feel powerless to help your dog flourish. You'll understand how to keep your dog's body functioning at its peak (whether your dog is a puppy, an adult, or a senior) so he or she stays in optimal health throughout their life. And, if your dog is facing some health issues, you'll have a better sense of how to address those issues in a natural, safe, but still effective way—without breaking the bank or running the risk of putting your dog through the potentially harmful side effects associated with most conventional medications. But before we get into all that, I want to take a little detour, because I want to make sure I really, truly, completely have your buy-in to what I'm going to share with you in the upcoming pages. Ready? Here we go!

Remember the movie *The Wizard of Oz*? I **loved** that movie. Flying monkeys…a walking, talking Scarecrow…Judy Garland singing "Over the Rainbow"…and of course, Toto! And their adventures! Dorothy believes the Wizard of Oz will help her get home. The Tin Man believes the wizard will give him a heart. The Scarecrow? He believes the wizard will give him brains. And the Cowardly Lion? He's visiting the wizard for a magical dose of bravery. Together, they (along with Dorothy's adorable little black dog Toto) journey down the Yellow Brick road until they get to the wizard's home: the Emerald City, the capital of Oz itself.

At first, the wizard appears as a giant face, surrounded by smoke and flames and mist. His voice is booming, intimidating. He sends the group away with orders to defeat the Wicked Witch of the West before he'll consider granting their requests. After they defeat the witch, they return to the palace and present him with her staff as proof she's been destroyed. The wizard, you may remember, appears again as a giant green face. He tells them to come back the next day, because he needs more time to consider their request. Understandably, they're upset—they trusted he would help them if they did what he asked, and now he appears to be breaking his word. Toto slips away from the group, runs over to the side of the room where a curtain is draped, and pulls the curtain back. Remember what he reveals? An ordinary man, using parlor tricks to appear to be a magical being. When this man—who is soon revealed to be the wizard—realizes he's been discovered, he first tries to pull the curtain shut again, and then, realizing they've seen him, says, "Pay no attention to that man behind the curtain!"

The Wizard of Oz was released in 1939, and it was popular among both viewers and critics. Released again for TV in 1956, it became wildly successful. Its popularity, of course, made the Ruby Slippers, the Yellow Brick Road, the Emerald City, and Munchkins familiar to audiences of all ages and backgrounds. But along with those things, the movie also introduced its audiences, in a very real way, to the "man behind the curtain."

Until Toto pulled the curtain back on him, the wizard had everyone in Oz convinced he was truly capable of magic. Through slick tricks and the power of suggestion, the people believed he had magical powers. They surrendered authority to him, making him ruler of all of Oz. And if someone ever doubted he was all he claimed to be, they didn't question it openly; after all, everyone they knew believed in the wizard, and a challenge to him would undoubtedly be met with resistance.

Once the wizard was revealed, though, there was no going back. Dorothy and her friends realized the magic they believed him to possess was fake. Once Toto exposed the man behind the curtain for what he was, they could nevermore believe him to be the "Great and Terrible" Oz he claimed to be.

The Wizard of Oz, of course, is a fictional story. But like any good story, it weaves together elements of reality to make the story more relatable and authentic. Those realistic elements are also a perceptive and insightful commentary on human nature and what's going on in the world, and the fact that the story continues to resonate with generation after generation is due in large part to the fact that the themes and insights in the movie continue to ring true.

The idea of the man behind the curtain is a perfect example of this. When it comes to our pets, the man behind the curtain is not a single, solitary man, easily sent away in a hot air balloon like the wizard in the movie. Instead, the man behind the curtain is the pet food industry. Using what seems to be magic, it's skilled at showing people what they want to see, even though, often, there isn't any substance to back it up. Now, depending on your past experiences and where you're at today, that notion might ring completely true for you, or you might be feeling skeptical. Either way, stay with me. I know, if you're reading this book, you've realized something is wrong with the "same old, same old" way we feed and care for our pets. You may not know exactly what to do about it (yet!), but you know something isn't right. And you are 100% correct about that—the approach we've taken to feeding and caring for our dogs over the past 50–100 years isn't working. They aren't thriving. They aren't flourishing. We can do better by them and for them. So in this book, we're going to look at exactly what's wrong and how to fix it. And we'll keep it interesting with real-life examples along the way.

Now, back to the man behind the curtain—or in our case, the industry behind the curtain. They use marketing—flashy images, slick words, pretty pictures—to convince pet owners the food in the bag is a healthy, balanced, nutritious choice for their dog. There's no Toto to pull this curtain back, though, so you have to do it yourself. How do you pull that curtain back? Well, reading this book is a great start. Doing research, using critical thinking, asking questions, and staying curious will get you there too.

When you start to look for yourself, you'll quickly find processed pet food (which I also refer to in this book as kibble, or in some cases, canned food) contains many ingredients that are either harmful to your pet, completely unnecessary, or both. And even the ingredients that may have once been beneficial have, in most instances, been rendered nutritionally worthless because of the processing that's been done to them.

When Dorothy and her companions first realized the wizard's magic wasn't real and they were on their own, they were disappointed. The wind was taken out of their sails. They'd put their faith in him, and they believed he would be able to help them. When they realized he didn't have the powers they ascribed to him, they went through a period of worrying about how to achieve their goals. But what they soon came to understand was that they were strong and self-sufficient in themselves. And the same pattern may hold true for you (it sure did for me when I started down this road!). When you first realize the pet food industry isn't really on your pet's side, you may experience feelings like Dorothy and her friends did. After all, we want to believe the industry truly has our pets' best interests in mind. But what we realize, after we pull back the curtain, is the answers are out there, and they really aren't as complicated as we've been led to believe. That realization can lead (as it did for Dorothy, the Tin Man, the Scarecrow, and the Cowardly Lion) to a sense of empowerment, and the added benefit is your pet will be healthier and happier as a direct result of your increased knowledge.

After the massive pet food recalls of the last decade, many more pet owners than ever before began to realize the pet food industry isn't the compassionate and caring entity it presents itself to be. The raw pet food movement is growing: There's been an explosion of small and large commercial raw food companies, and they're doing very well. The full-length documentary *Pet Fooled* exposed a great many of the issues of the pet food industry. There are blogs, articles, and books about how to feed your dog in a healthier, more species-appropriate way. The curtain is starting to be pulled back. For every single person that researches, investigates, and comes to their own conclusion independent of what the pet food manufacturers tell them, it's pulled back a little bit more. And every dog that thrives on a raw, species-appropriate diet helps to expose the charade for what it is.

Think about this: in America alone, we spend over $50 billion on pet food and pet health care every year[1]. And yet, dogs are dying younger than they used to. For example, according to one survey, dogs have had an 11% decrease in longevity in the past decade[2]. We're spending more than ever before on our pets' nutrition and health care, and yet they're dying younger and younger. I recently met a woman whose 1 ½ year old Yellow Lab had just been diagnosed with cancer. While shocking (he was only 1 ½!), that sort of story is becoming more and more common these days. Our dogs are dying of cancer, of diabetes—of any of a hundred chronic health conditions—and of being so run down and worn out (even before they hit late teens) that we consider it a mercy to euthanize them rather than watch them suffer any longer. It's an epidemic, my friends, and it's getting worse all the time.

But here's the good news: Dorothy and her friends eventually realized the answers to their wishes were within them all along. At the risk of being overly sentimental, I posit the power to help your dog be as healthy and well-balanced as possible is within you too. You don't have to rely on labels and marketing to determine what's best for your pet. By pulling the curtain back—by doing some research, asking some questions, and taking a cold, hard look at the facts—you can help ensure your own dog has the very best foundation for health possible. You don't have to go it alone…I'll be right here with you every step of the way. So, what do you say? Want to see how you can give your dog a better shot at a healthy, thriving life, and have some fun along the way? I thought so. Let's do this.

Chapter 2: The Breaking Point

Over the years, lots of people have asked me why they should consider switching their dog off kibble or canned food when their dog appears healthy. No diseases, no skin allergies, no lethargy...everything seems good. So why should they change? And I get it. I really do. When we're in the habit of scooping some kibble into a bowl and moving on, it may seem foolish to go through the transition process and upend the whole routine. It's not as convenient as just doing what we've been doing all along, right?

Unfortunately, it's not that easy. Each dog has what I've come to think of as the "breaking point." Think of a rubber band—it will stretch and stretch, but eventually, it snaps. Perhaps it got stretched too far, or perhaps it was stretched regularly over a long period of time. It's different for every rubber band, but all of them have a point where they break. It's the same for our pets. We don't usually know, just by looking at them, what their breaking point is. Will it come after years of eating processed food? Or will it happen much sooner, when they're still in what should be the prime of life?

Whether it's rubber bands or our dogs, by the time the damage shows on the outside, the inside is already affected. By the time the rubber band breaks, it's already been made weaker by microscopic tears and stretches we don't notice until it snaps completely. Similarly, by the time the hot spots appear on your dog, or he presents with cancer, or his teeth show a buildup of plaque and tartar, the internal damage has already happened.

I'm going to state it clearly for you right here and now: processed pet food is not a source of nutrition for your dog. Between the ingredients used and the processing itself, it's a source of toxicity, no matter how much you paid for it or how "premium" it claims to be. Now, if that comes as a shock to you, I understand. We've been trained to think about processed pet food—kibble and canned—as the best food to feed our dogs. But the facts tell a different story.

5

Fact #1: Cooked protein is denatured protein

Processed pet food is often cooked, which renders the protein unusable (or significantly less usable) by your pet's body[3]. Think of it this way. Imagine you're planning to build a wall, and you have all the blocks laid out, ready to stack up and form the wall. Then, imagine someone comes along and smashes the blocks with a sledgehammer. The blocks are still there, but not in any form that will allow you to build the wall, and even if you manage to piece the blocks back together, they're weak and won't provide any real strength or support to the structure. Because the blocks are broken, you isolate them and put them aside, and eventually you throw them away. Now here's the thing: The high heat and processing to which the proteins are exposed to make the kibble are like sledgehammers destroying the amino acids (which are the building blocks of protein). The broken, weak amino acids can't form strong proteins, just like the broken, weak blocks can't form a strong wall. And, since the body can't use the processed amino acids to form strong proteins, it isolates them and sets them aside. However, if they just sit in the body they become a source of toxicity, so they must be dealt with: the body must eliminate them. The problem arises when we continually flood our pets' bodies with these toxic and fundamentally unusable proteins (and this is part of the reason why, no matter what the pet food marketing departments tell you, no processed food will ever be a source of health for your pet). Their systems go into overdrive to shed out the toxins their bodies are encountering with every processed pet food meal.

Fact #2: Synthetic vitamins and palatants are bad for your dog

Kibble and canned food is sprayed with synthetic vitamins to increase palatability (and make it smell appealing enough to your dog that they'll eat it) and to give pet food companies the ability to say their food contains vitamins and minerals (which otherwise were cooked out of the food)[4]. This, of course, can cause a whole host of problems[5]: most of the synthetic vitamins are made overseas (mostly in China), and they often contain toxins that can be harmful or even fatal to your dog (remember the massive pet food recalls about a decade ago? In many cases, the synthetic vitamin packs—also called "premixes"—were to blame)[6]. But pet food manufacturers have to get your dog to eat the food, which means they have to trick them into believing it's food. And that's another place the synthetic chemicals come in: as a palatant. Pet food manufacturers know if the food isn't sprayed with this synthetic mixture, it won't smell like food to a dog. And, if it doesn't smell like food, dogs won't even try to eat it[7]. That's right—animals that are notorious scavengers and will eat just about anything won't eat processed food unless it's been sprayed. Says something about kibble, don't you think?

Fact #3: Toxic preservatives are found in kibble

We're going to discuss this in more detail in a little bit (I don't want to overwhelm you all at once), so for now, let me say processed pet food contains a myriad of preservatives that, unfortunately, are also toxic. And as you'll see in a little bit, those toxins have been proven to cause the exact same problems we take our dogs to the vet for. In other words, every time you put a bowl of kibble down for Fido, or slap some canned food in a dish for him, you're flooding his body with the same toxins that have been shown to cause allergies, cancers, tumors, and other chronic health issues. Eventually, it will catch up to your dog unless you start doing things differently.

So, whether your pet appears healthy on the outside or not, if they are being fed a processed food diet, they aren't in optimal balance. Think about when you get a cold or the flu. You were sick before you presented with full-blown symptoms, it just took a while to catch up to you. Same for our pets, but this is something that we can have an impact on.

To switch or not to switch? (Is that the question?)

If you're hesitating about switching your pet to a raw diet because you feel like they're healthy and it seems inconvenient to start doing something different when there doesn't seem to be any cause, I would invite you to look more closely at whether your pet is truly healthy. Look at their coat, their eyes, their body condition. Look at their teeth and smell their breath. Notice whether they have a doggy odor or not. Pay attention to their poop—the smell, the amount, the consistency. Are they hyperactive? Lethargic? How mentally present and alert are they? If they're a bit older (9, 10, 11, or even 12!) do they still seem like they're in their prime, or are they slowing down? These are all indicators of their overall health, and worth paying attention to. The diet I'm going to teach you about in this book supports your dog so he or she can live an optimal life. Truthfully, it's never too late to start your dog on the path to true vitality (check out "Cleo's story" later in this book for a real-life example of this!). If you've been feeding kibble, it's better to start as soon as possible, before the little issues you can't see snowball and become big—or even insurmountable—issues.

So, let's have some fun: Before you go any further, take this easy wellness quiz. Where does your dog fall on the spectrum?

Wellness Quiz

On a scale of 1 to 5 (5 being "completely agree" and 1 being "don't agree at all"), rate your answers to the following statements. There are no right or wrong answers, so be as objective as possible. At the end of the quiz, you'll be able to see if your dog is thriving, or if there are some areas where they might need a little help.

Coat: Look at your dog's coat, then rate your answers to the following statements:

My dog's coat is shiny and soft: _____
When I run my hands through my dog's fur, it doesn't leave any oily residue or gunk on my fingers: _____
My dog's coat doesn't feel dry or brittle: _____
When I look at my dog's coat, I don't see any skin flakes or discoloration/bald patches from excessive licking or chewing: _____

Eyes: Look at your dog's eyes, then rate your answers to the following statements:

The whites of my dog's eyes are clear: _____
The whites of my dog's eyes don't have tinges of red: _____
My dog's eyes don't have excessive discharge (they aren't "weepy"): _____

Parasites: Think about your dog's experience with parasites over the course of the past year, then rate your answers to the following statements:

My dog never picks up fleas and ticks, even when we go into areas where fleas and ticks are (such as out on hiking trails, etc.): _____
I feel comfortable not applying flea and tick preventives to my dog because they never seem to have a problem with parasites: _____

Body condition/weight: Look at your dog's overall body condition and feel their ribs and front of their chest, then rate your answers to the following statements:

I can easily feel my dog's ribs (and, if my dog has a short coat, I can see the outline of their ribs through their fur): _____
My dog's chest doesn't have an excess layer of fat on it: _____
When I look down at my dog from above, I can see a narrowing where their waist is: _____
My dog's hip bones don't jut out when I look down at my dog from above: _____

Oral health: Look at your dog's teeth and gums, then rate your answers to the following statements:

My dog's teeth are shiny and white: _____
My dog's breath isn't offensive: _____
My dog doesn't have tartar and plaque build-up: _____
I never have to get my dog's teeth cleaned because they're so sparkly: _____

Odor: Rate your answer to the following statements:

If someone walked into my house and my dog(s) weren't visible or making noise, they wouldn't even know I had dogs because they wouldn't be able to smell them: _____
When I pet my dog, I can't smell a "doggy odor" at all: _____
When I walk into my house, I don't notice a "doggy" smell: _____

Stool and anal glands: Think about your dog's waste, then rate your answers to the following statements:

My dog's stool is small and compact: _____
My dog eliminates waste infrequently (less than 2 times per day): _____
My dog's anal glands never get impacted or need to be manually expressed: _____
My dog's stool doesn't have a very strong smell: _____

Behavior: Rate your answers to the following statements:

My dog has energy, but isn't frenetic: _____
My dog doesn't have nervous energy, but also isn't lethargic: _____

Mental ability: Think about your dog's mental strength, then rate your answers to the following statements:

I'm constantly surprised at how smart my dog is: _____
My dog seems to learn new things quickly: _____
My dog is extraordinarily perceptive and able to focus: _____

Endurance: Think about when you take your dog for hikes, walks, jogs, or do any other type of play/exercise with them, then rate your answers to the following statements:

When I play with/exercise my dog, their energy lasts for a reasonable and appropriate amount of time: _____
My dog doesn't lose energy quickly under normal circumstances: _____
When I exercise my dog, they are ready for more by the next day: _____

Aging: Think about your "senior" dog (society deems a dog "senior" when they are 7 or older), then rate your answers to the following statements:

My "senior" dog still has a good amount of energy: _____
My "senior" dog is mentally sharp: _____
My "senior" dog doesn't exhibit excessive joint pain or stiffness: _____
My "senior" dog may have slowed down a little bit, but they're still thriving: _____

Now, total up your points and then check below for what your dog's score means!

144–180 points: Congratulations, your dog is thriving! It's important to support your dog's health and vitality throughout their life, so keep doing what you're doing. Re-take this quiz each year to make sure your dog is still flourishing.

108–143 points: While your dog is generally a relatively healthy individual, their systems and organs aren't as strong and balanced as they could be. The good news is there's still time to get them back on the road to thriving before big issues start to crop up.

36–107: Your dog probably needs natural support to help them get back on track to living a thriving life. You may already see signs of chronic conditions, and if you don't, there's a good chance that, unless action is taken now, chronic conditions will start to present soon. The good news is you can help them get back on the path to wellness with a common-sense, natural approach.

Please note: if you marked 1 or 2 to any statements, your dog's body may be deficient in certain areas, or overloaded with toxins, even if they were high scorers in other areas.

Barkley's Story

Throughout this book, I'm going to share real-life stories about dogs and owners that have, in one way or another, switched to a species-appropriate diet and seen fantastic results. Each of these stories is intended to show you there are lots of ways to feed a species-appropriate diet (I don't want you to start to think there's one "perfect" way, and if you can't do it that way, you're doing it wrong!). I hope they'll show you the power of a balanced, varied, species-appropriate diet and inspire you to get your own dog onto a healthy diet. Each story highlights a different dog—all of them are different ages, different breeds, and each of them have their own unique health situation. All of them, no matter what, were helped by a change in diet, just as I know your own dog will be. And, because there's so much more to dogs than just what they eat, lots of these stories also share (in their owner's own words) some of the ways these dogs impacted their people. If you're ready, let's kick things off with a story about one of my own dogs, Barkley.

There's a wonderful book by Marta Williams called *My Animal, My Self.* Throughout the book, Williams continually shows how our companion animals, be they dogs, cats, horses, birds, or another species of animal, mirror us and, in so doing, become our teachers and healers. Anyone who has shared their life with an animal can attest to this. In their own quiet way, they show us where we are mentally, spiritually, emotionally, and physically in need of support. By living in the now, they provide us with feedback, sometimes even before we are aware of it ourselves, of exactly how we are feeling. They show us areas in which we need to grow, and they do it all with unconditional love that makes it easier to accept the lesson.

While I think it's safe to say we love all the animals that pass through our lives, often there is one particular animal that seems to be our "soul" dog (or cat, or horse, or bird). This animal seems to find us at a time in our lives when we need them most, and they seem to know exactly what we need and then generously, unflinchingly, provide it wholeheartedly.

I would like to share part of the story of my soul dog, Barkley. He came to me almost 8 years ago, when he was (we think) about 3. I've always been a dog lover and grew up with dogs, but when I got into college and through most of my 20s, I didn't live anywhere I could have one. When I bought a house, I knew it was time to change all that: it was time to get a dog again. I contacted Best Friends Animal Sanctuary in Utah and told them I was looking for a very social, active dog that got along well with other dogs, people, cats, and enjoyed going to the dog park and going for runs. They told me to come visit and we would find the perfect match. I live in California, so a few weeks later, a friend of mine and I got in the car to take a road trip to the Sanctuary. When we got there, they told me there was a dog named Chad available that seemed to get along with cats. I asked them to show him to me, but they were a bit hesitant—warning me he might bark at me and not be friendly. How could I possibly decide to adopt him if I couldn't meet him, though? I told them I wanted to meet him and asked them again to bring him out. When he came out and our eyes met, there was an instant connection. He came right over to me and lightly leaned against me like we knew each other. I was hooked, and after taking him for a walk, I signed the adoption papers. My friend and I drove back home with my new dog, now named Barkley (after the dog in Sesame Street), in the back seat.

It soon became apparent that Barkley, while a complete angel with me, had not been properly socialized. He barked and snapped at strangers, lunged at anyone who got too close, tried to attack other dogs, chased my cat, and gouged chunks out of my door with his teeth whenever the mailman came. Essentially, he was the complete antithesis of what I had originally thought I wanted. And so, it fell upon me to figure out a way to work with him so we could all get along. During that whole, long, often frustrating, humbling, and slow process, I learned how to lighten up and be more welcoming to new people. I learned I tend to be a bit suspicious of strangers, and I also learned I have a habit of worrying—a lot. Through working with Barkley, I found he was an instant mirror for my emotions. On days I was frazzled and stressed, his reactivity would shoot through the roof. On days when I was calm, he was almost Zen-like. Of course, we worked on obedience, but all the obedience in the world didn't help if I wasn't under control first. I started meditating and clearly communicating my feelings and needs to people in my life, and found a state of calm I never thought possible. And as I grew, so did Barkley. His reactivity calmed down considerably, and now when he has an episode, I can stop it almost before it begins. And when I can't, it's a reminder to get myself back under control, because invariably it's tied to my moods and emotions.

My sweet boy is still a work in progress, but then, so am I. He's a source of inspiration to me, and a catalyst for much of the direction my life has taken. He didn't just teach me about finding calm in my own life (no matter what's going on around me), he also started me on the path of naturopathy and raw feeding. He'd always had problems with skin allergies, but eventually they got really bad. He was biting at his chest and legs so much all the hair was gone, his skin was raw and inflamed, he was crying almost constantly, and he couldn't sleep because he was so itchy. Vets couldn't figure out what the problem was, and their best solution seemed to be to suppress the symptoms. One vet suggested I keep him on steroids for the rest of his life. Another told me to give him 9 Benadryl a day, also for the rest of his life. They dismissed my questions about food allergies or environmental allergies out-of-hand. But, I wanted true healing for him, so I started doing some research. I found out about naturopathy and raw feeding, and enrolled in the American Council of Animal Naturopathy's certification courses. After an intense program, I got my certification as a carnivore nutrition consultant and a small animal naturopath. I've been feeding him (and all our other dogs) raw and learning everything I can about raw feeding and natural healing ever since.

Barkley. Photo credit Milton Clark

It took some time, but Barkley's allergies have mostly subsided, with only an occasional flare-up from time to time. When those flare-ups occur, I know how to address them and support him naturally, without harmful drugs with toxic side effects. I've helped many dogs since, but he was my first, and whenever I look at him—his healthy, shiny, soft coat; the bounce in his step; his strength and graceful movement (even though he's considered a "senior" now); his endurance (I recently took him on a 7-mile walk, and it didn't faze him at all); his overall vitality and health—I realize the power of the right diet. He continues to be my inspiration, and because of him, I've embarked on a journey I never could have foreseen.

Chapter 3: Pet Food, Then and Now

When my husband and I sat down to watch the documentary *Pet Fooled* for the first time, I was reminded once again of something I'd been thinking about for a long time. Essentially, this is what I've come to think of as the "diet" of the pet food industry.

My husband likes to say, "It's all in the sizzle." What does he mean by sizzle? The sizzle is the flash, the shiny thing, the slick words—it's the way someone chooses to deliver a message so someone else buys into that message. The pet food industry (a $28+ billion/year industry[8]) is built on sizzle. The flashy packaging, the smooth words, the pretty pictures, the implied and stated benefits...all the sizzle that makes pet owners trust the product in the bag or can is, first of all, food that can nourish their pet, and secondly, beneficial and nutritious instead of dangerous and devoid of any real nutritional benefit.

How do they do this? When you walk down the pet food aisle of a pet store or the supermarket, the choices can be overwhelming—there are so many of them! Your brain can't possibly filter through all the options, and so you get overwhelmed. When you're overwhelmed, you can't be as discerning. You step forward to look at a bag of food, and you see a picture of a dog or cat. They have a shiny coat, an alert expression, bright eyes. Maybe they're romping through a field or snuggling with a person. They look happy. Your brain downloads that image and associates it with that food. You see words like "natural," "balanced," "optimal," "thriving," or even "organic." Those words sound good, right? But what they don't put on the bag is that what they mean by those words is very different from what you understand those words to mean. For example, the term "natural" for pet food has been legally defined to mean: *A feed or ingredient derived solely from plant, animal or mined sources either in its unprocessed state or having been subject to physical processing, heat processing, rendering, purification, extraction, hydrolysis, enzymolysis, or fermentation, but not having been produced by or subject to a chemically synthetic process and not containing any additives or processing aids that are chemically synthetic except in the amounts as might occur in good manufacturing practices[9].*

When you look closely at this, you see that it can be subject to physical processing, heat processing, rendering, extraction, and so on. "Natural" does not, in fact, mean it must be in the same state as you would find it in nature, as you might assume. Additionally, if a pet food manufacturer uses "natural" to refer to a specific ingredient, they can add other plant, animal, or even mined products that don't fall under the definition of "natural" to the pet food. That's because the legal definition only requires them to use natural to refer to a specific ingredient, not the whole food. So, if you had a product called Fido's Treats with Natural Salmon Flavor, everything except for the salmon flavor would be exempt from the "natural" definition. And, the use of the word "flavor" means they don't have to have actual salmon in the treat (sneaky, huh?).

What about the term "holistic?" It has no legal definition when it comes to pet food[10], so pet food companies can use it on their packaging without actually meaning anything.

"Organic" is legally defined for human food, but not for pet food. The Association of American Feed Control Officials (AAFCO) states pet food "must comply with the USDA's National Organic Program (NOP) regulations (7 CFR 205)[11]. Remember, though, "AAFCO has no statutory authority to regulate pet products[12]."

What about "human grade" and "human quality?" These terms also aren't legally defined[13]. Pet food manufacturers can't use them on their labels (with certain exceptions), but they can (and do) use them on websites and in marketing materials.

I could go on, but you get the idea. Essentially, the pet food industry—an unregulated, multi-billion-dollar industry—is master of the sizzle. They're committed to making a profit, and they've figured out how to do that. Unfortunately, they aren't similarly committed to your pet's health.

In addition to the issues that arise from the ingredients (and quality of those ingredients) in processed pet food and the processing methods themselves, kibble and canned pet food also often contain toxic preservatives that can have a severely detrimental impact on your dog. Let's dive a little deeper into this, because I want you to get a good sense of what's in your pet's kibble and/or canned food and what it does to them.

Some of the most common preservatives found in pet food include (in alphabetical order): butylated hydroxyanisole (BHA), butyl hydroxytoluene (BHT), Ethoxyquin, Sodium Metabisulfite, Propyl Gallate, and Tertiary Butylhydroquinone (TBHQ). These are all preservatives added to food that have fats and oils so the food doesn't spoil. They can be found in many of the foods available from a myriad of pet food companies; if you buy kibble from your vet's office, or from large pet stores, the grocery store, or other retailers that sell processed dog food, there's a high likelihood the food or treat contains one or more of these preservatives. Because these preservatives are cheap and readily available, pet food companies can use them to help drive their profit margins up.

In case you're wondering—yes, there are natural, healthy, safe preservatives available, such as vitamin E, vitamin C, and herbs. Changing how the food is processed—for example, dehydrating it—also naturally preserves food without the addition of chemical preservatives. However, the natural alternatives aren't as cheap as the chemical options listed above, so pet food companies are reluctant to use them in place of the more toxic preservatives, side effects or no.

As you'll see in a little bit, pet food companies often use spoiled meat and rancid fats to make pet food[14] (shocking, I know, but it's true). That means they have to cover up the smell of the spoiled meats and fats, so you'll still feed the food to your dog. Preservatives like BHA and BHT are excellent at doing this. Pet food manufacturers can use 4D (dead, dying, disabled, or diseased) to make the pet food; while this practice is of course not allowed in meat and food intended for human consumption, the FDA's Center for Veterinary Medicine is aware of and does nothing to stop the practice in pet food[15]. And because processed pet food may sit on a shelf for a long time before it gets used, pet food manufacturers need to make sure that it stays smelling nice, and that it maintains the color we've come to expect, so that pet owners will continue to feed it. These preservatives do the job well—unfortunately, as we'll see, they also expose your pet to a whole host of health problems[16].

BHA

As previously discussed, BHA is a preservative. In addition to being used in pet food, it's also found in some human food, is used as a packaging preservative, and is used as a yeast de-foaming agent in food manufacturing. Studies have shown BHA to have adverse effects in many areas, including allergies, behavior, brain function, liver and stomach cancer, cell abnormalities, and increases in the formation of fatty tumors[17][18]. Like many toxins, BHA is what's known as a bioaccumulative substance, meaning that it's absorbed by the body at a faster rate than it's lost through the processes of catabolism and excretion. That means that, when it is fed over time, the body cannot flush it out, and it builds up and puts an additional load on the liver and kidneys.

BHT

Like BHA, studies have shown BHT can negatively impact the liver, lead to tumors, and may be carcinogenic. The MSDS (Material Safety Data Sheet) for BHT indicates it may be toxic to blood, the liver, and the central nervous system. It also warns against ingesting BHT or allowing it to come into contact with the skin or eyes. The MSDS also warns against inhalation of BHT, and states it may cause dizziness, weakness, headache, confusion, temporary loss of consciousness, respiratory depression; prolonged or repeated ingestion may affect the liver, kidneys, thyroid, adrenal gland, blood, and cause issues with behavior[19]. It may also lead to allergic reactions. Also according to the MSDS, it's classified as hazardous by OSHA[20]. I don't know about you, but it doesn't sound like something I want my pets eating! BHT is banned from baby food in the US, and it's banned from food completely in the UK and Japan[21]; this indicates to me it's known to cause serious issues. Vitamin E has been shown to preserve just as well, but as I mentioned above, it is much more expensive, which means pet food companies wouldn't make as much of a profit—so, in most instances, they choose not to use it.

Ethoxyquin

Ethoxyquin is another preservative pet food manufacturers regularly use in food and treats. However, unlike the other preservatives listed here, Ethoxyquin isn't added directly to the food, and therefore won't show up on the ingredients list. It is used by many companies as a preservative in fish meal. It has been used as a pesticide and is classified as a hazardous chemical by OSHA. The USDA lists it as a pesticide, and containers containing Ethoxyquin are labeled as "Poison" on the containers. This stuff is no joke! It can cause (again, in alphabetical order) allergic reactions, behavior issues, bladder cancer, deformity in puppies, infertility, kidney cancer, organ failure, stomach tumors, and skin issues[22]. Like BHA and BHT, Ethoxyquin accumulates in the body faster than the body can eliminate it, so when fed day after day, it can cause significant and severe problems.

Propyl Gallate

Propyl Gallate is generally used in conjunction with BHA and BHT. It has been shown to cause stomach irritation, liver and kidney damage, and it may be carcinogenic. It may also be an endocrine disrupter, and lead to thyroid tumors, brain tumors, pancreatic tumors, and adrenal tumors[23]. Just like with all the other preservatives I'm mentioning here, it just doesn't seem like anything I want to give my pets.

Sodium Metabisulfite

Sodium Metabisulfite (try saying that one three times fast!) is next on our list of preservatives to watch out for in processed pet food. In addition to being a food preservative, it is also widely used in commercial wine making. Among other things, it can depress the central nervous system, and it can cause abdominal pain, diarrhea, nausea, and vomiting[24]. Some dogs (and humans) are particularly sensitive to sulfites, and in those individuals, Sodium Metabisulfite can cause shortness of breath, wheezing, coughing, swelling of the skin, tingling sensations, and shock[25].

TBHQ

TBHQ, or Tertiary Butylhydroquinone, is a form of butane (butane!). Like the others, it's used in food to delay the onset of rancidness and extend shelf life—exactly what pet food companies need when making kibble and canned food. Ready for the laundry list of issues that TBHQ has been shown to cause? Delirium, dermatitis, DNA damage, stomach cancer, hyperactivity, nausea, restlessness, collapse, and vomiting, to name just a few. It has also been shown to be an endocrine disruptor[26][27].

There are some studies that have been carried out for some of these preservatives that did not find they caused the issues that other studies found. However, I question who funded those studies, and given there are lots of studies that showed these preservatives cause major health issues, is feeding them worth the risk? Not to mention, of course, is it worth the money you'll probably spend on vet bills trying to figure out what's wrong with your pet and treating it? I for one wouldn't expose my pets to risks like this when there are much better things for them to eat that I know are safe and support them in thriving and living optimal lives.

The preservatives I included here are common in many brands of pet food and treats. When you stop and think about it, it seems crazy they can go into the food of any living being, whether human or animal, and yet there they are. Feeding these things can cause a vicious cycle where your pet never thrives, no matter what you do or how well-intentioned you are. The best way to break the cycle and see your pet flourish is to avoid feeding these things to your dog and instead feed them what they're designed to eat—the very diet we'll go over in this book.

What did dogs eat in the past?

Before the rise of the modern-day pet food industry, dogs ate a variety of things depending on when and where in history they were located; often, they ate scraps from their owners and whatever they could catch on their own. Many pets that belonged to wealthy people were fed meat, while others, particularly those that belonged to poorer people, supplemented what they caught with whatever their owners had available.

I have a book from my great-grandmother called *Heather Jean: The Working Sheep Dog* (published in 1937). The author, Luke Pasco, a trainer, breeder, importer, and exhibitor of Border Collies and Associate Editor of *The Sheep Breeder*, says, "Perhaps the best way to understand the correct feeding of dogs is to go back to Nature and observe the dog in his wild state. In their natural environment they are hunters and depend upon their kill for sustenance[28]." He then goes on to say, "Best results are obtained by feeding dogs in accordance with their original native state habits. [...] A dog's digestive organs are such that they digest starchy foods, such as potatoes or white bread with difficulty. Hence, they receive little food value from them and the feeding of such feeds only aggravates frequent vomiting. Raw meat with milk and eggs is the best dog food. This provides variety. Where milk is fed regularly, the dogs must be wormed monthly, as a milk diet is conducive to worm growth[29]." This captures the way people used to feed their dogs to ensure vitality, optimal performance, and longevity. However, once people realized there was money to be made selling dog food, a new, multi-billion-dollar industry—the pet food industry—was born.

Retail pet food sales in 2016 were $28.23 billion. 2017 pet food sales were estimated to be $29.69 billion[30]. One of the factors industry experts feel contributes to the growth of the pet food industry is the rise of so-called "premium foods," especially premium dog food (and now I'm seeing more and more "super premium" foods, whatever that means). Clearly, pet food companies are hugely profitable. But despite what they would have you believe, the food they make—even the "premium" stuff—really isn't any good for your dog.

Processed pet food, whether it's "premium" or just regular old kibble, often is made by companies that are affiliated with (often by being owned by the same parent company) companies that also manufacture human food. This lets them use the waste products from human food production to make pet food (especially kibble). Whether someone is purchasing what they believe to be a high-quality pet food or not, it all boils down to the same thing—as Dr. Jeannie Thomason so eloquently put it: "kibble is kibble is still kibble[31]." To make kibble and canned pet food, companies use raw carcasses, many of which are "4D meat" (meat from dead, dying, disabled, or diseased animals). (As I mentioned earlier, the US Food and Drug Administration (FDA) is fully aware of this practice[32].)

4D carcasses are not the only things that go into the food; other waste products, such as supermarket rejects of meat (for example, expired or spoiled meat) are also included.

The process to make the pet food that eventually winds up in the bag or can at the grocery store or your local pet store is similar among most companies. First, the carcasses (including the 4D meat and/or supermarket rejects) are loaded into a hopper (essentially, a stainless-steel pit) that has an auger-grinder. There, the mass of carcasses are chopped into small pieces. Those pieces are then taken to another grinder and shredded. The shredded material is cooked to melt the meat off the bones and make a slurry that's the consistency of soup. The fat, or tallow, rises to the top and is skimmed off. Once the tallow is removed, the cooked meat and bone are put into a press to squeeze out any remaining moisture and get pulverized into a sandy powder. This powder is sifted to remove excess hair and large bone chips. Once the processes are complete, the final products are the tallow, the meat slurry, and the bone meal. The pet food manufacturers buy either the meat slurry or the dried meal for use in their pet food.[33]

It's important to remember canned food and kibble contain similar ingredients. What varies is the amount of fat, protein, and fiber. The quality and type of meat also varies across batches, so it's pretty much impossible to guarantee any kind of consistency.

Leaving aside the question of what 4D meat (the carcasses of which, in some pet foods, may also include our own euthanized companion animals[34] as well as things like medicines and antibiotics that were used to treat whatever diseases the animal in question might have had[35]) does to our pets, it's critical to understand the effect cooking has on protein, especially since so many people think it's safer to prepare home-cooked meals for their dogs than feed them raw. This, of course, is because they think of their dogs as little humans. We can't eat and digest raw meat and bone safely, so we assume our pets cannot. However, unlike us, they're carnivores, and so are equipped with all the tools they need to survive and thrive on raw meat and bones. Cooking denatures the protein. Put another way, cooking modifies the molecular structure of protein, which destroys or diminishes the protein's original properties and biological activity. This means it's unusable, or much less usable, by your dog's body. Essentially, denatured protein has had the secondary bonds that hold the amino acid chains in place broken, which causes the molecule to become a jumbled mass bereft of biological function. When protein is denatured by heat (and it takes very little heat, relatively speaking, to do this—cooking at 117°F for just three minutes is enough), the body doesn't have the ability to rebuild the damaged amino acids usable protein molecules. This is because the amino acid chains form enzyme-resistant links when cooking takes place. Because the body cannot separate the amino acids and use them, it eliminates them. The unusable protein becomes a source of toxicity rather than a source of health and energy because it is, in essence, dead organic waste material[36]. And this toxicity eventually presents in many of the diseases and ailments we see cropping up in younger and younger animals today, from obesity to pancreatitis, from liver and kidney disease to cancer.

I hope by now I've got your attention. Yes, we've taken for granted kibble and/or canned food are the best things to feed our pets, if we stop to think about it at all. But it's only relatively recently in our history we've started feeding our pets this way, and there are lots of downsides to it. We haven't even touched on the inflammation our pets endure because of eating the starches, carbohydrates, and sugars, and how that inflammation can ultimately cause so many chronic diseases (including cancers). No, we haven't touched on all that...but I don't think we need to. You know things in their current state aren't good, so now, let's turn our attention to how we can make them better.

Chapter 4: The Good News: What It Can Look Like on a Raw Diet

As I sit here writing this, I'm on day 3 of a 10-day juice fast. I don't know if you've ever done any kind of fasting, but I had never gone more than 24 hours without chewing something before, except for times I was really sick (stomach flu, for example), or when I was a baby and wasn't eating solid foods yet. I decided to embark on a juice fast for a few reasons. I wanted to do a little "reset" to my system, I wanted to give my system a break, and I wanted to experience what it would feel like to flood my system with nothing but juice for a set period of time.

The most fascinating part of the journey—and granted, I'm only at the beginning of the journey—is how well my body has adapted to just taking in juice for the past couple of days. I experienced a slight headache the first day, and I was really tired as well. The second day, I felt some cravings, some irritability, and some tiredness, but none of it was extreme, and in between I felt energized and happy. Today, I woke up full of energy. I tried to do my regular vinyasa yoga class (probably a bit prematurely, but you never know until you try, right?) and felt totally zapped, but a juice afterwards and some coconut water set me right. I did experience a tiny bit of nausea, but some warm water with a bit of fresh shaved ginger helped me get past that very quickly. Everyone told me the first three days would be the hardest, but they've been completely doable. I also found my creativity and focus increased, even during the first few days, and I'm excited to see what the next seven days will bring.

Yesterday and the day before, I was craving fried foods and bread and chocolate. Starting last night, I began craving vegetables, and today I've been daydreaming about a few vegetable soup recipes I recently saw that sound amazing—along with a beet and carrot salad a friend described to me that sounds truly delicious.

My point in sharing this with you is because, sometime yesterday, it occurred to me that the way I'm feeling right now is probably close to how our pets feel when we transition them from a processed-food diet onto a raw diet. Lately, I've been eating a lot of processed food, because I was feeling stressed and out of time and wanted to reach for the "convenient" answer. Our pets don't have a choice as to what we feed them, and often we decide to feed them what seems "convenient" to us at the time. That means that, just like me when I ate the processed food, they aren't getting good nutritional support from their food. Their bodies can continue in that fashion, at least for a while—the processed food will keep them alive, up to a point—but they can't thrive. Like I've been, they experience fatigue, never feeling completely full, weight gain, skin issues, mood issues, non-normal stool (bouts of either constipation or diarrhea), decreased cognitive function, and more. Yes, I was experiencing all those things, and our dogs do too.

I got used to feeling less than optimal, at least somewhat, but I realized it wasn't healthy and decided to change. Our pets don't have that option. They have to eat what they're given. And so often, what they're given is the equivalent to substandard, processed, fast-food junk, even if the bag says it's a balanced, whole, healthy meal. Truthfully, there's no such thing as healthy kibble or canned food, just as there's no such thing as a healthy Big Mac (remember the movie *Supersize Me*? The impact of eating nothing but McDonald's for just one month was profound, and that was for just one month. When we feed our pets kibble or canned food, it's like we're feeding them McDonald's, day in and day out, often for years.).

I fully anticipate feeling better and better over the course of the next seven days. And of course, for me, just like with my dogs when I first transitioned them off processed food and onto a raw diet, it won't end there. I will continue to eat whole, unprocessed foods, because I love how I feel when I eat in a healthy and natural way. Every single dog I have ever seen that's transitioned to a species-appropriate raw food diet also shows, in a thousand different ways, how much better they feel on their raw diet. It's so exciting for me to be able to experience how much better a radical (but still eminently doable and, yes, convenient, once you get the hang of it) change in diet, from an unnatural, man-made "convenience" diet to a nature-designed, species-appropriate diet, can make anyone—human or animal—feel.

Cleo's Story

My husband, Adam, adopted Cleo from a rescue group in Tennessee when she was 3 months old. When she was about 15, we switched her to a raw diet. Prior to that, she was eating what we considered to be a "premium" kibble. It was close to $70/bag! Cleo was getting frail—her joints ached, she was grumpy (probably because she was in almost-constant pain), and when she stood for any length of time, her head would hang until her nose was almost on the floor. She didn't seem as sharp mentally either. We put it down to advancing age. After all, she was in her teens! But then, when I learned about raw feeding (for Barkley) we decided to switch our other dogs over to a raw diet too. After all, we figured it's never too late to choose healthier habits. While we were hopeful it would make a difference, neither of us had any idea what a profound impact it would end up having on Cleo.

Remember, Cleo was already 15 when we switched her off kibble—she was no spring chicken! Despite that, she started to get stronger, almost overnight. She was much less grumpy, although she still didn't tolerate dogs getting in her face. In fact, I remember one time (she must've been about 16) I took her and the rest of the gang to the dog park. A young and boisterous Husky kept bouncing up to her, trying to get her to play. She growled at him to warn him off, but he didn't take the hint. Suddenly, she lunged at him and nipped him on the nose. He yelped and ran off, and Cleo took off after him, staying right on his heels. She chased him around the entire perimeter of the dog park twice before coming back to stand with me. Her owner looked at her for a minute, then looked at her Husky, who was standing a little distance away from us trying to figure out what just happened. Then, she looked at me, and said, "He just turned 1. How old did you say your dog is?"

The longer we fed raw, the more noticeable the changes got for Cleo. She stopped drooping her head on the ground when she stood. She started going back out on hikes and walks with us. Her cognition improved. At mealtime, she raced down the hallway like a puppy, jumped around, twirled in circles, and relished every bite with gusto. She could still get up and down with relative ease on her own, even at the very end, and while it sometimes took her a bit to work out the kinks, she remained relatively strong and supple throughout her golden years.

Cleo, our beautiful Canaan dog, passed away on April 26, 2017 at the age of 19. She died as she lived—completely on her own terms, at the time and place of her choosing. Both Adam and I had a sense she was going to pass on the evening she did, and I know the dogs all knew too—they were sad and completely dispirited the day before, especially Barkley. They, like Adam and me, grieved Cleo after her passing. She was a friend and a teacher to each one of them. On her last evening with us, I made sure she was comfortable in her bed, as I always did, and I spent some extra time with her and gave her extra kisses before going to bed myself. I felt a huge surge of love from her that evening just before I fell asleep. And in the morning, she was gone.

My heart will always hold an incredibly special place for Cleo. Even as I write this, I feel tears, but they are tears of joy, joy that I got to know such an incredible soul and joy that she is running free and wild somewhere. I don't feel any guilt, or wonder if there was anything else I could have done for her to make her life better or keep her here any longer. Because of how we fed her and cared for her, I know we made her life as optimal as it could be, right up until the end. And to have 19 years with her—with any dog—what a blessing, and almost unheard of these days. I miss Cleo deeply, but in a way I can't explain, I feel her presence near me. I know we will meet again, and until then, I carry her lessons and her unconditional love with me.

Cleo on a hike at 17. Photo credit Kristin Clark

Chapter 5: What Exactly Do We Mean by a Raw Diet?

Up to this point, we've talked about diets that aren't optimal for your pet. You know I'm hoping you've decided to switch your pet from a processed-food diet and onto something healthier and much more supportive of their overall vitality. What is that something? A raw diet.

What do we mean by a raw diet? Simply put, when I talk about a raw diet in this book, I'm talking about a diet of meat, bones, and organs, which haven't been cooked. Similarly, they haven't had toxins added to them. A raw diet can mean a commercial raw diet, whole prey, prey model, or some combination thereof. It can even mean freeze-dried raw. In general, it includes an 80/10/10 ratio (more about that later).

Unlike processed-food diets like kibble, raw diets are highly usable by your dog. Protein sources like rabbit, chicken, turkey, pork, lamb, beef, egg, and sardines—all readily available protein sources—are packed with Vitamin A, Vitamin B (Thiamine), Vitamin B2 (Riboflavin), Vitamin B3 (Niacin), Vitamin B5 (Pantothenic Acid), Vitamin B6 (Pyridoxine), Vitamin B9 (Folate and Folic Acid), Vitamin B12, Vitamin C, Vitamin D, Vitamin E, Vitamin K, Calcium, Copper, Iodine, Iron, Magnesium, Manganese, Phosphorous, Potassium, Selenium, and Zinc. These vitamins and minerals support and promote a myriad of essential functions in your pet's body.

Things like probiotics, enzymes, chondroitin, and glucosamine are found in raw, species-appropriate foods, such as raw green tripe, chicken, and eggs. Your dog can use the nutrients in species-appropriate foods, and because the foods are raw, synthetic vitamins don't have to be added (as they are to processed food) to try and replace what was lost in the processing. Thinking about what you now know about processed-food diets, is it any wonder to you that pets fed a processed diet eventually reach a point where their bodies are so overloaded with toxins and starved for essential bioavailable nutrients they begin to present with issues that get progressively worse, until eventually their bodies shut down altogether? Pets fed a species-appropriate raw diet, on the other hand, can pull every bit of nutrition possible out of their food, and they're not flooded with more toxins. I sometimes think of pets fed a processed food diet as taking two steps backward for every step they take forward. Eventually, it catches up to them. Pets fed a raw diet, on the other hand, are supported and re-balanced with each meal.

Types of raw diets

Commercial raw

Commercial raw diets are generally complete and balanced raw diets you buy premade, rather than putting them together yourself. Some examples of commercial raw companies include Vibrant K9, Primal, Small Batch, Vital Essentials, and Answers. These diets include meat, bones, and organs, come in a variety of different proteins, and are generally grinds. They may include fruits and/or vegetables as well. You purchase them frozen (or in some cases, freeze-dried) and defrost them before you feed them.

Prey model raw

Prey model raw diets fall under the "DIY" category. In general, if you're feeding a prey model raw diet to your dog, you should aim to include about 80% muscle meat, 10% bone, 5% liver, and 5% non-liver organs each week. Some people include fruits and/or vegetables in these diets (when fruits and veggies are included, it's known as a biologically appropriate raw food (BARF) diet), and some don't (when fruits and veggies aren't included, it's known as a species-appropriate raw food (SARF) diet). These diets may also be referred to as "frankenprey" diets, because they include a wide variety of meats, bones, and organs to make up (over time) a complete and balanced diet. It's important to remember, if you're feeding a prey model raw diet, that you're aiming to achieve a balance of meats, bones, and organs over time, rather than in each individual meal.

Whole prey raw

Like prey model raw diets, whole prey raw diets fall under the "DIY" category. When most raw feeders refer to whole prey, they're referring to the complete animal—for example, a whole prey chicken means a chicken that still has its organs, head, feet, wings, and sometimes even feathers (although some people do not include feathers or fur in their definition of whole prey). Another example of a whole prey meal is rabbit; again, this would include the head, feet, organs, and possibly even the fur. Many do-it-yourself raw feeders feed a combination of prey model raw, whole prey raw, and possibly even raw grinds.

Motley's Story

I wasn't looking for another dog. We already had three amazing dogs and a wonderful cat. In terms of pets, my life was rich indeed. The last thing on my mind was adding another one. But sometimes, fate intervenes and brings us what we need, whether we're conscious of wanting it or not. And so it was on April 10, 2015, when I first met Motley.

He wasn't called Motley then, of course. He was Donald, a scruffy little tan and white dog stuffed into one of the crates at Riverside Animal Control's booth. I was with my mom at America's Family Pet Expo, about 60 miles from my house, and we were trying to find the booth where SoCal Aussie Rescue was located. We were there as volunteers to educate people about Aussies, promote the breed, and give information about how to adopt one if they were interested in doing so. To get to that booth, we had to walk through the huge tents filled with dogs that had been picked up by animal control, or surrendered by their owners, and were now waiting in shelters across the region in the hopes of finding homes. The din was incredible—hundreds of dogs were barking madly, or whining and crying, and it was impossible to hear what my mom was saying to me. I was walking quickly, but suddenly I sensed someone looking at me. I turned my head, and there he was. He was the only dog in the whole place that wasn't making any noise. His eyes were at once scared, sad, and wise. Drawn by some implacable force, I went over to his crate. His little tail thumped once, twice, and then was still. He seemed hesitant, but he didn't growl or bark. He just stood there, watching me, allowing me to put my finger through the bars of his crate, but not moving closer to my hand.

As much as I love dogs, and as often as I've fostered and assisted with rescues, it is rare I meet a dog I fall in love with instantly—at least, the kind of love that makes me want to adopt the dog and give it a forever home. I love them all in their own way, but for most of them, my home is a stopping point on their journey, not their forever home. That attitude is what allowed me to foster, because otherwise I would end up adopting all of them and wouldn't be able to open my home to others—I'd quickly run out of room! But this little guy was different. I fell for him instantly, and I wanted nothing more than to help lift the fear and sadness from his eyes. However, the decision wasn't mine alone. My then-boyfriend (now husband) Adam and I lived together, and I couldn't bring home a dog without talking to him first. So, I decided if the little dog got adopted that day, then it wasn't meant to be. If he didn't, and if Adam was agreeable, I'd come back and get him later that weekend.

That evening, when Adam got home, I asked him if he would be open to getting another dog. Initially, he wasn't too keen on the idea, but we talked it over again the next day, and after calling the shelter that evening, I found out "Donald" was still available and would be back at the Expo on Sunday. We resolved to go down there and adopt him. And just like that, Motley's first lessons were upon me. I have a tendency, especially when I really want something, to become so focused on that thing I have a hard time going with the flow. The experience of getting Motley, because it couldn't, of necessity, happen instantaneously, and because the outcome wasn't guaranteed, gave me an amazing opportunity to practice being OK with whatever happened. It let me practice trust that whatever happened would be for the best, which helped me practice looking at a situation as an opportunity for growth rather than stress.

The journey for getting Motley also helped me continue to develop my communication skills. So often I have a hard time really communicating what I want and why, and I shut down and withdraw when I feel like I can't make my point. It's sometimes hard for me to compromise, which can lead to feelings of resentment or even helplessness. In navigating the topic of getting Motley with Adam, I had to trust our communication and trust how that communication would go. I also had to be empathetic to his point of view while expressing my own. Adam was wonderful throughout the process, and I emerged from it with a deeper understanding of how to communicate in a healthy and productive way. Two major lessons, and we hadn't even adopted him yet? What a dog. What an incredible little dog!

When we got to the Expo that Sunday to get Motley, he was right there, waiting for us (in fact, they told us he was the first adoption of the day!). I signed the paperwork, Adam and I wandered around the Expo for a bit, and then it was time to take him home. He was so terrified to walk across the Expo grounds that his legs were shaking, his tail was tucked, and his whole body was completely shrunk in on itself. Nevertheless, step by slow step, we made our way to the car. He elected to huddle in the backseat, as far from us as he could get, but he rode quietly and with no accidents for the entire 90-minute car trip back.

When we first introduced him to the other dogs, it was clear he didn't have much experience as part of a pack. All of them were patient, but he was scared and wanted them to keep their distance. Whenever any of them got anywhere close, he would growl and tense, ready for a fight. They ignored that, though, sensing it was insecurity that caused him to act like that, and eventually, he began to relax around the pack.

This is not, of course, to say that there weren't a few little skirmishes, but overall, he settled in incredibly well because of the power of the pack. Our dog Elle was especially good at guiding him; it was Elle that first showed him how to play, and it was Elle he first snuggled against. He seemed to trust me, but he was also nervous about Adam handling him, reacting in fright and then aggression when Adam petted him. Adam, though, also understood it was insecurity on Motley's part that made him act that way, and he slowly but surely worked with him. It was beautiful to see, and I came to realize, over and over again, how much can be accomplished when you have a strong support system. This support system was there for me and for Motley, and it impacted both of us. So often, I feel like I need to do everything myself. I guess it's a way of proving I'm competent and independent, but sometimes it gets in the way of asking for help. But the pack and Adam were able to help me with Motley and were able to help him in ways I couldn't, because they brought up issues in him that I never would have been able to. There was no way I could really help him work through his fear of men, because I'm not a man. But Adam could, and did. And I couldn't teach him how to be in a pack—but Elle, Cleo, and Barkley could. So, both Motley and I learned, and grew, and eventually Motley was able to play with the other dogs, and sniff them and be sniffed, without resorting to reactivity and aggression. And faster than I could believe, he came to accept and love Adam too.

Mots was in rough shape, physically, when we first got him from the shelter. He had been there about 6 weeks, and had received myriad vaccinations as well as being neutered. His coat was coarse and dry, his nose was cracked, he shrieked in pain when his ears were touched, and he often limped. We immediately set about transitioning him to a species-appropriate diet. By the time we got Motley, I was experienced at switching dogs from kibble to raw, so we jumped right in. I fasted him for a day, then offered him a chicken drumstick. The first few days he didn't know what to make of it, and in fact, he refused to eat anything for the first few days. But by the third day, he seemed to figure it out, and he made short work of the chicken he was offered. He has since proved himself to be a hearty eater, and I haven't yet found anything that he'll turn down. He's happily eaten chicken, duck, goose, turkey, rabbit, lamb, goat, alpaca, muskrat, venison, elk, bison, beef, pork, sardines, Cornish hen, guinea fowl, and quail, to name just a few. Eventually, as his system began to recover from the assault it had undergone, his nose began to soften and get cold and wet again. He started to be able to go for walks and runs without limping, and his coat became shiny and his fur softer. His ears no longer caused him pain. As his system detoxed, his zest for life came out more and more. He turned out to be a high-energy dog, excitedly and busily racing from here to there whenever we went on off-leash walks and setting the pace when he was on-leash, and happily running around and playing with Elle and even Barkley when we were at home. Mealtimes are one of his favorite times of day, and when I carry his bowl out to him, he races as fast as he can to his eating spot, then dashes towards me, springing up to walk backwards on his hind legs to where I set his bowl down. He's more athletic and stronger than I could've ever imagined when I first saw him—raw feeding and natural, healthy, holistic living will do that though.

In the time we've had him, Motley's come an incredibly long way, physically, mentally, and emotionally. He has grown into the potential I saw when I first laid eyes on him. He's a happy go-lucky guy for the most part, and he throws his entire being into whatever he's doing, whether it's eating, or walking, or cuddling. He has captured my heart, and that is, perhaps, one of the greatest lessons I learned from him: that our hearts have an infinite capacity to love, and just when you think your life is full and your cup overflowing, you may find your heart swelling with even more love than before. For that is what happened to me—I learned there's always a way to love even more than I thought possible. And that is a phenomenal gift indeed.

Motley. Photo credit Kristin Clark

Chapter 6: How to Start Your Dog on a Raw Diet

A wise man once said that a journey begins with a single step. This is true whether you're starting a physical journey or a journey into feeding your dog a raw diet. It can be easy to get overwhelmed, particularly when you're starting out. Because many of us didn't grow up feeding this way, we have a hard time imagining what it looks like and what to do. But don't worry! At heart, it's very simple. Let's look at how to get started together.

Making the switch

To start, you can take one of two approaches. The first approach, and the one I usually favor, is to start the journey to raw feeding with a quick, decisive step. Wait 12-24 hours from the last feeding of kibble (this gives the system a chance to digest and pass out the processed food), then start feeding raw. If your dog doesn't eat that meal, it's OK to let them fast and try again at the next meal. It's fine if they miss a few meals (remember my story about Motley?), and eventually healthy dogs will start eating the food you're offering. And, the chances are good your dog may just dive right into the raw food, like they've been waiting for it all along!

The other option is to transition them slowly. If you go this route, feed them 75% of their daily kibble in the morning, then 25% of their total daily raw allotment in the evening. Do this for a few days, monitoring their stool to make sure it's firm and regular. If everything is fine, move them to 50% of their daily kibble in the morning, then 50% of their total daily raw allotment in the evening. Again, monitor their stool to make sure everything is staying regular and firm. If so, you can move them to 25% kibble in the morning, 75% raw in the evening. Once their stool is firm and regular, you can move them to 100% raw and no kibble. The whole process could take up to a few weeks.

I haven't had much problem with diarrhea or other digestive issues when transitioning using the first method, but some dogs do have trouble, so the latter method is probably safest if you're concerned about your dog's ability to handle the transition without digestive upset. Either option will get you there, so do whichever you feel most comfortable with. Just remember, if you use the first method, your dog may have some diarrhea or other issues. It's important not to panic if that happens. You can slow the transition down, but make sure you keep transitioning. You've got this!

What proteins should you start with?

Many people prefer to start their dog off on a raw diet of chicken, because it's relatively inexpensive, easy to find, easy on the stomach, and full of soft digestible bones. It's very bony[37], which helps firm up stool that may be softer due to the diet change and resulting detox. However, you don't have to start with chicken—if you have access to a different protein source (beef, for example), start with that. Try to get organic or pasture-raised animals. Make sure they're antibiotic- and hormone-free. And if you can't find organic/pasture-raised, at least get a brand that isn't enhanced (injected with saline and/or flavor enhancers).

Transitioning to new proteins and organs

Whether you're feeding commercial raw, prey model, or whole prey, try to feed the same protein source for at least a week, and preferably two, before you switch to a different protein source. Watch the stool to make sure it's firm. You will notice your dog's poop is much smaller, breaks down more quickly, and your dog doesn't poop as much as they did when they were kibble-fed. Once the stool is consistently, but not overly, firm, start slowly introducing in organs (unless you're feeding a commercial raw, which should already have organs in it). Start with liver and then start adding in other organ meats and glands. Basically, this includes all the parts that secrete and are squishy (more about organs in a bit). You can feed all kinds of parts, such as liver, kidneys, blood, eyes, testicles, lungs, brains, and so on. You can also start introducing other protein sources, but make sure to monitor your dog's reaction to these changes. The key here is moderation, and there is no need to rush the introduction of new proteins or organs. Your dog will achieve a balanced diet over time, so whatever nutrients it doesn't get in its meal today it will get tomorrow, or the day after that. This is the way animals in the wild also eat—with balance over time. If they required all their meals to be balanced in and of themselves every single time, they wouldn't be able to function at an optimal level consistently. Our carnivore pets are the same way.

How much should you feed your dog?

When figuring out how much to feed your dog, aim to feed about 2-3% of its ideal body weight per day. For puppies, aim to feed about 2-3% of their ideal adult body weight. If you have no idea what your puppy's ideal adult body weight will be, you can aim for 10% of their current ideal body weight, but monitor their weight changes and adjust the amount given as they grow (see the chapter "Feeding Puppies Raw" for more information). If your dog is underweight or overweight, you can adjust the amount you're feeding to help them achieve their optimal weight. Keep in mind that many kibble-fed dogs are overweight, and as a society we are used to seeing animals that are too heavy. When you look at your dog, you should be able to easily feel their ribs but not see them (unless their fur is very short). When you look down at your pet from above, you should see a narrowing where their hips are. If you cannot easily feel their ribs or see this narrowing, they are too heavy. If their ribs or hip bones jut out sharply, they are too thin. If their weight does need adjusting, do it slowly (balance over time!), and remember it's better to have an animal that's slightly thin than slightly heavy.

The 80/10/10 ratio

When you feed raw, you're attempting to mimic what carnivores in the wild, particularly wolves, eat. The prey animals typically consumed by wolves and other predators in the wild are generally about 80-85% meat (including muscle meat, fat, connective tissue, skin, heart, lungs, and so on), 10-15% edible bone, and 5-10% organs. Therefore, general guidelines for a raw diet (both commercial raw and prey model) are about 80% meat, 10% bone, 5% liver, and 5% non-liver organs. If you feed a prey model diet, remember this is achieved over time, so if, for example, you feed a lot of meat with less bone for several days in a row, aim to feed a bit more bone at the next meal. Aim to achieve these percentages (the 80/10/10 ratio raw feeders often refer to) over the course of a week.

Doing the calculations

To calculate how much to feed your dog, figure out how much they weigh (or what their ideal weight is). Let's assume you have a dog that weighs

40 pounds and you want to feed them 2% of their body weight per day. To get the total amount of meat, bone, and organs to feed, convert the percentage fed into a decimal: 2 ÷ 100 = 0.02. Then, to figure out the total weight in pounds your dog should eat per day (including treats!), multiply your dog's weight (or ideal weight) by the decimal: 40 pounds x 0.02 = 0.8 lbs. You can then convert this to ounces to make it easier to figure out how much bone, meat, and organs to feed. To do this, multiply the pounds your dog should eat per day by 16: 0.8 x 16 = 12.8 ounces. Then use the 80/10/10 guideline to determine about how much meat, bone, and organ to feed.

Meat/day: 12.8 ounces x 0.80 = 10.24
Bone/day: 12.8 ounces x 0.10 = 1.28
Liver/day: 12.8 ounces x 0.05 = 0.64
Non-liver/day: 12.8 ounces x 0.05 = 0.64

If you want to figure out how much you should be feeding per week (in case some meals are larger than others per day), you can just multiply the above amounts by 7 (the number of days in a week):

Meat/week: 10.24 ounces x 7 = 71.68
Bone/week: 1.28 ounces x 7 = 8.96
Liver/week: 0.64 ounces x 7 = 4.48
Non-liver/week: 0.64 ounces x 7 = 4.48

Using this same method, you can also figure out an appropriate range for your dog (for example, figure out the uppermost range they should eat in any given week based on feeding 3% of their body weight per day, and the lowermost range they should eat based on feeding 2% of their body weight per day). You can use these figures to make sure your dog gets the proper amount of meat, bone, and organ each week.

Feeding organs

Ok, so now we've looked a little bit at how to get your dog switched over to a raw diet. If you're going to feed prey model raw, you'll also have to make sure you feed them organs regularly. The organs can come from a wide variety of animal species (I feed chicken, turkey, rabbit, and beef organs regularly, and other organs when I can get them), which makes things a little easier. About 5% of your dog's weekly food intake should be liver, and about 5% should be non-liver (what some people refer to as offal, or secreting organs). With that in mind, let's take a closer look at organs, both what options you can feed and what they can do for your dog.

Liver

First and foremost, let's talk about liver. Liver is one of the few organs you absolutely must feed regularly. Compared to most other organs, the liver is large both in terms of volume and weight (the stomach and the lungs are bigger, but more about them and where they fit into a raw diet in a bit). Liver contains lots of nutrients, including vitamins A, B1, B2, B5, B6, B9, B12, C, D, E, and K; iron; zinc; calcium; phosphorous; magnesium, potassium; protein; essential fatty acids; and CoQ10. Interestingly, researchers that have observed wild carnivores eating their prey have found that often the liver is eaten first.

Because liver is such a nutritional powerhouse, it's possible to give too much of it (and since many of the vitamins it contains are fat-soluble, not water-soluble, too much of them can lead to problems for your pet). Liver should make up about 5% of your dog's weekly total intake. For a 50-pound dog being fed 3% of their total body weight per day, that's only 8.4 ounces per week. For a 10-pound dog (again, being fed 3% of their total body weight per day), that's only 1.7 ounces per week.

If you're new to raw feeding, particularly if you're following a prey model diet, introduce liver slowly. It's quite rich, and introducing it too quickly can lead to diarrhea and gastric upset. Additionally, if you feed beef liver, be aware that it may make your pet's stool dark and runny. If your pet seems sensitive to liver, try feeding it in smaller amounts over the course of a week rather than feeding their entire weekly portion all at once.

Kidneys

Along with the liver, kidneys are also nutritionally important. Kidneys are a common choice for raw feeders to go towards making up the "5% non-liver organs" requirement. The kidneys are nutrient-dense and full of vitamin A, B2, B5, B6, B12, C, D, and E. And, some of the nutrients found in the kidneys are more highly concentrated there than in other parts of the body.

Spleen

While some raw feeders don't regard spleen as a vital organ to feed, it does provide high levels of iron and vitamin C (when it's raw and fresh). The spleen is a large organ that looks a bit like the liver and kidneys—they're all a dark reddish-purple color and very squishy. Spleen is a great organ to feed, but it isn't vital if you can't find it.

Pancreas/Thymus

The pancreas and the thymus are what're known as "sweetbreads." They have lots of vitamins and minerals, but you certainly shouldn't panic if you can't find them. Both the pancreas and the thymus are fatty, so you should feed them in moderation if you do feed them. If you can get your hands on them, they're a great way to include some variety in the raw organs you're feeding.

Brain

Like the kidneys, the brain is another organ that has some nutrients that muscle meat and bone don't, or at least that they don't have to the degree you find it in brain. However, much like the pancreas and thymus, if you can't find brain, it's not a real cause for concern. If you feed whole prey, you will obviously feed it, but if you feed prey model raw or you feed a commercial raw food, you may not be able to find it. The brain is relatively small compared to the entire animal, so if you are feeding prey model and you have access to brain, it's great to feed in moderation. If you don't have access, don't stress out over it.

Heart, Stomach, and Lungs

For purposes of raw feeding, we consider the heart, the lungs, and the stomach to be meat, not organs. While they're technically organs, they're considered meat for the purposes of raw feeding. That's because when it comes to classifying organs vs. meat, we're talking about nutrition, not function. In other words, from a nutritional standpoint, body parts like the heart and the stomach are more of a muscle (even though functionally they're organs).

Green tripe

Often, people ask me if there's any particular food I recommend most for raw diets. While I always advocate variety—various protein sources, such as rabbit, beef, pork, turkey, sheep, and so on—I also highly recommend feeding green tripe regularly.

What is green tripe, you ask? Tripe is another name for the stomach of ruminating animals, such as cattle, sheep, and goats. You may have seen bleached, processed tripe at the grocery store, but when you're feeding tripe to your carnivore pets, use green tripe, which is the raw, unbleached tripe. Once the tripe is processed and bleached, it has almost no nutritional value whatsoever, but green tripe has a myriad of benefits. Interestingly, green tripe is more brown than green, but it often has a greenish tint from the hay or grass that the animal was digesting. And, because this vegetation has already been broken down and digested by the herbivore, it doesn't stress the carnivore's body to consume it.

When we look at the nutritional analysis of pasture-raised, organic green tripe, we see the ratio of calcium to phosphorous is about 1:1, which is exactly what our dogs need. And, the calcium and phosphorous are also bioavailable to your dog, which means they can use all the calcium and phosphorous supplied by the green tripe. Additionally, green tripe's overall pH is 6.84, which is slightly acidic and good for digestion. Green tripe contains iron, potassium, zinc, and selenium, along with several other important nutrients. It also contains a large amount of *Lactobacillus Acidophilus* (a probiotic). Green tripe contains the right proportions of Linoleic and Linolenic acids, which are essential fatty acids (meaning your dog can't make them on her own and must get them from her food)[38]. Green tripe also contains digestive enzymes and amino acids, both of which are vital to supporting the health and vitality of our carnivore pets.

Tripe has a strong smell, so you may want to store and thaw it outside your house, or in an airtight container if you have to put it in your refrigerator. Add green tripe into the rotation of meats you feed your carnivore pet (you can include it in the meat portion of their weekly meals); its nutritional value is excellent, and the probiotics, digestive enzymes, essential fatty acids, and other nutrients it contains will greatly benefit your dog.

Mixing kibble and raw

One of the things people sometimes ask me (especially if they're transitioning their pet to a raw diet, or want to feed a combination of raw and kibble) is whether it's OK to mix kibble and raw together. I've done a lot of research into this topic, and what I've found is a lot of conflicting information. Of course, in my ideal world, people wouldn't feed their pets kibble ever, but still, when multiple people ask me about it, I do get curious. *Side note: I hope in this book to give you ways to feed raw that work for your budget and your lifestyle. But, I still want to address this question, since so many people have asked me about it.*

Multiple vets and other researchers believe dogs process raw foods and kibble very differently. Raw food is processed as a protein and held in the stomach to be dealt with by the stomach acids. Kibble, on the other hand, is processed as a starch[39]. That dogs process kibble and raw differently makes sense to me: our dogs have evolved to eat raw meats, bones, organs, and glands, and their bodies don't recognize kibble as food, particularly because of the way that it's processed and the ingredients it has.

Other research I've read also mentions kibble can affect the gut and metabolism negatively, slowing the metabolic rate down and making it more difficult to digest the food[40]. In both situations, mixing kibble and raw food together can result, for some dogs, in digestive upset, including gassiness, burping, and digestive discomfort.

Then there's the anecdotal evidence. When I reviewed forums and other sources of anecdotal evidence as to whether there was a problem with mixing raw and kibble, I found an almost 50/50 split of people who said their pet had no issue when they did that, and people who said it caused diarrhea, gas, vomiting, and other digestive issues.

While the research isn't definitive, I tend to think it's not worth the risk. I wouldn't want to run the risk of subjecting my dogs to any digestive discomfort, and I think most pet parents feel the same. If you're feeding a mix of kibble or raw, it's worth examining your reasons for doing so: are you doing it because raw is too expensive? Or is it because you're worried the raw diet isn't "complete and balanced," and you want to feed some kibble as a back-up?

If it's the first situation and you find raw feeding to be too expensive, look at my "Feeding raw on a budget" chapter for some tips on how to make raw affordable. And remember, when you feed raw, you generally don't have to spend nearly as much in vet bills, which is another great savings.

If you aren't feeding 100% raw because you're worried the diet isn't complete, it's important to remember our dogs are carnivores. They're designed to have their nutritional needs met through their natural diet of raw meat, bones, organs, and glands. I know it can be hard to wrap your head around this, because we think of our dogs as members of our family (which they most assuredly are). However, we should bear in mind they aren't humans. We are omnivores. They are not. They don't have the same ability to break down and use all the foods we can, and in fact, they get all that they need through species-appropriate raw food diets. It's similar to herbivores, who don't need to eat meat to have a well-rounded, complete, balanced diet. Our carnivore pets don't need carbohydrates for a complete meal, and they don't need their meals cooked (in fact, cooking renders the proteins unusable and eventually leads to problems). So, feeding them kibble as a sort of "insurance policy" is counter-productive.

If you're just dipping your toes into raw feeding and want to continue feeding kibble a bit longer, ask yourself why. If you're moving to raw, you've obviously educated yourself and are taking a huge step towards helping your dog live their most balanced, thriving life. Trust that, when done properly, a species-appropriate raw food diet is all they need (and can be affordable!), and give up kibble for good. If you do that, you'll never have to worry about whether it's safe to feed kibble or raw together. You can rest assured you're feeding your dog exactly what they need to thrive.

The logistics of raw feeding

If you're like I was when I decided to make the switch to feeding a raw diet, you may be a bit overwhelmed by the logistics of it all. I had lots of questions, and it was sometimes difficult to find suggestions and answers to some of my most basic questions. There are lots of conflicting opinions out there, and if I'm being brutally honest, unfortunately not everybody is patient with or kind to newbies. And so, I thought it would be helpful to describe the nuts and bolts of raw feeding for you. Of course, there's more than one way to do it, and what works for one person may not work for another, but hopefully we can take some of the mystery out of the process.

First, let's look at the tools and equipment that will make the process much easier.

A freezer

One of the most crucial items in your raw toolkit is a deep freezer. If you don't already have one, you will want to get one. They come in various sizes and have various features; you can decide what's important to you. To give you a sense of size, I have three dogs (ranging from 16-50 pounds), and we have a 20.2 cubic foot upright freezer. About 90% of the freezer is devoted to food for our pets, and I regularly order 100–150 pounds of food at a time, usually when I have about 40 pounds of food left. Prior to this freezer, we had a 5.1 cubic foot chest freezer (which I gave to my mom when she made the switch to raw feeding—yay, Mom! I'm so proud of you!). It wasn't as convenient as our upright freezer, but it did the job for years. With that freezer, I would order food every 4–6 weeks: more frequently than I do now, but not super often.

Keep your freezer between -1 and 0° F (-18° C) to halt the activity of any microorganisms in the meat, and stop (or nearly stop) any potential degradation of the meat by the naturally occurring enzymes in the whole food.

To help avoid feeling overwhelmed, I recommend purchasing a large amount of food at once, particularly if you get it shipped. Stocking up will allow you to settle into the rhythm of feeding a varied, balanced, raw diet in a convenient way. It may seem initially expensive, but it will also help you get the most bang for your buck in terms of shipping costs.

A kitchen scale

When you first start feeding raw, especially if you're feeding prey model or whole prey, it's important to make sure you're feeding the right amount of meat, bones, and organs for your dog's weight (or ideal weight). The best way to do this is by weighing the food you're giving them using a kitchen scale. Now, I know lots of raw feeders scoff at the idea of using a scale and weighing their dog's food; I still think when you're starting out, you should do what you need to do to make sure you're feeding the right amount. This is especially true since so many of us tend to overfeed, at least a little bit, and we aren't good at judging how much food we're giving (or eating ourselves!)[41]. Eventually, you'll probably get to the point where you can "eyeball" the food; you may also get to a place where you know your dog so well you can use their energy level and physical appearance to judge how much to give them. But, especially when you're starting out, weigh your dog's food. Scales also come in handy if your dog doesn't finish everything you've given them. If, for example, you give them a pound, but they consistently only eat about 12 or 13 ounces, you can adjust how much you feed each meal to fit their pattern.

A good cleaver, a rubber mallet, and some poultry shears (sounds like the start of a bad joke, doesn't it?)

If you feed prey model, or if you have a smaller dog, you'll run into instances where you have to cut your dog's portion up. Investing in a high-quality meat cleaver makes this so much easier. Poultry shears can also be handy (although if you're only going to get one, get the meat cleaver). My husband, bless him, came up with a great method for how to cut up bone-in pieces: holding the cleaver where I want to make the cut, then using my other hand to forcefully tap (OK, it might be a bit more than a tap) the cleaver with a rubber mallet. It really helps me get the force and leverage I need to chop up even bone-in pieces (boneless pieces, of course, are easy to cut with just the cleaver). He's strong enough to cut bone-in pieces with just the cleaver, but for me, the rubber mallet method works really well.

Remember, I have 3 dogs ranging in size from 16 pounds (Motley) to close to 50 pounds (Barkley); they all eat different amounts, so I have to cut up different sizes for different dogs. To be perfectly honest, my favorite meal days are whole prey days where I don't have to cut anything, but with my cleaver and mallet, even days where I need to cut through bone are pretty simple.

On a side note, many supermarkets will sharpen your knives for you for free; talk to the butcher at the market to see if this is an option. They'll also be able to tell you the best way to care for your cleaver. I always hand-wash mine, and I hone the blade each time after I use it. You can also find information about how to properly care for a knife online.

A raw food journal

When I started feeding raw, someone suggested I keep a raw food journal. I don't use it anymore (I've been feeding this way for years, and I just pay attention as I go), but I found it helpful when I first started feeding raw. Now, I'm a lists-and-planners sort of gal, so I loved the raw food journal. If you aren't that into keeping track of every little thing, it may not appeal to you; if that's the case, skip it. But if you do enjoy that sort of thing, get a notebook or create an Excel spreadsheet and track (by date):

- What you fed
- How much your dog(s) ate
- How your dog(s) reacted to the food

My raw food journal showed me some valuable patterns, like the fact Barkley has very dark, runny stool after I feed him beef liver, or that Elle shouldn't have more than 1 ½ pounds of food at a time, or that Cleo didn't like fully feathered quail.

The process of feeding

When I first started feeding DIY raw, I wasn't sure the best approach to take. When I fed kibble, I just scooped it into the bowl and put the bowl down. Each animal had their special place to eat inside, and they would run to that spot and wait for me to put the bowl down. They would scarf it down, and I wouldn't give it any more thought until the next meal. It was pretty much the same with commercial raw (although I did have to factor in the defrosting time).

When I switched to prey model and whole prey, I knew I wanted to feed the dogs outside, because I wasn't sure if they would keep the meat and bones and organs in their bowls or take them out and drag them around. But beyond that, I didn't know what the best way to do it was. What I soon figured out, though, was that each dog has their own special approach to eating a raw diet, and it wasn't nearly as hard to adapt to feeding in a way that works for them and us as I had thought.

In general, my feeding routine goes like this: I portion out the food for each dog for the day, put it in that dog's bowl, carry it outside, and put the bowl down to the cement. Each dog has their own special place, and I always put the bowls down in the same order. It makes it easier to do it that way, because the consistent routine means each dog knows their food is coming, and they don't try to steal it out of someone else's bowl. I usually stay outside with them while they eat (which could take anywhere from a few minutes to half an hour, depending on what they're eating). That way, I can make sure Elle and Motley don't steal food from anyone else. Plus, it's fun for me to watch them eat, because they have such blissful looks on their faces. When they're done, I get the bowls and bring them inside to clean them, the cutting board, the countertop, and the cleaver and/or shears. Cleanup generally takes me about 10 minutes total (it takes much less time to clean up after the dogs than it does to clean up after cooking dinner for us!).

The question of bowls

I know some people say you shouldn't use bowls for raw-fed pets. I'm of the opinion, though, that you should do whatever works best for you. I find bowls handy to carry food outside without dripping anything on the floor. I also find them useful if I'm giving a mix of things—for example, some liver along with a chicken back, a few whole eggs, and some green tripe. If you do use bowls, opt for stainless steel rather than plastic. Stainless steel is relatively inexpensive, very durable, won't harbor bacteria or leach anything into the food (plastic can leach and because it is porous, bacteria can linger even when you wash it), and you can find bowls in all shapes and sizes.

Where to feed

I feed my dogs outside on the cement for several reasons:

1. My backyard is mostly cement, with a large wooden deck and a swimming pool taking up most of the remaining space
2. The food doesn't seem to stain the cement
3. The places I feed them get full sun throughout the day. Sunlight acts as a natural disinfectant, so this helps keep it clean and disinfected without having to use any chemicals.
4. I don't like feeding them on the deck because they lick up miniscule bits of blood and meat, and I don't want them to ingest any of the stain that's on the deck or get splinters in their tongues.

Some people feed their dogs on grass. If you want to feed your dog inside (in case of really bad weather or because you don't have a backyard), you can feed on a mat or an old towel or blanket. You can also feed in a crate if you live inside and your dog drags food around everywhere. If you feed inside and your dog does drag the food onto the floor, it's not a big deal; just disinfect and clean it up after.

Preparation is key

Once you establish a routine, you'll find feeding raw is as convenient as feeding kibble was. However, I can give you one last tip: Plan ahead. Set a reminder or get in the habit of pulling food out of the freezer to defrost in enough time so the food is completely thawed out when it's time to feed. If you forget to pull food out (which happens to everyone at some point), you can either fast your dog (more about that later) or feed them some frozen sardines while you wait for the food to defrost. If you absolutely need to, you can thaw the food in a bowl of warm water for a few hours to defrost it more quickly.

Red meat versus white meat for dogs

At some point during your raw feeding journey, you might come across people who have very specific ideas about feeding red meat versus white meat to dogs. There's a lot of debate and confusion about this topic, so I wanted to take a minute to break it down from a common sense, species-appropriate perspective.

White meat and red meat?

Like literally **everything** else in the raw feeding world (seriously—spend some time on Facebook watching raw feeding discussions, and you'll see what I mean), there are people with very strong opinions about red meat and white meat for dogs. Why? Some people are adamant dogs should eat a diet almost exclusively comprised of red meat. Their rationale is wolves adapted to eat deer, elk, caribou, bison, and so on, and we should mimic that with our domestic dogs. They also point to the nutrient profiles of red meat versus white meat, saying red meat contains more nutrients vital for dogs. Finally, they also frequently argue that many dogs (if they're going to have trouble with a protein) seem to have adverse reactions to poultry.

While some of these arguments have some truth to them, they don't really hold up when you look at them from a holistic, common-sense perspective. Let's take the first argument—that wolves adapted to eat deer and other large four-legged mammals, and we should feed our domestic dogs the same thing. Wolves do eat deer and other large mammals, no question about it. However, without taking away from the veracity of that statement, what's really important—for all canids, wild or not—is variety. Wild canids such as wolves (which have virtually identical digestive systems to the domestic dog) did adapt to eat diets of primarily red meat when it was available, but they will eat white meat as well when they catch it. Feeding a variety of red meat, white meat, and the occasional fish (or if not feeding fish, supplementing with quality fish oil) mimics what happens in nature far more closely than feeding a diet of red meat exclusively.

Additionally, different meats have different amino acid and nutrient profiles, and by feeding variety, you help ensure your dog gets all the amino acids, vitamins, and minerals they need. Different meats also contain different types of fat: poultry is high in polyunsaturated fats (especially linoleic acid) and low in saturated fats and docosahexaenoic acid (DHA), ruminants are high in saturated fats and low in polyunsaturated fats and DHA, and fish is, typically, rich in DHA. Feeding your dog a variety of different protein sources will help balance the fats in her diet. It's important dogs consume a balanced spectrum of fats; to do this, they should consume a variety of red meats and poultry supplemented with fatty fish or fish oil.

Finally, while it's true many dogs seemingly have problems with poultry (especially chicken), what they're often reacting to are the hormones and antibiotics in the poultry. When those same dogs are fed antibiotic- and hormone-free chicken that was free range and raised on organic feed (and allowed to roam and supplement their feed with bugs and other species-appropriate food), the problems the dogs were presenting with often disappear.

What makes meat "red"?

According to nutritional science, red meat is meat that is higher in myoglobin than white meat from chicken or fish[42]. For example, according to the USDA, chicken breast (which is white meat) is 0.005% myoglobin, while beef (which is red meat) ranges from 0.40–2.00% myoglobin, depending on the age of the beef. In general, we tend to classify red meat as meat from mammals and white meat as meat from fowl, but there are exceptions to this (aren't there always?).

Red meat has lots of iron, phosphorous, zinc, and B vitamins[43], all of which are important for our dogs. It's also a good source of lipoic acid[44], which is important in aerobic metabolism/cellular respiration.

When looking at meat for the purposes of raw feeding, it's generally safe to assume meat from mammals, whether livestock or wild game, is red meat. Alternately, poultry and fish are generally considered white meat. However, there are some exceptions to this: goose and duck, for example, are considered red meat. If you want to get complicated, you can also find definitions that look at the cut of meat or the age of the animal when slaughtered to determine if it's white meat or red meat. For example, many consider pork to be red meat if the animal was slaughtered as an adult, but white meat if the animal was slaughtered when it was young. Sometimes people classify wild game as "dark meat" that's in a category all its own. And some people consider chicken breast, for example, to be white meat, but chicken thigh to be red meat.

I share all this to show you that, if you really want to get into it, even a simple question like "Is this meat considered white or red?" can get extremely convoluted. But it doesn't have to be this difficult. If you feed a variety of meats, and make sure to include mammals, poultry, and fish in your dog's diet, you go a long way towards ensuring your dog receives all the nutrients he or she needs to thrive.

To make things easier, I've included a list of various proteins you can feed your dog, as well as indicating which of them are red meat and which are white meat (in general, anyway—as I mentioned, it often depends on which definition you use).

Red meat proteins

- Alpaca (very lean)
- Antelope
- Beef
- Bison (leaner than most beef)

- Caribou
- Deer
- Duck (red meat, even though it's poultry. Relatively fatty)
- Elk
- Goat
- Goose (red meat, even though it's poultry. Very fatty)
- Kangaroo
- Llama
- Moose
- Pork (depending on age and cut)
- Sheep (depending on age and cut)
- Squirrel

White meat proteins

- Chicken
- Emu
- Fish, such as sardines, herring, mackerel, trout, and anchovy
- Ostrich
- Pigeon
- Pheasant
- Pork (depending on age and cut)
- Sheep (depending on age and cut)
- Quail
- Turkey

As you can see, you have lots of options when it comes to both white and red meats you can feed your dog. Aim for variety, and experiment with different proteins. As long as you do that, your dog will get all the nutrients they need, and the variety will also help keep mealtime a fun and novel experience for them.

Canine Health Promotion's

Prey Model Raw Cheat Sheet

Feed as meat (80% of diet):

Muscle meat

Heart

Stomach

Gizzards

Tongue

Trachea

Green tripe

Gullets

Fat

Connective tissue

Feed as organs (10% of diet):

Liver (should be approximately half of organ meat fed)

Kidneys

Spleen

Sweetbreads (Pancreas and thymus)

Brain

Testicles, uterus, and other reproductive system parts

Eyes

Skin

Bone should form the other 10% (approximately)

Where do we get these percentages from?

They are modeled after the general composition of members of the deer family: mule deer, elk, caribou, moose, white-tailed deer, and so on.

These animals are approximately 70–80% meat, fat, skin, fascia, and connective tissue; 10–15% edible bone, ligaments, and tendons; and 10–15% organs and glands.

In PMR, we attempt to recreate this natural balance, using various types of animals.

Dealing with a picky eater

Sometimes, when we decide to make the switch to feeding a raw diet to our dogs, they seem to have other ideas. I've heard things like, "My dog just won't eat raw," "My dog only likes cooked chicken," or even, "My dog refuses to eat anything other than her kibble." Nobody wants their dog to starve, but we do want to make sure they're eating the best thing possible, so what do we do?

The first thing to keep in mind is that, unlike cats, it's perfectly fine to fast healthy dogs for several meals, and even several days (we'll go over fasting in a bit). Remembering that can help when you're dealing with a picky eater, especially if you're in the process of switching your dog from kibble to raw. In fact, if you decide to switch your dog "cold turkey," it's a good idea to fast them for at least 12-24 hours to flush out the processed food (do a little reset, if you will) and build up a hearty appetite. That's true whether you're in the habit of feeding your dog once per day, twice per day, or even if you free-feed. Remember Motley? He refused to eat the chicken he was offered for several days before he finally got hungry enough and ate it. It was important to me he learn right from the get-go he would need to eat what he was offered, because (just like dealing with a child) I didn't want him to think he could start turning his nose up at everything I gave him. But I digress...back to our picky eater that we're transitioning from kibble to raw.

Once you've fasted your dog for 24 hours, offer her a raw meal. Give your dog her space; in other words, don't hover nervously, anxiously watching for her to take a bite. Keep an eye on her from a bit of a distance—after all, would you want someone looming over you while you ate, intently watching your every move? Dogs are sensitive, and this is even less appealing to them than it would be to us. If your dog doesn't seem very interested in the food, that's fine. Leave it down for 15 or 20 minutes, then pick up the food bowl and put the food away. Of course, if your dog is still working on eating after 15 minutes, give her a chance to continue, but if she's not interested, calmly take it away.

If your dog is a healthy adult, wait another 24 hours before you try again. Put the same amount of food down, and give her another 15 or 20 minutes to eat. You can encourage your dog to eat, but again, don't hover anxiously. If your dog refuses to eat, pick the food up as you did the day before and put it away.

After a few days of this, healthy adult dogs will realize this is the food they're now getting, and will eat it from that point on. Oh, but that reminds me of something...let's jump back to our example dog, Motley:

54

Once he finally ate that first raw meal, another issue cropped up, and it's one you might notice too. Because his teeth and gums were in such poor shape from all that kibble (yes, it's a myth that kibble cleans teeth[45]), it took about a week before he was able to eat without his gums bleeding a bit, but we continued to give him chicken meat and bones, which are quite soft and easy for dogs to eat, until his teeth and gums got stronger and healthier. Fast forward a few months, and his teeth were pearly white and his gums were strong.

If you have a dog that eats most everything in his raw diet but doesn't seem to like a certain part of it (for example, he doesn't like to eat the organ meat), there's something else you can try to entice him to eat. If he has some obedience training and you've used treats to train him, you can ask him to do some obedience (sit, stay, come, down, shake, etc.) and then use the meat he didn't want as his "treat." My husband, Adam, came up with this idea, and we used it to great effect the first time or two we gave Barkley liver, as he didn't really want to try it but did seem to feel he had earned it when it was given as a treat. I asked him for a series of more difficult obedience maneuvers so he'd expect a "high-value" treat, and when he successfully performed them I praised him and gave him a bit of liver. Then we did more maneuvers, until eventually all the liver was gone. After a few times of that, he seemed to have no problem eating the liver.

You can also try putting a small piece of whatever they don't like on top of or layered in a large amount of what they do like to eat. This is useful when you're trying to get your dog to eat something they are reluctant to try, such as organ meat or a new protein type. Generally, once your dog has grown used to eating lots of variety, it's no longer an issue, but when you first start out, they may be hesitant to try a wide variety of things.

You can also lightly sear the meat or organ they don't like at first—no, it's not, strictly speaking, "raw," but it may help entice them. Just make sure you only do this for a few days, then get back to feeding raw. If they refuse to eat it, it's time to get creative, or just outwait them. Think back to your childhood: would your parents have catered to you if you only wanted to eat French fries for dinner, day in and day out, instead of whatever the rest of the family was eating? Probably not. Be like them, and don't cater to your dog's insistence that he only be fed a particular protein served a particular way. Remember, this is the same dog that will happily eat rotten food out of the trash can. He can certainly eat the nutritious and species-appropriate food you're offering him.

Now, all that being said, if your dog hates a particular protein but enjoys lots of other proteins, you may want to consider not feeding that protein. Just like us, dogs have food likes and dislikes, and as long as they get a wide variety of proteins, it may not be worth trying to force them to eat that one protein they despise. For example, in our pack, Motley positively adores rabbit, Elle will eat it, but Barkley won't touch it except very reluctantly, and sometimes not even then. He dreads it. So, because he gets such a wide variety of other proteins, we don't force the issue. It's a genuine dislike for the rabbit that leads him to avoid it, and he eagerly eats everything else. There are things I don't like either (hello, dill pickles), so I can relate.

Finally, if your dog's been eating a raw diet happily for a while, and then doesn't seem to want to eat for a day or two, I would suggest keeping an eye on him or her but not forcing the issue too much. Just like us, sometimes they may feel a bit under the weather and may not be interested in eating. The digestive process takes quite a bit of energy, so if the body is out of balance, it's often better to let that energy go towards healing than towards digesting. Continue to offer the food, but don't force it. We went through a period of 4–5 days one summer when Cleo wasn't interested in eating at all. We monitored her, but everything was normal except she wasn't interested in eating and she slept a bit more. After 4 or 5 days, her appetite returned, and she went back to happily eating whatever was placed in front of her with gusto. If this occurs and you're concerned about it, you can set up an appointment with a holistic veterinarian or a certified animal naturopath to discuss it, but generally speaking, in a healthy dog, it's not a cause for concern.

Above all, remember this is a journey, and relax and trust the process. Have fun with how you feed your dog, even if it requires you to get a little creative at first with how you get them to eat.

Feeding a commercial raw diet

There are many people who want to feed their dogs something other than kibble or canned food, but aren't yet ready, for whatever reason, to make the switch to prey model raw or whole prey meals. For these pet parents, commercial raw may be a great way to go.

Commercial raw is a great way to transition to a prey model or whole prey way of feeding. And just to be clear, by prey model, I mean a diet that includes about 80% muscle meat, 10% raw bones, and about 10% organ meat (5% liver and 5% non-liver organs). In other words, it attempts to mimic what your dog might eat in the wild, and it also is a diet that you prepare yourself (rather than buying it pre-made at a pet store). In this context, I'm referring to a diet that includes pieces of various animals put together to form the whole meal (for example, maybe a turkey neck, some chicken liver, sheep ribs, and some green tripe). Feeding this way is sometimes also referred to as *frankenprey*. Whole prey refers to feeding the same proportions as prey model raw, but in whole prey form—in other words, giving your dog a whole chicken, or rabbit, and so on. Many people who feed a raw, species-appropriate diet feed both ways, depending on what's available, but there are many who just stick with a prey model raw diet that doesn't include whole prey.

Commercial raw, on the other hand, will still generally consist of the same percentages that prey model raw consists of, but may include veggies, fruits, and even dairy. The bone contained in commercial raw is generally ground, and the entire meal is usually either ground or chunked. Because it generally comes frozen in a bag, you can simply defrost it and feed it to your dog, similar to how you feed kibble.

I find most commercial raw is relatively expensive compared to prey model raw or whole prey, and because I'm feeding 3 dogs, I find it easier and less expensive to prepare their meals myself. However, I did transition everybody but Motley by feeding commercial raw, and it worked quite well to help ease me into the concept of feeding raw food (notice I said it was helpful for easing **me**, not my dogs, into the idea of raw feeding).

Commercial raw isn't just valuable as a transition food. Remember kibble and canned foods contain toxic preservatives, fillers, sub-par meat, and other things that can cause your pet harm. Almost any commercial raw food out there will be better to feed than kibble or processed food, and there are many dog owners who keep their pets on commercial raw for their whole lives (check out "Peanut's story" for one such example). They enjoy the convenience and knowing their pets are still getting (in most cases) a high-quality food, and they also find comfort in knowing they don't have to balance their pet's meals themselves.

So, let's say you want to feed commercial raw. How do you know what to look for to make sure you're making the best choice? When I discussed this with someone who's quite knowledgeable about the industry and commercial raw manufacturers, she said the number one thing to check for is where the meat is sourced. You want to make sure the meat used to make the food is high-quality. It should be hormone- and antibiotic-free. Grass-fed and/or pasture-raised is very important. You should also know exactly where the meat is coming from—make sure no 4D meat (meaning meat that comes from animals that are dying, diseased, desiccated, or disabled) is used. If you can't find the source of the meat, don't use it. Unfortunately, it's not enough to just call the manufacturer to ask, either. The pet food industry is not regulated, and unscrupulous manufacturers may not tell you the whole story, even if you ask them directly. So, be ready to do some research, or talk to someone who's knowledgeable about the commercial raw pet food industry.

Another major thing to consider when picking out a commercial raw food for your pet is the amount of veggies and fruit in the food. Remember your dog is a carnivore, designed to eat and thrive on raw meat, bone, organs, and glands. When a commercial pet food has a high percentage of fruits and vegetables, that means part of your pet's diet will be things that aren't truly needed. It's good the fruits and vegetables are generally not fed whole in these types of diets, which spares your pet from having to tax their pancreas and other organs trying to break them down, but you still want to limit how much fruit and veg they're getting. Chances are you're paying top dollar for a commercial raw diet, too, so make sure you're getting the most bang for your buck by picking a food that wholly or mostly consists of exactly what your pet truly needs: meat, bones, and organs.

Remember, too, your dog needs variety. Different proteins contain different nutrients, and by giving them a variety of proteins and organs, you help ensure all their nutritional needs are met. Make sure you include red meat along with poultry (if you choose to feed poultry at all), and again, try to limit how much fruit, vegetable, and dairy is included. You may even want to feed several different brands of commercial raw along with different formulas within each brand to increase variety. If you need to supplement, do so mindfully, and as your pet gets healthier, consider trying to replace the supplement with a whole food that supplies that nutrient.

Some raw food manufacturers use high pressure pasteurization (HPP) to process their raw food. This is done to eliminate bacteria. Unfortunately, HPP denatures the proteins, making your pet's body much less able to use the amino acids to build new proteins, and it also destroys a lot of the good bacteria that're so beneficial in raw food. When choosing a raw food for your pet, make sure you know whether the commercial raw has gone through HPP. If it has, you may want to strongly consider getting another food, unless there's a specific medical reason you need a sterile pet food.

Feeding a commercial diet can be a great way to get your dog off processed pet food, whether you move on to a homemade diet or keep them on it forever. Make sure you do your research when picking out your raw commercial food, though, so your dog gets the highest quality food possible. Once you've decided on what food(s) you'll be buying your pet, continue to monitor the manufacturer. They can and do change their sources and practices, so it's in the best interest of your pet to stay on top of it.

The omnivore myth

At this point, you might be wondering if raw meat, bones, and organs are enough to satisfy your dog's dietary needs. So, let's take a moment and address that question.

As science has shown, our dogs are—you guessed it—carnivores[46]. The evidence of this can be seen in their bodies and physical makeup. Our dogs' stomachs have a pH of about 1–2 (if they've been eating processed food, it will take a little time to get to this pH), whereas ours (for comparison) have a pH of between 6 and 7. What this means is their stomachs have way more hydrochloric acid than ours do. Their teeth, from the canines to the molars, are sharp. In contrast, omnivores and herbivores have flat molars that allow them to grind their food. Look at your own teeth— sharp canines that let you eat meat, but flat molars that let you grind plant matter. Or look at the teeth of a horse—every tooth is flat, enabling them to powerfully grind plant matter. Now look at your dog's mouth. Those pointy teeth are designed to handle meat and bone, not plants. And it doesn't end there. Our carnivore pets have powerful jaws that are designed to move in a scissor-like motion, which allows them to rip, shred, tear, and finally gulp their meals. Dogs have carnassial teeth: only found in certain carnivores, they enable the animals that possess them to shear meat[47].

Left: Dog skull (© Gavran333). Notice every tooth, even the molars, are sharp.
Right: Pig skull (© Kornilovdream). Notice this omnivore has lots of flat, small teeth.

Unlike omnivores and herbivores, dogs can't move their jaws from side to side to chew and pulverize plant and grain matter. Our dogs can regurgitate food that didn't get mashed up enough the first time around and then eat it again (gross to us, delicious to them). Their intestines are shorter to allow their food to digest and pass through quickly and to help prevent "bad" bacteria from gaining a foothold. Carnivores, including our pet dogs, don't have amylase in their saliva, and their pancreases produce only trace amounts of cellulase. This means they lack the ability to break down the cellulose in plant matter and extract the simple sugars (and therefore energy) from it. In other words, unlike herbivores and omnivores, they cannot break down and digest plant matter.

Some people have asserted wolves and other carnivores end up eating plant matter when they eat the stomach contents of whatever animal they have brought down. However, researchers have observed carnivores shaking out the stomach of an animal before eating it[48]. Their bodies cannot digest the plant nutrients, so they don't consume them. Other people point to dogs eating grasses as a sign that they need plant nutrients. What they're really working on getting is the soil-based organisms that come along with the plant matter. And if you look, you see the plants come out the same way they came in when carnivores eat them. Wolves and other canines have been observed eating berries out in the wild, but this is only when food is scarce. They will eat anything to stay alive, but this doesn't necessarily mean it's good for them (case in point—think of the number of dogs that are taken to the vet each year for eating chocolate. Also not good for them, but they will eat it!).

Since a carnivore's system is not equipped to digest plant matter, when we feed vegetables and grains to them, they can't process it and it ends up, at best, passing through with no benefit. At worst, it ferments in the stomach and over time, when such things are fed repetitively, causes major issues. In a nutshell, just as you would never try to feed a horse a piece of steak, it doesn't make physiological sense to feed your dog a diet predominantly made up of starches, vegetables, or fruits.

Now, if you really feel you should feed your dog fruits and vegetables, you can: Just understand that, from a physiological perspective, they aren't necessary. Feed them in small amounts, and try to feed items low in sugar. I think feeding a raw diet with some fruits and vegetables is still miles better than feeding any sort of processed food diet, so if feeding that way works for you, go for it.

Is freeze-dried raw food good for your fur baby?

I used to work for someone who would advise us to "take a squinty-eyed look" at all the data when we were trying to solve a problem or answer a tough question. The mental image that phrase evokes always makes me laugh—and it also perfectly captures the essence of what we have to do when we're trying to figure out the answer to any tough question. Wondering whether freeze-dried raw is a good choice for your dog? If so, you're not alone. Lots of people have asked me about this, and I want to address it here. What do you say? Want to join me in rolling up your sleeves and taking a squinty-eyed look at the pros and cons of freeze-dried raw? Thought so! Let's do it.

The spectrum of diets

I tend to think of the food options we have for our dogs on a spectrum. At one end, there's kibble. And at the other, there's whole prey our dogs have caught themselves. While most pet owners feed kibble, luckily more and more are moving along the spectrum and starting to feed some form of raw (cheers to you, dear reader, for joining this ever-expanding tribe!). Take a look at my representation of the spectrum of ideal food for our dogs. The further right you move on the spectrum, the more ideal the food is.

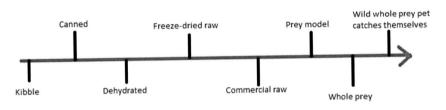

Many of us, myself included, feed some combination of the spectrum (as I've mentioned, I feed a combination of prey model and whole prey to my dogs). And as you can see, I think (for lots of reasons) commercial raw, prey model, and whole prey diets are the most ideal for our dogs. However, freeze-dried raw is another great option to consider, particularly in certain situations.

What is freeze-dried raw?

When a food is described as freeze-dried raw, it means its ingredients started out raw and then had the moisture removed through a process of freezing and then drying (in low heat). Freeze-dried is different from dehydrated (which, as you can see, is less ideal of a food than freeze-dried), because dehydrating typically uses higher heat to remove the food's moisture. When a food is freeze-dried, it usually needs to be reconstituted with water (either hot or cold is fine) before feeding.

So why, if freeze-dried raw uses low heat, is it considered less ideal than fresh or frozen raw? Mostly, it's because some of the nutrients in raw food are destroyed in the drying process, even though that process uses low heat. While freeze-dried raw retains more nutrients than dehydrated food, it doesn't retain all of them, making it a less-ideal option than the other types of raw.

Freeze-dried raw benefits

Despite this, freeze-dried raw may still be worth considering, particularly for pet parents in certain situations.

Situation 1: You're hesitant to feed fresh raw
If you're currently feeding kibble or canned, want to switch to something better, but don't feel comfortable feeding a fresh (or frozen) raw diet, freeze-dried raw is a great choice. It's way better than either kibble or canned; your dog will get significantly more nutrients and benefits out of their food without as much harm being done to their bodies. And, it may help you get used to the idea of feeding raw, until eventually you begin experimenting with feeding commercial raw, prey model, or even whole prey.

Situation 2: You're traveling
Because freeze-dried raw doesn't need to be kept frozen, doesn't take up much space, and is so light (it's lighter than both kibble and fresh raw), it's a great option for when you're traveling with your dog. Generally, you can keep it at room temperature, reconstitute it with water when it's time to feed, and you're ready to go. So, whether you're taking a road trip, camping, or doing some other type of travel with your four-legged friend, freeze-dried raw can be a lifesaver. And, the same benefits that make it great for traveling also make it a great option for inclusion in an emergency preparedness kit.

Situation 3: You don't have much space
If you don't have a lot of freezer room, it may be difficult to feed a raw diet effectively. Because freeze-dried takes up relatively little space (compared to both kibble and raw), it can be an awesome choice if you need to save space.

In any of these situations, freeze-dried raw might be a great choice for you. It's becoming more and more widely available, making it easier than ever to come by. And in many instances, the commercial freeze-dried raw food that is available is extremely high quality. Because it has a long shelf life (it can last for years in the package, although it should be fed promptly, with whatever your pet doesn't eat refrigerated, once it's been reconstituted), is less messy than fresh raw, and is still nutritious compared to kibble, canned, and even dehydrated, freeze-dried raw is worth considering.

Are there any downsides to freeze-dried raw?

While freeze-dried raw can be a great option, there are some downsides to consider.

It's not as nutritious as other types of raw
Like I've said, freeze-dried raw is more processed than other types of raw, and there are some nutrients delicate enough to be destroyed in the preparation process. However, it doesn't use chemicals or high heat, which makes it a better option than kibble, canned, or dehydrated. If you're already feeding commercial raw, prey model, and/or whole prey, best to stick to those. However, you may still want to keep some freeze-dried raw on hand for emergency situations or for when you're traveling with your pet.

It can be expensive
Depending on what type of freeze-dried raw you get, you might find it to be expensive. If you're looking to switch to raw and you're discouraged by how expensive it seems, you might want to forego the freeze-dried option and get right into doing it yourself. Check out the chapter about feeding raw on a budget for tips on making raw more affordable.

Some dogs don't like the taste and/or texture
Because freeze-dried must be reconstituted, it's a different texture than either raw food or kibble. And, the process of removing the moisture can also affect taste. You might have to experiment a bit to find a freeze-dried raw that your pet will eat. If you're going to go this route, be patient and persistent. Eventually, you should be able to find some your dog will eat.

Some freeze-dried raw takes a long time to reconstitute
Check the packaging, because while some brands of freeze-dried can be reconstituted in just a few minutes, others take longer. If you're in a bit of a hurry, you can break the food into smaller chunks to help speed up the rehydrating time. Just make sure to plan ahead and know how much time you need, so you aren't caught off-guard when dinnertime rolls around!

Bottom line

In this reporter's opinion, freeze-dried raw can be a great choice for you and your furry family member. It has a lot of benefits, and it's significantly better than kibble or canned. If you're looking for something that's convenient, easy to take when you travel, or even less messy than raw, freeze-dried may just be your answer.

Elle's story

One of the things I love most about animals is that every single one of them has the capacity to teach us something. Our beautiful dog Elle is a perfect example of this.

Elle, our 5 ½-year-old Lhasa Apso mix, is one of those dogs that always seems to have a bounce in her step, a twinkle in her eye, and a smile in her heart. Most dogs I know are happy, but Elle takes it to another level. She has an incredible knack for finding the fun in any situation, and the look on her face when she's inviting you to a fun new game always elicits a smile in return. Elle is a born peacekeeper and is highly intuitive when it comes to sensing when someone—dog or human—is feeling a bit down. She always seems to know when a game will cheer someone up, or when quiet companionship is needed. She's not what I would call a lap dog, but she has a tender way of being that at once comforts and soothes.

My husband, Adam, got Elle from a local shelter when she was 3 months old. He started taking her to the dog park, letting her explore and learn how to relate to dogs of all sizes, ages, and dispositions. She is one of the best socialized dogs I've ever seen, and many is the time I've watched her at the dog park, leading a game of chase with so many dogs involved that it's a blur. She's inclusive and seems to instinctively know how to draw dogs out of their shells. She hasn't quite managed to figure out how to get our cat, Gryphon, to play, but I'm confident she'll crack the code someday.

Elle leads by example, and that's how she taught me valuable lessons. Two different situations will illustrate what I mean.

After my dog Guenivere (Gwinnie) passed away, I was broken-hearted. Gwinnie was one of the most loving dogs I've ever known, and her loss left me reeling. One afternoon, several weeks after she was gone, I was sitting on the bed, feeling absolutely bereft. Gwinnie was the one who had always comforted me when I was feeling lonely or sad, and now Gwinnie was gone, and her loss, along with the thought that I wouldn't know that gentle, unconditional, loving companionship in quite that way again, was so hard to bear. Suddenly, I felt a gentle pressure against my leg. I looked down, and saw Elle leaning against my leg. She was, quite literally, leaning—she would have fallen over if I had moved my leg. She was gazing up at me, and wagging her tail in a slow, steady rhythm. I put my hand down, and she nuzzled her face into my hand. And she stayed there until I moved, her weight against my leg a tangible symbol that she would be by my side, supporting me, for as long as I needed. She was only a year and half or so at the time, and generally very high energy, but she knew instinctively that what I needed was a gentle love, not a game, and she offered me that unconditionally. The gift she gave me that day was incredible.

I was able to witness firsthand how she offered the gift of unconditional love to another creature that needed it, with finesse and insight. When we first adopted Motley, he was suspicious of other dogs and, it was clear, had never learned how to play. He would growl and snap if another dog came close, and if one touched him, he would erupt. The other dogs gave him a wide berth, for the most part, but Elle took it on herself to teach him that he could have friendships with other dogs. It started slowly—she would come up to him and then lay down so that he didn't feel vulnerable (he's shorter and lighter than she is). She got closer and closer, and would sometimes come up and play bow and then dash away. At first, he just stood there and growled, but eventually, he started to run after her. She would let him chase her, moving slower than her usual speed because at that point, he couldn't keep up with her. When he caught her, she would fall down on the ground and roll over, tail wagging, with a big smile on her face. Once he got used to the concept of play chasing, she started to wrestle with him a bit, always being mindful of his limits. She refused to be put off by his posturing, but she never pushed him to the point where he actually felt cornered. Eventually, after a few months, the two of them were playing together daily, and Motley was able to start learning how to transfer those skills to other dogs. When he and Barkley started playing together, Elle would stay close by, watching. If it got rough, she would bounce in between the two of them in a playful way, defusing the situation, and then step back when they were calmer and let them play again. It was skillful and amazing to witness, but it was no surprise. She's an amazing dog.

So, what is the lesson for me in all of this? Elle taught me that tuning in to what another being is feeling, and understanding where they're at, is absolutely imperative if you're going to reach them. She also taught me the value of paying attention to what others need. This sounds simple, but it's so profound. How many of us do things for others because they're things we want, or because we've been told that's what we're supposed to do? Gary Chapman wrote a book called *The Five Love Languages*, and it touches on this. We all have a "love language" (and often more than one), and we tend to try to show our love to those around us using our own primary love language. If, for example, our primary love language is gifts, we feel we've received love from another when they give us gifts. If the person we're expressing love to, though, has a primary love language of words of affirmation, giving them gifts doesn't have the same impact for them as it would for us. So many of us, though, default to showing our love based on our own love language, and then we are confused when it isn't received in the depth or way we intend. Elle, though, doesn't do that. She observes what the dog, or person, needs and wants, and then moves to give it to them. She was able to show Motley love, friendship, and inclusion in a pack through play in a way that he could receive. She was able to give me comfort in exactly the way that I needed it most. If she weren't aware of that, she probably would have approached me much differently—perhaps with an invitation to play a game, which is her favorite thing. But she sensed that wasn't what I needed, and she was able to selflessly give me what I needed. Same with Motley. She restrained her own normal way of playing until he was able to understand that she was a friend and could accept full play. I've seen her do this countless times with other dogs and people…watching them, gauging what they need, and then providing that to the best of her ability.

This lesson has helped me learn how to feed and care for my dogs in the way they need, even when it's not necessarily the way society has taught me to do so. Raw feeding is a prime example of this: it's not how most dogs are fed, but then again, most dogs today aren't living optimally balanced and flourishing lives. She, more than any other dog, taught me to read what my dogs, as individuals, need. Sometimes one dog needs a bit more bone, or a little less organ. Sometimes they need more food, sometimes less. Sometimes they need their space. Sometimes they need more cuddle time. Through her beautiful example, I learned to tap into the nuances of what they needed, and then do what I could to give it to them.

Elle was young enough when we switched her to raw that she wasn't showing any real problems. She hadn't been exposed to many toxins, either externally or internally, and her health was good. And she continues to thrive on her natural regimen. Plenty of exercise, a diet as optimal as we can make it, pure water, quality rest, and lots of love from her people and her pack have (probably unsurprisingly) proven to keep her at her peak. It makes me so happy to look at her, because I know in a very real way we've helped each other to grow further than either of us could have alone.

Elle has taught me, and continues to show me, how to be better. She embodies a way to really touch those around us in a way that's more about them than ourselves. She has an empathy that is rare and wonderful, and I am inspired each day by her. She is at my feet right now as I write this, quietly sleeping. I know that if I needed her and woke her up, she would immediately assess the situation and move to give me whatever she thought I needed. She epitomizes selflessness and unconditional love. I treasure her, and each day, I strive to be that much more like her.

Elle. Photo credit Kristin Clark

Chapter 7: The Benefits of Raw Feeding

We've spent quite a bit of time talking about the different types of raw, how to feed raw, and more. Now for the fun part (oh, who am I kidding? It's all fun, right?!): the benefits of feeding raw. While it may take some time, feeding a high-quality, balanced, varied raw diet can have incredible impacts on your dog. Take a look at some of the benefits (and this is just a sample—there are lots more!):

- Shiny teeth and strong healthy gums (no tartar or plaque, and no periodontal disease either!)
- Shiny coats and flake-free, non-itchy skin
- No "doggy odor"
- Bad breath becomes a thing of the past
- Improved energy
- Huge reduction in quantity and size in poop
- Increased cognitive ability
- Better health and vitality
- Resistance to parasites like fleas and ticks

Remember too, raw feeding is not just about the physical benefits (although that's a huge part of it). It's also about the emotional and mental benefits. When you feed your carnivore pet a diet they have evolved to eat, it taps into something primal. If you watch a dog crunching through bone or enjoying raw meat, you'll notice the same ecstatic look on their face as we get when we're eating a delicious meal at a fine restaurant. Imagine the bliss you felt the last time you had an extraordinary meal. Even before you started eating, the scent of the food reached your nostrils. In anticipation of the feast to come, your mouth started watering, you felt pampered and relaxed, and when you did bite into your food...well, at that point, your meal became a delectable journey of culinary ecstasy.

Our dogs feel the same way. A species-appropriate raw diet—providing as it does the chance to use their powerful jaws for the exact purpose for which they were designed (that is, to rip, tear, and shred their food) and providing variety, enticing smells, various textures, and what must, judging by the looks on their faces when they are eating, delicious taste—is one of the most beneficial but also joyful experiences you can give your dog. As pet owners, we've turned treats and toys and other pet accessories into a multi-billion-dollar industry, but from what I've seen, showing love to our dogs starts with feeding them in a way that supports and benefits them physically, mentally, and even emotionally.

Even when she was 18 and 19, Cleo still got excited and started bouncing up and down and barking when it was time to eat. (If you've never seen an 18-year-old dog hopping up and down, bumping you with her nose, and chattering her teeth and barking at you to *hurry up!*, you're missing out.). She would race outside and twirl around while she waited for us to set her food down. Our littlest dog, Motley, walks on his hind legs backwards to his eating spot when it's mealtime because he's too excited to keep all four feet on the ground. Barkley jumps straight up in the air, the top of his head rising above mine (and I'm 6 feet tall) in excitement and anticipation for his food. Elle races to her food spot, then races back to me, and repeats this until we get to her area. When I set the food down, they almost always bury their noses into the food for just a moment to inhale it before they dig in—I liken that moment to the appreciative sniff we sometimes take before we start to eat...it enhances the pleasure we know is about to come. And once they do dive in, they look like they've been transported to an amazing place. There's such joy on their faces as they settle in with their food.

For me, the benefits of a species-appropriate raw food diet and the disadvantages of processed food make my choice to feed my animals a raw food diet very easy. But the icing on the cake for me is seeing their joy during each meal. They are carnivores, and by feeding them the way nature intended, I'm honoring not just their species, but their essential natures as individuals.

Chapter 8: What About Treats?

Many of us love giving our pets treats. We do this when we're training them or just to show a little extra love. But it can sometimes be hard trying to figure out an easy treat that fits into the raw dog's diet. Since it's not always easy to give pieces of raw meat or organs as treats, what should you do? Well, here are a few options to consider.

Sardines

One of the best (and easiest) treats to give is frozen, whole sardines.

Sardines are packed with Omega-3 fatty acids. In fact, according to the website raisinghealthydogs.com, an average sardine has about 175 mg of Omega-3s. Sardines are also full of protein, can help with skin and coat issues, can help animals with allergies, and support proper brain function. They contain bones and organs, so your dog gets a nice blend of meat, organs, and bone in each little fish.

Because the sardines are frozen (there's no need to thaw them or debone them), they have very little smell. Dogs can eat them relatively quickly because they're small, and they're a nice supplement to a raw diet. While in normal circumstances you shouldn't feed them every single day, feeding them a couple times per week is perfect to give your dog the benefits of sardines without overdoing it.

When buying sardines for your dogs, I suggest getting wild-caught, flash-frozen, whole sardines. I buy them in 5-pound boxes for around $9/box. Each sardine weighs around 3-4 ounces, with an average of 20-25 per box. Pretty inexpensive treats that last for quite a while, even with 3 dogs! If you can't find sardines, mackerel are another great option.

We get our sardines from the local Asian market. If you have an Asian or other ethnic market close by, check there first. They may have exactly what you need at a much more reasonable price. Otherwise, your local grocery store should carry it (if you don't see it, ask the manager, as they may be able to order them for you).

Hare of the Dog Rabbit Treats

Hare of the Dog Rabbit Treats (go for the 100% rabbit options, not the rabbit and sweet potato blends) are made with a single ingredient—rabbit—and come in a variety of sizes and shapes. They make great training treats, or just a nice little goodie to give your dog. Rabbit is lean, full of nutrients, and is an "exotic" protein that generally doesn't cause allergic reactions. Bottom line: if you're looking for a fun new treat to give your dog, these might be just the ticket! You can get them on Amazon, and you can also find them at www.hareofthedog.com.

Bully sticks

Variety is the spice of life, and that goes for treats too. So, here's another treat idea for you: Bully sticks. They come in a wide variety of sizes, and can be straight, braided, rounded, and so on. They're made of 100% beef pizzle, are high in protein, and they're a big hit with every dog I've ever seen. You can find them at pet stores or online. One great resource is www.bestbullysticks.com.

Chapter 9: Feeding Puppies Raw

Feeding puppies a raw diet is fairly similar to feeding adult dogs a raw diet, but there are some differences to keep in mind if your dog is less than a year old. As Dr. Jeannie Thomason noted in her book, *Breeding and Raising Dogs the Way Nature Intended*, "No special ingredients, "protein," or calcium are needed in [the puppy's] diet [once they've been weaned]. They require the same calcium and phosphorus levels as an adult dog—1:1 and 2:1 parts calcium to phosphorous ratio. They do, however, require up to 10% of their body weight in raw meat, bones, and organs compared to adults who only require 2.5-3% of their body weight[49]".

Also, unlike adult dogs, puppies under 1 year of age should never be fasted, and in fact, may need to eat 4 meals per day when they're less than 4 months old, 3 meals per day when they're between 4 and 6 months old, and 2 meals per day when they're 7 months to 1 year old.

Dr. Thomason goes on to point out that:

A raw prey model diet is biologically appropriate for the puppies. The levels of protein, fat, and calcium are naturally balanced and suitable for a young dog's growing bones and muscles. Kibble contains too much fat, protein, and synthetic calcium. It is cooked so is not easily digested and contains other synthetic vitamins and minerals. Kibble causes fast, uneven growth, and too much synthetic calcium interferes with the absorption of other essential vitamins. The raw bone in a species appropriate diet provides essential calcium, but won't interfere with vitamin absorption. If the dog ingests too much bone, it is just eliminated in the feces. I also feed raw green tripe, which is a great natural probiotic and digestive aid. Do not feed cow yogurt or fermented dairy products as they are not easily digested[50].

To give your puppy the best chance at optimal vitality, it's of the utmost importance to feed them a raw diet. Nutrition is the foundation of good health, and providing that strong platform early in life will help set them up for a lifetime of vitality and thriving.

So, what does a raw meal for a puppy look like? Pretty much the same as it would for an adult dog, with adjustments made for the smaller size of your puppy. You might give your puppy a little bit of liver, gizzard, heart, and a chicken drumstick in one meal, then give them a sheep or pork rib and a little bit of green tripe at the next meal. Remember, just like adult dogs, they should get organs, bones, and muscle meats, in an 80/10/10 ratio.

Because puppies can grow so quickly, it's important to keep an eye on them from day to day and adjust how much you're feeding them if they start to get too thin or too heavy. Feel your puppy along with looking at them. Do they seem more roly-poly than the day before? Are they looking a bit thin and gaunt? While you want your puppy to be relatively lean (they shouldn't be fat), you also don't want to let your puppy get too thin. So, adjust based on what your puppy's body is telling you, and adjust daily if needed. For an in-depth look at feeding puppies raw appropriately, check out "Onyx's story."

Onyx's Story

The following story is from Dr. Erin O'Connor (an animal chiropractor and certified naturopathic carnivore nutrition consultant), about her puppy, Onyx. I am grateful to her for allowing me to include her story in this book, because it's a perfect demonstration of how to feed and care for a puppy naturally.

My Story

I found that I love German Shepherd Dogs from working and interacting with them at my clinic. I knew one day I would have one of my own. However, I wanted to find a naturally reared puppy. I wanted him to be raised as close to how nature intended as possible, so I could have a puppy with an excellent foundation in health from the start.

This means I was searching for a breeder who was breeding quality, health-tested dogs, feeding a species-appropriate diet, and following a natural lifestyle. I wanted the puppies to nurse as long as possible and, when they were ready for solid food, to be weaned onto raw food. I didn't want the puppies to ever be fed kibble, canned food, or anything processed. I also only wanted them to use natural methods for health care when indicated, rather than traditional medications, vaccinations, and preventatives. I wanted a breeder who provided a loving environment with lots of physical and mental stimulation, playtime out in nature, and the opportunity to soak up lots of fresh air and sunshine. I wanted to make sure that any allopathic treatments used were minimal and only used if necessary. After much research, I found a breeder in Montana who was doing everything I had wanted for my puppy and had been truly following a natural rearing protocol over the past 20 years.

Onyx's Story

My puppy, Onyx, was born July 22, 2016. He came to me "au naturel," just as I wanted, weaned onto raw food and without any vaccinations (note: he did receive his rabies vaccine as required by law in my state, but not until he was older).

Over the past 50 or so years, we've been convinced that getting a puppy with the above "health background" is not the right way of doing things. However, our pets are not living as long. It is common to hear about dogs that have allergies, autoimmune conditions, itchy skin, gastrointestinal problems, and more. Why aren't we looking into ways of doing things differently? They say the definition of insanity is doing the same thing over and over and expecting a different result. I chose to find another way.

Onyx is the very first naturally reared dog I have had. Several years prior to getting him, I did a great deal of research into dog nutrition and then continued my education in naturopathic carnivore nutrition with the American Council of Animal Naturopathy. I also took their immunology course to be sure I was making sound decisions regarding health choices for my puppy.

I flew out to Missoula, MT from Chicago, IL to pick up Onyx. The breeder's home was surrounded by gorgeous mountains. I found her, as well as Onyx's mom, dad, and his litter playing in a field on her property. It had to be one of the most adorable sights to see. As I got out of my car, I saw a bunch of tiny German shepherd heads bopping up and down, as they jumped and ran around the field. Their parents were proudly watching over them. I was first greeted by Onyx's parents who happily came over to me. Then, Onyx was the first puppy to run right up to me, almost as if it was meant to be! We flew home the next day. Onyx traveled in-cabin with me to Chicago and was a very good boy for both of our flights. During our travels, he ate freeze-dried raw. It was the closest to the real thing I could bring along. I was able to easily pack this with me and feed it to him at the hotel and in the airports.

When we finally arrived home, Onyx enjoyed a raw meal in his new home: ground chicken. He was so excited and ate it all. The next day I fed him a turkey wing…it was about as big as he was! He happily ate it for as long as he could, and he ate as much his little puppy teeth would let him. Everything I offered him, he loved. He seemed like a bottomless pit! Even now, he eats everything he is offered.

Starting Your Puppy on Raw

If you are starting your puppy on raw, you will feed the same amount as an adult. Hopefully, you have an estimate of about how much they will weigh as an adult. You can always use that as a starting point and adjust accordingly, based on if they are still looking hungry, not finishing, or visibly looking like they can use some extra. A good starting point is to feed 3% of your puppy's estimated adult body weight daily.

Onyx is estimated to weigh 85 lbs. as an adult, so his daily intake is 2.55 lbs. a day. However, when he was going through major growth spurts, he sometimes ate double that amount. This is okay. You can feed your puppy extra if they seem overly hungry. Every dog is different, so you may or may not need to do this. As your puppy begins to mature into their adult features, watch for signs of a healthy weight, such as an abdominal tuck, a waist that tapers just before their hips, and being able to feel their ribs as if there is a thin blanket over them. Almost every other raw feeder I know has told me that their puppies ate more than expected during rapid growing phases.

With eating such a large amount of food, you will need to divide this up into more frequent meals in a day:

Under 4 months = 4 meals per day
4–6 months = 3 meals per day
6 months–1 year = 2 meals per day

Please note this is a guide; you may need to alter it somewhat for your puppy. I found Onyx needed to stay on 3 meals a day until about 7–8 months. When I tried 2 meals a day at 6 months, even though it was the same amount of food in those 2 meals, he would vomit bile, which is a sign of an empty stomach anticipating food. We went back to 3 meals per day for a while, and when we tried 2 meals per day later, he was ready.

If your puppy isn't finishing their meals and losing weight, add in another feeding time per day to help create smaller portion sizes. If they are maintaining weight and not finishing all meals, you can eliminate a feeding time.

Raw Feeding Puppies

A species-appropriate raw food diet is a diet that strives to come as close as possible to the diet of a wild canine without going into the woods to hunt wild prey animals. It is based on whole meats, connective tissues, fat, organs, blood, and so on from a variety of prey animals to achieve balance and to feed all the nutrients in whole prey.

Essential components of a species-appropriate raw food diet include meat, bone, and organ. As a rule of thumb, the "right proportions" tend to fall close to 80% muscle meat, 10% bone, and 10% organ, with an emphasis on including liver in organ content.

Observe your puppy while they eat. Become familiar with their eating habits. This will allow you to learn what you can safely feed them, whether they need to be in a crate, sent outside, away from others, etc. No matter how well you know their habits, always keep a watchful eye when they are eating.

Types of Raw Foods

I put types of raw foods into 3 categories: "whole prey," "chunks," and "grinds." I feed all the categories to all 3 of my dogs. If your dog has all their teeth, they should be able to eat from any category just fine.

Grinds
If you have a small or medium breed dog, you can do fine grinds. Medium, large, or giant breeds can do course grinds. Be sure that these grinds are including the proper amounts of muscle, bone, and organ.

Chunks and Whole Prey
Chunks are part of a whole carcass. For example, a whole chicken can be cut into smaller (but large enough to not be gulped) sizes and fed in that way. Fish are great soft "starter" bones. Puppies are thrilled to be able to work their tiny puppy teeth through the entire fish. Chicken, duck, and rabbit are also easier for them to gnaw through.

You can give other proteins like turkey, lamb, goat, and pork; however, they may not be able to get through these bones completely until their adult molars come in. It still will give them great physical and mental exercise to try and gnaw their way through these bones. A happy puppy, sleepy from lots of gnawing and a happy belly = a good puppy!

Watch the Stool
If you are feeding too much bone, your dog's stool will be powdery or have a very hard consistency. If you are feeding too much organ, their stool will be dark and tarry.

Give a Dog a Bone

It is very beneficial to give your dog raw meaty bones to gnaw on and eat. They are good for dental hygiene as well as providing natural exercise to the muscles and bones of your pet's jaw area, and they provide great mental stimulation. Decide what will work for you; however, if you choose not to feed raw meaty bones for your dog to gnaw through, your dog will be missing out on some of the great benefits.

Be sure bones are size-appropriate. You want to be sure they are larger than their mouths so that they do not swallow them whole. Puppies are growing and hungry. They will try and get food down as fast as they can. With Onyx, he learned that some pieces he swallowed were too large. He would then regurgitate that piece back up, crunch as fast as he could, and re-swallow.

If your puppy is trying to gulp or eat bones quicker than the speed of light, like Onyx, you can feed partially frozen. Feeding partially or fully frozen can slow your dog down and force them to take more time, so you can implement this to teach your dog if needed. Besides, they may enjoy a duck neck "popsicle" on a hot day!

Variety

With a raw diet, balance of nutrients is achieved by feeding a variety of proteins; rotating 3–4 proteins is ideal. With puppies starting on raw, unless they spent some time on kibble, you can typically do much more variety from the very start. Onyx did great with every protein, even the fattier ones like duck and lamb. When starting so young, there's no having to "get used to" raw... their system is ready!

Transitioning a Puppy from A Processed Food

If your puppy came to you on a processed food, try to feed their first raw meal 4–5 hours from their last kibble meal. Then, stick to the same protein for a couple weeks. Chicken is a great starter protein. If gas and stool are normal, you can start introducing more variety. Puppies tend to be better at handling more variety at the start, as the processed food hasn't had a long time to cause imbalances in their gut or the rest of their body yet. If your puppy was on a very poor diet previously, their body will purge it out very quickly once introduced to raw, so you may see some interesting stool at the beginning.

Treat and Chews

Be sure you are also feeding species-appropriate treats. These are found as freeze-dried or dehydrated and typically single protein or single ingredient, such as freeze-dried rabbit nibs that are only rabbit meat, bone, and organ; or dehydrated beef liver.

It is also beneficial to have some appropriate chews around your house. For Onyx, I used large split elk antlers and water buffalo horns. This gives more gnawing opportunities for whenever they should need it with teething. Know your puppy and what will work for them.

Natural Choices for Your Puppy

As mentioned previously, Onyx came to me naturally reared and raw fed. This was continued throughout his puppyhood and will continue throughout his entire life.

With choosing natural options for your puppy, you want to be sure that what you are choosing will have a high success rate. I find that where problems occur is when pet owners read something on the internet and simply throw whatever is suggested at their dog to try and get their desired result. This can be compared to having a nail sticking out of a board and trying to get it in by throwing a large rock at it in the dark. It may work, it may not, but it certainly will not be specific to the problem. I highly recommend working with a reputable professional, whether that be a holistic veterinarian or animal naturopath.

If needed, there are also many very effective treatment options to look into, such as animal chiropractic, veterinary acupuncture, canine massage, animal reiki, canine physical therapy, homeopathy, micro-biome transplant therapy, herbs, therapeutic laser, swimming, underwater treadmill, and more.

Concluding Thoughts

I can't believe how fast the first year with Onyx flew by. He is in such great health that he serves as a micro-biome fecal transplant donor. He fit 100% of the strict criteria and lab testing. His micro-biome is transplanted by a local veterinarian into unhealthy dogs to restore health. We are currently still training him into becoming a well-mannered boy, and soon we plan to figure out what activities he'll enjoy. I am very happy with every choice I made for him, and he is loved more than he'll ever know. I plan to continue to use him as a role model for health and wellness in dogs.

Remember, you are always going to be your pet's best advocate. What is right for me may not be something you are comfortable with. Health is not black and white, and you will have to decide what is right for your individual puppy. Take time to make educated choices for them.

Onyx. Photo credit Dr. Erin O'Connor

Chapter 10: Overcoming Common Raw Diet Fears and Problems

While raw diets are picking up steam, there are still lots of people who are resistant to feeding raw, mostly for one simple reason: fear. I can relate: for me, the anxiety was strongest the first time I gave my dogs bones. There are a few common fears that can crop up, but at their heart, all of them are based on either misinformation or a lack of knowledge. If you have some anxieties about switching your dog to a raw diet, read on! This chapter discusses some of the most common concerns about the raw diet and should ease your mind about them.

Feeding bones

One of the most common fears people who are new to the idea of feeding a raw, species-appropriate diet to their pets have is a fear of feeding bones (that was definitely me, the first few times I fed bone). I can't tell you how many times people have asked me if (or told me) feeding bones is dangerous, and I've heard from many other raw feeding proponents and guides that they get the same question. In fact, other than a fear of bacteria, the fear of feeding bones seems to be the most prevalent concern people have about the diet—even more than the fears the diet might not be balanced or could make their dog aggressive.

If you're concerned about feeding bones to your dog, you're not alone. The good news, though, is there are things you can do to make it much safer for your dog—which is a carnivore and adapted to eat raw bones—to eat and digest bones. In fact, when you follow a few simple guidelines, you significantly reduce the risk associated with feeding bones to your pet.

It's important, for optimum vitality, to feed raw meaty bones to your dog. Dogs evolved to eat prey animals (which of course includes that prey's muscle meat, bones, organs, and glands), and they need the calcium, phosphorous, and other minerals they contain. Whole bones also act as toothbrushes and floss for them, helping to keep their teeth and gums clean and healthy. Bones are a vital part of a balanced diet, and chewing and crunching on raw bones also helps exercise the jaw muscles (as well as tapping into a primal joy that's evident on a dog's face when they're eating bones).

You can see feeding bones is very important to your dog's overall well-being. So how to go about safely feeding them?

Rule #1: only feed your dog raw bones. The first, and perhaps most important point to remember, is dogs should **only** be fed raw bones, never cooked ones. Cooked bones become very brittle and can easily splinter, perforating their stomach linings or causing other damage to their digestive tracts, causing blockages, and so on. Raw bones, however, are pliable and soft, and much less likely to splinter.

Rule #2: Avoid feeding the weight-bearing bones (i.e. leg bones) of large ruminants, such as sheep or cows. This is because these bones are incredibly dense, and dogs, especially those that are enthusiastic chewers, can crack a tooth on the bones. Bones from birds and rodents are perfect to feed, and I also regularly fed beef and sheep ribs with great success to my dogs.

Rule #3: Feed the right size bone to your pet. For dogs, this means offering pieces that are bigger than their mouths until you know how they'll handle the bone. Any smaller, and your dog may try to just swallow the bone whole, especially if they're novice bone chewers.

Rule #4: Offer bones that have meat attached to them. When you offer raw meaty bones (which is exactly what our dogs evolved to eat), you give your pet a chance to eat a balanced, species-appropriate meal, while at the same time increasing the safety margin of that meal. When meat is still attached to the bone, your dog must work to rip, shred, and tear the meat off the bone, and this slows them down from just trying to swallow the bone in one gulp. It's especially important to do this with novice raw eaters, as they may not yet know how to eat bone properly. Feeding this way gives them a great chance to learn what to do, while still providing mental stimulation and all the other benefits that go along with eating the diet they were designed for. Plus, to our carnivore friends, raw meaty bones are pretty tasty, and who doesn't want to enjoy a meal that appeals to them in every way?

Rule #5: Monitor your pet at all times when they're eating, especially eating bones. Even for experienced chewers, it's important to keep an eye on your pet when they're eating (and by the way, this goes for everything, not just bones—monitor them when they're eating meat, organs, even kibble and canned food). If your pet chokes or has some other kind of problem, you want to be able to help them immediately. I will say that, particularly if you have a dog you're transitioning from kibble or canned food over to a raw, fresh, balanced species-appropriate diet, you may see a little bit of blood in their mouths or on their food for a few days at the beginning of the transition. Because the bones act as floss and a good toothbrush, if they have a build-up of tartar and plaque (and most animals on a processed-food diet do), there will be a very small amount of blood until their gums are tougher and healthier and the tartar and plaque are reduced (generally only a few days). It's nothing to be concerned about, just as you wouldn't be concerned if you started flossing your teeth after a long period without flossing and saw a small amount of blood. However, if you see a large amount of blood, you need to investigate and help your pet immediately.

Rule #6: Separate and monitor your pets when feeding bones (or anything else, for that matter). If you have a multi-pet household, make sure you keep your pets separate when feeding them. This prevents squabbles from arising because somebody got too close to somebody else, and it also prevents one pet from swallowing a bone or other food before they've had a chance to properly cut, tear, or crunch it to the right size, just to prevent someone else from taking it. Everyone should be allowed to eat in peace, and you will need to monitor them to make sure they get this opportunity.

Rule #7: Keep in mind that bone marrow is fatty and a higher-caloric food, and can cause diarrhea until your dog is used to it. You can certainly feed your dog a bone with marrow, but if your dog is overweight or not used to marrow, you may want to limit it or forego it altogether.

Rule #8: Feed bones in a place that's easy to clean. Because raw bones can make a big mess (trust me on this one!), it's a good idea to feed them outside, in a crate, or on a towel or mat. We feed our dogs outside, which makes clean-up a lot easier.

Bacteria

Sometimes, people worry raw diets carry a high risk of salmonella and e. coli infection (or possibly some other bacteria). Bacteria such as salmonella and e. coli are naturally present in both us and our carnivore pets. The issue only arises when there is an imbalance and the salmonella or e. coli numbers get out of control, which creates an imbalance in animals or humans with weak immune systems. While raw meat and bones do contain these bacteria, kibble—and the meat you may prepare for your own meal—also do. Normal precautions, such as washing your hands thoroughly after preparing your dog's meal and cleaning anything that came into contact with the meat, will ensure these bacteria don't become an issue.

Disease

Another fear I've heard expressed is a raw diet will cause pancreatitis (or some other disease, such as kidney disease). However, dogs are hardwired to eat raw meaty bones, and switching to a raw diet does not cause these diseases. Healthy animals will not present with disease when switched to a raw diet. If a dog does exhibit disease symptoms when switched to a raw diet, it means disease was already present in the body and presented as pancreatitis or kidney disease (or whatever disease it is) when the body began going through detox and throwing off the toxins. If this happens, it's important to stay with the diet to start giving the body the nutrients it needs to heal itself. If necessary, other modalities may be used to lend the body additional support, but as mentioned before, proper nutrition is at the heart of health. If your dog does present with a disease, whether they're on raw or not, consult a holistic veterinarian or a certified animal naturopath.

Aggression

Some people have told me they think their dog may become vicious and aggressive eating a raw diet. They seem to think their pet will develop a taste for blood and turn into a dangerous killer. However, raw-fed dogs are generally much calmer than their kibble-fed counterparts. This is because they're getting the nutrients they need (and none of what they don't need, including high amounts of carbohydrates, which can cause the equivalent of a sugar rush), they're burning energy eating their food (they have to work at getting the meat off the bone and crunching through the bone), and the very act of eating taps into something primal and satisfying for them. There are plenty of reports of raw-fed dogs peacefully co-existing with other animals, even animals of the same species they're eating.

Expense/Inconvenience

Some people are initially reluctant to start their pets on a raw diet because they worry it may be too expensive or because they think it may be inconvenient. However, most people find, after some practice and experimentation, feeding a raw diet is just as easy as feeding kibble. There are lots of resources available for finding a good source of quality meat at reasonable prices (check out our chapter about feeding raw on a budget for some tips). And because your pet won't have many of the health issues that a kibble-fed animal will, you save money in the long run on vet bills, teeth cleaning, and even things like anal gland expression. Remember that health is not about convenience, it's about providing the body with the support it needs to keep itself in optimal health. It's much more convenient to feed a raw diet than to constantly take your pet to the vet to deal with the issues feeding a processed diet causes. And ultimately, because raw meat, bones, and organs are essential for carnivores such as your dog, feeding a raw diet will allow your pet to live longer and have a much better quality of life while it's here.

Diarrhea and constipation

Diarrhea and constipation can both occur when you switch to a raw diet. Diarrhea often comes during the detox phase, but it also occurs if a dog isn't getting enough bone or is getting too many rich organs before his or her system has adapted to handle them. Constipation can occur in the detox phase or if our pets are fed too much bone. In the case of constipation, decrease the amount of bone you are feeding. In the case of diarrhea, increase the amount of bone. If one of these problems presents when you're transitioning from kibble or canned to raw, slow down the speed of the transition. (Also note we have more information about how to handle diarrhea in Chapter 21, "Dealing with Diseases Naturally".) Remember, one of the tenets of a successful raw diet is balance over time, which means you can feed a bit less bone for a few days and then increase the bone percentage if needed when your pet's stool has returned to normal. Similarly, the idea of balance over time can help when transitioning a dog to rich organ meat or a new protein source. Until your dog has gotten established on a raw diet, introduce new proteins and organs slowly. And if your pet is transitioning from a processed diet, again, go slowly (for example, feeding only chicken for the first couple weeks) to allow their body time to start shedding out the toxins present because of feeding kibble. Give them a chance to detox and move through the healing response before introducing new and richer protein sources. Once the raw diet is established, though, you will find you can introduce variety more quickly. And remember the adage "Know thy dog." Watch their stools, watch their demeanor, and watch how they react to various proteins and sizes of meals. While you may still see occasional tummy upsets, you'll be able to adjust what you're feeding to assist your dog through those upsets while still achieving balance over time.

Bone shards in your dog's stool

If your dog is coming off a processed-food diet (kibble or canned), there's a high likelihood they're low in digestive enzymes. It takes time to build the enzyme levels back up, just like it takes time to get their stomach pH back to where it should be. Until everything is back to normal (which can take anywhere from 10 days to a few months), you may notice bone fragments in your dog's stool if you feed whole bone. As long as everything else looks normal (no blood, dog isn't in discomfort, and so on), this is no cause for concern. Once your dog's stomach pH is correct and they have a healthy amount of digestive enzymes, they'll be able to fully break down those bones and you won't notice them anymore. If you're really concerned about it, you can start out with ground bone (for example, in a commercial raw or a commercial grind) while your dog's system realigns, but in most cases, a bone shard here or there is really nothing to worry about.

Alf's Story

I worked with Alf, an adorable American Staffordshire Terrier, and his owner to get Alf transitioned over to a raw diet after his owner lost her previous dog to cancer. While he didn't have any major health issues, she wanted to move him to a raw diet to keep him healthy. She had known about raw for a long time, but she told me she'd resisted transitioning because she felt like it would be an enormous amount of work to sustain; she also thought the learning curve would be prohibitively steep.

I started working with her and Alf when he was about 4 years old. Soon after she switched him, I asked her what changes she noticed. She said the first thing she noticed was his coat had never looked brighter or felt softer. She also pointed out he seemed relaxed and wasn't on edge about everything anymore (when he was eating kibble, he had major problems with anxiety and reactivity).

She chose to feed a prey model/whole prey raw diet rather than commercial raw, and I remember she was very pleasantly surprised to see how many local farmers were around her (she lives in Indiana). She quickly found affordable sources of raw for Alf, and subsequently went on to help her parents and one of her friends switch their dogs to raw.

She told me Alf's favorite meal is chicken, but she mixes and matches proteins and organs depending on what's available that week from her suppliers. She feeds him once daily (she had been feeding twice per day on kibble) and fasts him 2x/week.

Now, lest I make it seem like everything was peaches and cream from start to finish of the transition process, she did face some challenges. The detox phase was tough, because he had lots of diarrhea. She did point out, though, that the detox-phase diarrhea was a lot different than the diarrhea he got from eating processed treats or eating kibble. He still had lots of energy and was never listless or lethargic. She also said (I love this!) that it was a learning experience that really enabled her to tune in to what Alf's body was telling her. She learned pretty quickly how much bone vs. meat to feed, when to lay off on one over the other, when to give organs, and when to fast. The most important lesson she learned was to be patient with Alf (and herself!) and not rush into everything all at once. She went from being totally overwhelmed the first time she walked into a butcher shop to learning what worked for her and her cutie.

Her favorite part about the raw diet is seeing Alf thrive. She told me several times that watching him eat what he loves and feel great afterwards is incredibly rewarding. Alf is no longer plagued with hot spots and dry patches, and he no longer shows anxiety and aggression.

Alf loves hiking, especially off-leash, but before switching to raw, he had problems with aggression towards other dogs and couldn't be allowed off-leash. She told me since switching him to raw, they have a closer bond than ever. She is a professional dog trainer, but she did say that even though she worked hard to overcome Alf's anxiety and aggression towards other dogs, the raw diet was the missing link to allow him to do that.

I asked her what her #1 piece of advice would be for someone thinking about switching their dog to a raw diet. You know what she said? "Do it! This is the best thing I've ever done for my dog! He's more alive than I've ever seen him. He plays harder and faster, sleeps more soundly, and wakes up full of life. His coat is beautiful, and his eyes are bright. This was life-changing for me and obviously for my dog. He is thriving and happy and that's all I can ask for."

Chapter 11: Feeding Raw on a Budget

By this point, hopefully you're ready to dive into feeding raw (or maybe you've already started!). But perhaps you're still reluctant; maybe something is stopping you. Something that, if we're honest, most of us have struggled with at some point in our raw feeding journey. And that something, my friends, is the cost of feeding raw.

While the number of raw feeders is (thankfully) on the rise, there are still lots of people—most pet parents, actually—that don't yet feed raw. And often, it's because they just aren't sure if they can afford it. And I get it. I really do. Raw feeding can be an expensive way to go. But, here's the good news: there are ways to feed raw without going broke. And in this chapter, I'm going to talk about a few of them.

Before we dive in, a caveat: most of the methods I'm going to share may take some work, at least initially. You'll have to do a bit of digging. The good news is once you have some sources lined up, you won't have to do any more work than you would if you were using more expensive sources. So, grab a cup of coffee (or a glass of wine!), settle into your favorite chair, and let's figure out how to make raw affordable for you.

Affordable Raw Way #1: Co-ops

One of the most recommended (but unfortunately, not always practical) ways to feed raw affordably is by finding a local raw feeding co-op. Because co-ops can buy large quantities of food at one time, they can get volume discounts. This results in significant savings for you.

Pros:

- Co-ops are crazy affordable. Case in point: my local co-op offers beef for less than $3/pound, lamb for about $3.25/pound (sometimes less!), and chicken for about $0.80/pound. Like I said: crazy affordable.

- They offer variety. For example, my local co-op offers beef, chicken, duck, pork, turkey, fish, lamb, rabbit, Cornish game hen, and more. They also offer various organs, along with supplements.
- Because they're local, you don't have to pay for shipping (which is one of the things that can make raw food so expensive).

Cons:

- Co-ops don't exist everywhere. If you don't have one close to you, you won't be able to take advantage. And finding them can be tough. I recommend googling "raw feeding co-ops <your city, state>" and seeing what comes up.
- Often, they have limited ordering timeframes and pickup days each month (remember, they rely on being able to place large orders to get volume discounts, so they need everyone to order at the same time to take advantage of this). If you run low on food, or if you're not available on the pickup days, it can be hard to order and/or pickup when it's convenient.
- Depending on the co-op's suppliers, the meat may not be pasture-raised/hormone-free/antibiotic-free.

Bottom line: if you have a co-op within driving distance, it's worth checking them out. You may save a ton of money while still getting the variety and quality your dog deserves.

Affordable Raw Way #2: Hunters

If you know a hunter, you might be able to get wild-caught game. If you don't know a hunter, don't let that stop you: I've known people who've had a lot of success putting up Craigslist ads before hunting season asking for frozen meat. More people than you might realize have to clear out their freezers to make room for whatever their latest catch is, and let's be honest...dogs don't mind freezer-burned meat. If you aren't comfortable placing a Craigslist ad, you might be able to find some hunters by contacting a local hunting club (one club to check is the North American Versatile Hunting Dog Association, at http://www.navhda.us/chapterinfo.aspx).

Pros:

- Wild-caught game is free from antibiotics, hormones, or other toxins, and it grew up in ideal natural conditions. Wild-caught game is free of any weird antibiotics, hormones, or other toxins, and it grew up in ideal natural conditions.
- You can vary what you feed based on what's open for hunting at the time, which will increase variety and ensure your dog is getting a good assortment of red meat, white meat, and different nutrient profiles.
- It can be a great way to feed whole prey: if you're comfortable with it, leave the fur or feathers on and let your dog eat those too. It's how wild canids get most of their fiber in the wild (fiber also comes from bone and cartilage), and it's great for your dog too.
- It can be a great way to get meat scraps for free (or very cheap): Ask the hunters to give you whatever they don't want for themselves. This often includes various organs and scrap meat. This is especially true for large animals like elk or deer, which are amazingly nutritious for our dogs.
- If you find a hunting club, you may be able to get birds for free. Often hunting clubs throw the birds away after they've shot them; you may be able to take them for free and feed them to your dog. Added benefit: the bird's life doesn't go to waste.

Cons:

- You may have to do some digging to find a hunter/hunting club. It can take some time, but I think it's worth it in the long run.
- If it hasn't already been done, you'll need to remove the shot or bullet from the animal before you feed it.
- Because you don't always know how much meat you'll get from a hunter, or when, you may have to use this to supplement your other meat suppliers. Unless you or someone you know hunts consistently, chances are hunting won't be the primary way you get meat for your dog.

Bottom line: Hunters and wild-caught game are a great option if you can find them. Not only is the meat affordable, but it's often some of the healthiest and best food you can give your dog.

Affordable Raw Way #3: Meat Processors

Companies that process whole animals usually have to pay to get rid of the unwanted parts, like meat scraps, bones, fat, and organs. While it may seem kind of gross, in reality it can be a great way to get meat for pretty cheap.

Pros:

- Often you can pick up the meat and other parts they don't want for free (or a nominal fee)
- As you develop a relationship with the company, they may be willing to separate out certain items for you for a small fee.
- Because these companies generally process more than one kind of animal, you might be able to get a lot of variety from them.

Cons:

- You'll have to do a Google search to find companies that process meat locally to you. And once you find some, you'll have to call around to see if they're willing to let you take the unwanted meat.
- They usually store their meat scraps, etc. in barrels or large bins. You'll have to go down there and dig out what you want, which can be a time investment (and can be messy as well).
- You'll need to check with them to make sure their meat is antibiotic- and hormone-free.

Bottom line: Meat processors may take some work, but they're a great way to find affordable meat if you're willing to do what it takes.

Affordable Raw Way #4: Farmers

I had no idea there were so many farmers and ranchers within driving distance of me (I live in the suburbs of Southern California), but thankfully, there are. And chances are there may be some by you too! And if so, they may become one of your greatest resources in your quest to feed raw affordably.

Pros:

- Many small local farmers raise meat for their own table, and they don't pump the animals they raise full of antibiotics and hormones.

- They're often willing to let you take stillborns, animals that had to be dispatched due to injury, and unwanted parts from animals they butchered for free. After all, it saves them having to pay to have the animal or the parts hauled away. And, because they know their stock so intimately, they can tell you exactly how and why the animal died, so you can decide if you're comfortable taking it or not.

Cons:

- Like all the other options listed here, you'll have to do some legwork to find farmers. A good place to start is your local farmer's market: if people are selling eggs, ask them what they do with the old hens. If people are selling goat's milk, ask them what they do with stillborn babies or culled goats. And so on.
- You have to do a bit of sleuthing to make sure they don't give their animals antibiotics or hormones.

Bottom line: While it may take some work, farmers are—in my opinion—one of the best places to find raw meat at reasonable prices. And what's even better is that often when you meet one farmer, they may introduce you to other farmers. The network can grow organically and quickly... which means inexpensive (or maybe even free!) quality raw food for your four-legged friend!

Affordable Raw Way #5: Ethnic grocery stores

I've heard from lots of raw feeders that they turn to ethnic grocery stores to find affordable meat. We buy sardines for our dogs at our local Asian market, and there are tons of other meats there that are inexpensive as well.

Pros:

- Ethnic grocery stores often carry a wide variety of meat (both various types and various cuts).
- They are generally much cheaper than larger, more mainstream grocery stores.

Cons:

- You need to pay attention to the meat you buy and make sure it doesn't contain hormones or antibiotics. You will also need to make sure the meat isn't enhanced (high in sodium), marinated, or otherwise processed.

Affordable Raw Way #6: Local butchers

Speaking from personal experience, you may find some butchers are more than happy to work with you in getting inexpensive meat for your dog. I've had some really positive experiences, and while it can take some legwork to find someone who's willing to work with you, it's worth it. My best advice when trying to find a local butcher you can work with? Appreciate the ones who help you, and let the other ones roll off your back.

Pros:

- Lots of times, you can get meat at a substantial discount from your local butcher if it's close to expiration or if it was a custom order that didn't get picked up (or they made a mistake in the meat cutting). These are things that might stop people from buying the meat for themselves, but don't make any difference to a dog.
- Often you can talk with them and get on a "list" (or just have them keep you in mind) to be notified when they have excess, close-to-expired, or mistakes that you can get at a reduced price.
- They often have ground and whole options, and they may have everything from beef to chicken to turkey and more.

Cons:

- You've probably guessed it by now: it can take some research and digging to find local butchers willing to offer you meat at a discount.
- You'll need to check and make sure the meat is hormone- and antibiotic-free.

Here's the bottom line: If you take a bit of time to implement some (or all!) of these suggestions, you'll find that feeding raw is financially doable. Doing it yourself is usually significantly less expensive than feeding a commercial raw. Take your time, do some research, and then sit back and enjoy the ride. After all, you're feeding your dog in a way that helps them live their optimal lives, and you're doing it affordably. And my guess is that'll keep you, your dogs, and your bank account thriving.

Chapter 12: How to Find Meat Suppliers

One of the most common questions I hear from people who are starting to feed their dogs raw is, "What's the best place to get the food from?" Lucky for you, there are lots of options, so no matter where you live, you should be able to find some feasible places. (Note that for this section, I'm talking about how to find suppliers for prey model and whole prey meals. There are also lots of commercial raw companies: to figure out how to find good commercial raw manufacturers, check out the section "Feeding a commercial raw diet" in Chapter 6, "How to Start Your Dog on a Raw Diet". You can also see recommendations for some commercial raw companies in Appendix A.) Now, if you just read the chapter about feeding raw on a budget, some of this will sound familiar. I'm including both chapters because I want you to have a solid plan for how to feed raw affordably, and I also want you to consider some sources you might not otherwise have.

Wild-caught game

If you know anyone who hunts, you may be able to get wild-caught game. This is far and away the best option, because wild game is the closest thing possible to what your dog is designed to eat. You can vary the meal plan based on what is open for hunting at the time; in other words, feed elk or deer during their hunting season, feed quail more during quail season, feed duck or pheasant when that's an option, feed wild-caught rabbit when possible; and so on. Do make sure, of course, that you don't feed the shot or bullet—this must be removed before you can feed the game. When you are feeding wild-caught game, leave the fur or feathers on if you can, and feed the entire animal (head, feet, etc.). This is a supremely balanced meal. If the animal is larger than your dog's daily allotment, you can feed a bit less the next day. Also, watch your dog's body condition and adjust how much you feed according to his needs (he may need more at certain times of the year because of activity level, for example).

Additionally, if you know anyone that hunts elk or deer, ask them to give you any of the parts they don't want for themselves. This is a great way to get organ meat and so on. Your dog can eat almost any bone, except for weight-bearing (leg) bones of larger animals such as sheep, goats, cattle, deer, or elk. Avoid these, as your dog may crack a tooth if they're a particularly enthusiastic chewer—those bones are dense!

If you have any local hunting clubs that run field trials or hunt tests for dogs, check with them about taking the birds they've hunted after they're done. Often, they just throw the birds away, and they're happy to give them to someone for free (or for a very nominal fee). You just need to contact the head of the local hunting chapter. One club to check is the North American Versatile Hunting Dog Association (http://www.navhda.us/chapterinfo.aspx).

Getting meat delivered from a supplier

There are reputable companies that will ship food for your dog right to you. All of them have great products:

Greentripe.com (source for ground raw green tripe, beef gullets, whole beef trachea). Find them at www.greentripe.com.

Rabbits4U (source for whole prey and processed rabbits, as well as sheep (boneless and bone-in), beef (boneless and bone-in), whole prey and processed chickens, various organs, and other proteins as available). Find them at www.rabbits4u.com.

My Pet Carnivore (source for whole prey and processed proteins). They have a wide variety of proteins and are a great option. Find them at www.mypetcarnivore.com.

Hare Today, Gone Tomorrow (source for whole prey and processed proteins, including whole prey quail, chickens, rabbits, guinea pigs, and fish). Find them at www.hare-today.com.

Layne Labs (source for various sizes of quail, rabbits, and other proteins). Find them at www.laynelabs.com.

Raw Feeding Miami (source for whole prey and processed proteins). They have a wide variety of proteins you can order. Find them at www.rawfeed-ingmiami.com

Simply Rawesome (almost like a co-op, but they ship. Great source of all sorts of proteins. You do need to pay attention to the ordering dates, however.) Find them at www.simplyrawesomeus.com

Local resources

Farmer's markets: These can be a great resource for eggs. If you're feeding whole prey, you may also be able to find farmers willing to sell the chickens that are no longer laying (I've gotten them as cheap as $1/bird). Just make sure they're not giving their birds any antibiotics or hormones.

Local butchers: Some butchers may grind up leftover meat and organs for pet food, or they might have whole bones (remember, your dog should not be given leg bones of larger animals), organs, and chicken and turkey backs/frames. If the meat is close to expiration, it may be available at a substantial discount. Additionally, custom meat orders that don't get picked up by the customer and meat-cutting mistakes may also give you the opportunity to purchase good meat at a reasonable price. It's worth talking with them and seeing if you can get on a "list" or have them keep you in mind when they have excess, close-to-expired, or mistakes that you can get at a reduced price. Make sure the meat is antibiotic- and hormone-free, and preferably organic/pasture-raised/grass-fed.

Raw food co-ops: If you have a raw food co-op near you, check with them about how to participate in ordering food for your dogs. Because raw dog food co-ops order large quantities at a time, they can generally get their meat wholesale, thereby reducing costs significantly. To find co-ops, google "raw dog food co-ops <*Your city*>".

Farmers: They may have animals available at reduced prices, including culled animals, injured animals that they had to dispatch, or stillborns. If you go this route, make sure to ask them if they have given any medications to the animal recently, and make sure the animal didn't die of illness.

Peanut's Story

Unlike Alf, whom we met earlier, Peanut (a Dachshund mix) is on a commercial raw diet, and has been for several years. His owner decided to switch him to raw when he was 3 ½ years old. She had been feeding him kibble for about 3 years, but learned about raw from the pet store she takes Peanut to. After switching him to a raw diet, she said she noticed his coat became very shiny and soft. She also noticed how clean his teeth became.

She told me one of her favorite parts of the switch to raw is Peanut poops less than he did when he was on kibble (I'm telling you: raw feeders love the change the new diet makes to their dog's stool!), and overall, he's in great health. She told me that's in stark contrast to when he was eating kibble—those days, little Peanut was super gassy and had very little energy, even though he wasn't very old. Now that he's on raw and has tons of energy, she takes him to the dog park regularly, where he runs around with his buddies and plays fetch with her.

Peanut's owner says the pet store she goes to offers three different brands of raw food. She tried them all before settling on a brand Peanut loves. They have lots of proteins, and she gives them all to him—from turkey, to beef, to bison, chicken, and fish. She feeds little Peanut twice per day: once in the morning and once at night.

She said she ultimately decided to make the switch to raw after learning about the natural ingredients in the food. While she did say the price of raw cuts into her financial situation, because she sees an improvement in her dog's health, she pays the extra amount. And, she finds raw very convenient, saying she loves how easy it is to defrost the food and serve it to Peanut. Because of that convenience, she said she'll probably stay on a commercial raw diet forever instead of doing prey model or whole prey. And that's perfectly fine: she's happy and Peanut is thriving!

Like so many people who've made the switch, she says she highly recommends feeding a raw diet. As she told me, now that she's moved Peanut to a raw diet, she'll never go back to dry kibble again!

Chapter 13: Feeding Your Dog Raw Even if You're a Vegetarian

Those of you who read my last book, *Let Food Be Their Medicine: Using Nature's Principles to Help Your Dog Thrive*, already know what I'm about to say. But for my new friends, I think it's time I make a confession: I'm a vegetarian. I don't eat cheese or most dairy products either, although the occasional butter sneaks in, and I do enjoy eggs (one of my friends has chickens, and those beautiful ladies lay the most delicious eggs I've ever had). So why am I mentioning this now? What place does this have in a book about caring for dogs? I mention it because more and more frequently, I'm hearing vegetarians and vegans say they don't want to feed their pet raw meat and bones because they themselves are vegetarian/vegan, and I hear those who aren't vegetarian/vegan disparaging those who are for that attitude. It seems to be widespread on both sides, and I thought it was important, as a vegetarian, to share some information about raw diets and why it's important to feed your carnivore pets a raw diet, no matter how you decide to nourish yourself. For simplicity's sake, I'm just going to use the term vegetarian here, but please understand I'm referring to vegans as well.

Many of us vegetarians make the choice to be so for health reasons or because we're concerned about animal welfare and the environment (or perhaps a combination of the two). I made the decision to be vegetarian years ago, and I did it for both reasons I just mentioned. I'm an omnivore; physiologically, I can take in both plant and animal matter for nourishment. However, my dogs are carnivores. They can only thrive on a diet appropriate for carnivores, which boils down to meat, bones, and organs/glands.

As a vegetarian, I'm concerned with animal welfare. Of course, this includes animals like cows, sheep, chickens, and turkeys (all animals that at one point in my life I ate), but it also includes the welfare of companion animals like my dogs. This is an important point to remember—the welfare of our own pets is as important (not more important, perhaps, but certainly not less) as the welfare of other animals in the world. Loving our pets as we do, it's important to take care of them and give them what they need to thrive and flourish. And one of the fundamental ways to do this is by making sure they have the proper nutrition—in other words, feeding them a raw diet. Nutrition is the cornerstone of health, because it gives the body the support it needs to achieve harmony and balance, which leads to and maintains good health.

I recently saw something that said the life expectancy of Golden Retrievers is half of what it was in the 1970s[51]. I don't know if this is accurate, but what I do know is that all dogs (not just Golden Retrievers) are presenting with instances of diabetes, cancer, and other serious issues at younger and younger ages. When I talk with people these days, they tell me their pets are passing away at 8, 9, and 10 years old. This is due in large part to the processed food diets we feed them, because those diets don't give our pets what they need to maintain true health. Considering this, I think it's imperative, as the custodian of my pets' health, to feed them what they're designed to eat so they stay strong, fit, and healthy.

So how do I reconcile my dogs' welfare with the welfare of the animals they're eating? For me, it boils down to being mindful of the suppliers I use. I look to make sure they're treating the animals humanely and giving them access to plenty of fresh air, sunshine, and species-appropriate food. I look for meat that's pasture- or grass-fed and doesn't have added antibiotics or hormones. Some suppliers I have seen include information about how they treat their animals. For example, Layne Labs, which sells quail, rabbits, rats, and mice, includes an "Animal Bill of Rights", which states:

All Animals Born in Our Facility Have Certain Inalienable Rights. These Include:

- A Stress-Free Living Environment
- A Constant Flow of Fresh Air
- Clean Drinking Water
- Fresh Food, Available at All Times
- Clean, Dry Bedding
- Peace and Quiet
- Natural Day and Night Light Cycles
- To Be Treated Humanely, With Compassion and Respect

I also look for information on how the animal is dispatched. It is important to me this is done in a humane manner. By making sure I support the farms, ranches, and suppliers that raise their animals humanely and compassionately, I am helping to make sure those are the farms and suppliers that will thrive. I believe one of the best ways to show support (or lack thereof) in our society is through where we spend our money, and each time I buy from these businesses rather than a big factory farm, I further the ability of those farms to keep raising animals in a sustainable and compassionate way.

One thing to keep in mind, if you're a vegetarian struggling with feeding your dog a raw diet instead of kibble, is that just because kibble looks like a dried nugget that's meat-free doesn't mean it is meat-free. It does contain meat, but that meat (protein) has been denatured by the cooking process. This means your dog can't utilize the protein effectively to thrive. Also, much of the meat that is used is not raised with any concern for the meat animal's welfare, and frequently the animals the meat comes from have been treated with hormones and antibiotics (and after slaughter, the meat has been enhanced with sodium and other things), which are then passed on to your pet. If you're looking to feed your pet a vegetarian diet, you are not achieving that by feeding kibble or other processed food.

Most of the vegetarians I know respect and honor other species. I think, as I said earlier, it's just as important to honor the carnivores that share our lives as it is to honor the herbivores they've evolved to consume. Honoring and loving them means honoring and loving the essence of who they are. This includes feeding them according to the needs of their species. To do otherwise is to disregard the essence of our pets and instead try to turn them into little versions of us.

In truly understanding our pets, perhaps the most important thing is to understand they're different than us. They share their lives with us, and the love and joy we get from them and they get from us cannot be questioned. However, they are not humans. We tend to think of them as little people. My animals sleep in bed with us, share adventures with us, make us laugh, and provide us with comfort when we're going through a rough time. I know there's a movement to refer to people who have pets as "pet parents" instead of "pet owners" (heck, I regularly refer to myself as a pet parent). I think, considering how integral they are to our lives, and how close they are to our hearts, it's perfectly normal to think of our pets as little people. But they aren't: They are dogs. By keeping that in mind, we can more easily remember they have needs that are different than ours, and treating them as little people, especially in how we feed them, doesn't do them any favors. They are family, but of the four-legged kind. And we should feed them as such.

Finally, I know some vegetarians are uncomfortable handling raw meat. Because I chop meat up almost every day for my dogs, I don't have any issue with it. However, at the beginning, it did take a little getting used to. I would suggest using gloves and an apron if you don't want to touch the meat (just make sure the gloves don't have any chemicals on them). I have a separate cutting board devoted to meat for the animals. And I make sure after each feeding to thoroughly clean the cutting board, cleaver, poultry shears, countertops, and bowls, so no meat or blood smell lingers and so everything is clean when I prepare my food.

It is my sincere hope you'll stop and think about how you feed your dog, whether you're a vegetarian or not. If you're struggling with feeding your pet a raw diet because you're a vegetarian, think about why you became a vegetarian in the first place. If it was for health reasons, remember feeding your dog a raw diet is critical to maintaining their health. If it was for animal and environmental welfare, keep in mind your dog's welfare is just as important as the welfare of other animals, and feed them what they need to thrive. Do everything you can to find meat suppliers that treat their animals with compassion, dignity, and respect, and you'll be helping to ensure the lives of those animals, as well as the health and well-being of your beloved dog, are the best they can be.

Chapter 14: A Month's Worth of Raw Meals: Weekly Sample Meal Plans

If you feed commercial raw, rotate through the various protein options they have over the course of each month to ensure your dog is getting enough variety. You can also try feeding a few different brands, which can help with the variety as well.

If you're feeding prey model or whole prey, you'll have to figure out your own meal plans. Here is a sample of some meal plan ideas: remember, you're aiming for balance over time rather than balance each day. You can mix and match according to your dog's needs and preferences, but this is a good start to get you going. I include some recipes here too, which you can find in Chapter 15, "Recipes for Meals for Your Dog". Take a look at those for inspiration.

Understanding the sample meal plan

Throughout the meal plan, I make suggestions of types of proteins to feed each day. Remember we want the majority of what your dog eats to be meat, not bones or organs. When it comes to whole prey, you can feed it with the feathers and fur on or off. Feathers and fur provide fiber, but some people are uncomfortable feeding them. I find whole prey is more convenient to feed, so I feed it whenever I can (and it provides a balanced meal in terms of organs, glands, bone, and meat), but you don't have to feed it if you can't/don't want to.

Also, because I don't know how big your dog is, I can't say how much of each thing to feed. Use the 80/10/10 guideline as a base point, and adjust as needed.

Note: When feeding eggs, crack them once into the bowl to eliminate any mess. Feed yolk, whites, and shell.

The sample meal plan

Week 1:

Monday	Tuesday	Wednesday	Thursday	Friday	Saturday	Sunday
Chicken (bone and meat)	"Where's the beef?" (Recipe example 2)	Whole rabbit (organs, fur, head, feet intact)	"Meal on the hoof" (Recipe example 6), non-liver organs	Boneless beef, 1-2 whole eggs	Turkey neck, green tripe, liver	Chicken (bone and meat)

Week 2:

Monday	Tuesday	Wednesday	Thursday	Friday	Saturday	Sunday
Frozen whole sardines, boneless sheep	"Duck, duck… turkey?" (Recipe example 1)	Pork ribs, liver	Whole rabbit (organs, fur, head, feet intact)	Green tripe, ground venison or bison, 2 whole eggs	"Venison, anyone?" (Recipe example 5)	Turkey breast (bone-in)

Week 3:

Monday	Tuesday	Wednesday	Thursday	Friday	Saturday	Sunday
Beef chunks, whole eggs	"Got calcium?" (Recipe example 3)	Sheep ribs, duck head, frozen whole sardines	"Rabbit and green tripe" (Recipe example 4)	Ground chicken	Beef (ground)	Ground venison or bison

Week 4:

Monday	Tuesday	Wednesday	Thursday	Friday	Saturday	Sunday
Beef or pork ribs	Chicken quarter, liver, green tripe	Frozen whole sardines, 2 whole eggs, Sheep ribs	Ground venison or bison	Green tripe, chicken breast	Sheep or goat chunks	Whole prey chicken (feathers, head, feet intact)

Chapter 15: Recipes for Meals for Your Dog

Following are some "recipes" for raw meals you can feed your dog. While they don't all represent "balanced" meals in and of themselves, they're great recipes to include in a meal plan. In fact, we include some of them in the sample monthly meal plan in this book. Depending on what you have access to, your dog's tastes, and what your dog needs, you can adjust these recipes to fit your needs. You can switch out proteins and/or organs, or you can use these as is. Watch your dog's stool, body condition, energy level, and overall vitality as you get used to feeding him or her raw, and adjust what you're doing as necessary. For example, do you notice they're slightly constipated? Decrease the amount of bone you're feeding. Are they having diarrhea? Increase the bone and/or decrease the organs a bit until they've adjusted. And so on…

Before you know it, if you're feeding prey model and/or whole prey, you'll be putting together your own combinations. Have fun, give them lots of variety, and keep that overall weekly balance of 80/10/10 in mind— you'll be just fine!

Note: Since I don't know what size your dog is, I'm not including specific "amounts" in each recipe. Instead, I'll list types of things in the recipe, and you can adjust using your dog's weight and the 80/10/10 ratio.

Recipe example 1: Duck, duck…turkey?:

- Ground boneless turkey
- Duck wings (feathers on or off)
- Duck hearts
- Duck feet
- Duck or turkey liver
- Duck or turkey gizzards

This recipe gives you a good mix of boneless meat (ground turkey, gizzards, and duck hearts), as well as bone (duck wings and feet) and organs (liver). Remember hearts and gizzards are fed as muscle meat, even though technically they're organs.

Recipe example 2: Where's the beef?:

- Boneless beef chunks
- Beef tripe
- Whole eggs

This recipe has very little calcium (which is mostly coming from the eggshells here). However, it's a good example of what you can feed if you've been bone-heavy the past few meals.

Recipe example 3: Got calcium?:

- Sheep or pork ribs

or

- Turkey necks

or

- Chicken or duck frames

and

- Green tripe
- Beef heart
- Beef liver

This recipe is mostly focused on calcium: In other words, upping the percentage of bone your dog gets in a given week. You can use it, or some variation of it, if your dog needs more calcium (which you'll see in their stool).

Recipe example 4: Rabbit and green tripe:

- Rabbit quarters
- Rabbit heart
- Rabbit liver
- Rabbit kidneys
- Green tripe (ground)

You can replace the rabbit in this recipe with another protein source. If you can, go for an "exotic" protein source to give your dog a wider variety of nutrients.

Recipe example 5: Venison, anyone?

- Venison (chunks or grinds)
- Sheep rib (for bone)
- Liver
- Non-liver organs of some sort

When I serve this to my dogs, I usually include some sort of rib because giving them a lot of organ can soften their stool. If you just wanted to feed them venison for one meal, you certainly could do that (and skip the bone and/or organ). Remember, it's balance over time, and we're looking at getting close to 80/10/10 over the course of a week. So, if you feed a meal of just ground or chunked venison (or beef, or turkey, or rabbit, or chicken, or any other protein source), consider feeding a good dose of bones in the next meal: maybe "Got calcium?" or some variation thereof.

Recipe example 6: Meal on the hoof

- Goat, sheep, bison, or beef (chunks or grinds)
- If above is boneless, include some bone: ribs are a great choice (even our 16-pound-dog, Motley, can eat sheep ribs), but if your dog is too small to eat ribs, go with a poultry back, a duck or turkey neck, or a chicken wing or two

Whole prey:

If you're looking for a supremely balanced meal, as close as possible to how our dogs were designed to eat, you can feed whole prey. No preparation (other than defrosting) is necessary: You just put the whole animal (fur, feathers, organs, and all) down for your dog. If he's new to whole prey, you might have to cut it open the first time so he realizes it's food. Otherwise, just thaw and serve!

Some great options are quail, rabbit, chicken, duck, sardines, mackerel, and even goose. I've also known people to feed muskrat, beaver, pigeon, squirrel, and Cornish game hen.

Bone broth (supplement)

Some people swear by bone broth. It can be an incredible source of additional nutrients and calcium. If you want to make your own, here's a recipe I've used in the past (note that poultry bones are best, but you can also use ribs from hoofed animals as well):

1. Put bones in a Crock pot (or other slow cooker) and cover with water.
2. Add a generous pour of apple cider vinegar.
3. Bring to a boil, then set your Crock pot's temperature at simmer for as long as possible. Keep an eye on it: if the water drops below the top of the bones, add more.
4. Simmer for about 36 hours (you may need to restart your Crock pot timer at least once, and maybe twice, to get to 36 hours).
5. Once the concoction has simmered for about 36 hours, put all the now-soft bone chunks and "floaters" into a blender (a high-powered blender like a Vitamix or a Blendtec is best) and blend on high until it's a smooth, paste-like consistency. Put the remainder of the broth from the Crock pot into a container and refrigerate.
6. Put the paste into containers. Freeze all but one of the containers (refrigerate the remaining one).
7. Add the paste to your dog's meals as needed. At first, only add a small amount, and only increase as you see how your dog handles it. If the paste is too thick, stir in some of the bone broth you retained.

Chapter 16: Vitamins, Minerals, and Where to Find Them

After a long day at work, you finally get home, finally walk through the door. Deep brown eyes look up at you. A tail wags frantically, happily. A doggy mouth smiles a greeting at you. And you feel the weight of the world lift, just a little bit. Bending down, you caress her velvety-soft ears, give her a quick kiss on her nose. She whines, just a little, and lifts her foot in that adorable way she has. You smile, and putting your stuff down, you move towards the refrigerator, where her food is ready and waiting.

You pull out her dinner: tonight, beef is on the menu, and she thumps her tail in recognition and excitement. Putting the meat in her food dish, you take the bowl outside. She's spinning around, dashing forward and then back to you, eyes twinkling all the while. She's overjoyed...you're home, her food is here, and all is well with the world again! You put the bowl down, and she immediately sets herself to the business of eating.

Settling down to watch her eat, you wonder whether she's getting all the vitamins and minerals she needs. You know that what's important is balance over time, but still...is her nutritional intake complete and balanced? Does she get everything she needs? You feed her a variety of proteins, but sometimes you read things that say homemade diets are lacking in vital nutrients. Your dog is your baby, your best friend, your world, and you want her to have everything she needs. She's sleek, soft, beautiful...no outward sign anything is wrong, but still, you wonder.

Wonder no more, my friend. While it's true we don't know, beyond a shadow of a doubt, how much of every single trace nutrient our beloved dogs need, we do have a good understanding of what vitamins and minerals they should be getting and what those nutrients do. And as you'll see, if you're feeding a balanced raw diet rich in variety (especially if that diet consists of pasture-raised, hormone- and antibiotic-free meat), chances

111

are pretty good you're giving your dog all the vitamins and minerals her body requires.

MINERALS

Calcium — Builds and maintains strong bones. It also aids in blood clotting, muscle contraction, and the ability of nerves to send messages

Copper — Helps make red blood cells and keeps nerve cells healthy. It is known to help form collagen, and may act as an antioxidant

Iodine — Used in the production of thyroid hormones

Iron — Important in the production of red blood cells

Magnesium — Regulates muscle and nerve function, blood sugar levels, and blood pressure. It's also important for protein, bone, and DNA production

Manganese — Vital to the formation of connective tissue, bones, blood clotting factors, and sex hormones. It's necessary for normal brain and nerve function, and aids in calcium absorption, the regulation of blood sugar, and more

Phosphorous — Works with calcium to build strong bones and teeth

Potassium — Vital to proper heart function. It also plays an important role in skeletal and smooth muscle contraction

Selenium — Important in reproduction, thyroid gland function, DNA production, and protecting the body from damage caused by free radicals and from infection

Zinc — Aids the immune system in fighting off invading bacteria and viruses. It's also important in protein and DNA production, wound healing, proper brain and thyroid function, and more

FAT-SOLUBLE VITAMINS

Vitamin A — Supports normal vision and the immune system. Helps the heart, lungs, kidneys, and other organs work properly

Vitamin D — Primarily aids with absorbing calcium and supporting normal bone growth

Vitamin E — Primarily aids in protecting cells from damage caused by free radicals (it's an antioxidant)

Vitamin K — Regulates blood clotting. It's also vital in transporting calcium through the body, which makes it very important for maintaining good bone health

Fat-soluble vitamins are stored in the body. Because of this, they can build up in excessive amounts if too much is given.

WATER-SOLUBLE VITAMINS

The B vitamins — The B vitamins are made up of 8 different vitamins: B1, B2, B3, B5, B6, B7, B9, and B12. Together, they support a myriad of functions in the body.

Vitamin C — Helps the body form and maintain connective tissue (bones, blood vessels, skin, etc.). It's also a powerful antioxidant

Water-soluble vitamins aren't stored in the body. That means they should (in general) be replenished each day. The body will take what it needs and excrete the rest through the urine. Because of this, excesses of these vitamins generally don't occur.

WHERE TO FIND VITAMINS AND MINERALS

Beef Vitamins: B1, B2, B3, B5, B6, B9, and B12. Minerals: calcium, copper, iron, magnesium, manganese, phosphorous, potassium, selenium, and zinc

Brain Vitamins: A and E

Bison Vitamins: B1, B2, B3, B5, B6, B9, B12, and E. Minerals: calcium, copper, iron, magnesium, manganese, phosphorous, potassium, selenium, and zinc

Chicken Vitamins: A, B1, B2, B3, B5, B6, B9, and B12. Minerals: calcium, copper, iron, magnesium, manganese, phosphorous, potassium, selenium, and zinc

Egg Vitamins: A, B1, B2, B3, B5, B6, B9, B12, D, E, and K. Minerals: calcium, copper, iron, iodine, magnesium, manganese, phosphorous, potassium, selenium, and zinc

Goat Vitamins: B1, B2, B3, B5, B6, B9, and B12. Minerals: calcium, copper, iron, magnesium, manganese, phosphorous, potassium, selenium, and zinc

Fish Fish includes raw sardines, haddock, halibut, salmon, etc. Vitamins: A, B1, B2, B3, B5, B6, B9, B12, C, D. Minerals: calcium, copper, iron, magnesium, manganese, phosphorous, potassium, selenium, and zinc

Heart Vitamins: B2, B5, B6, B12, and C

Kidney Vitamins: A, B2, B5, B6, B12, C, D, and E

Lamb Vitamins: B1, B2, B3, B5, B6, B9, and B12. Minerals: calcium, copper, iron, phosphorous, potassium, selenium, and zinc

Liver Vitamins: A, B1, B2, B5, B6, B9, B12, C, D, E, and K

Ostrich Vitamins: B1, B2, B3, B5, B6, B9, B12, and E. Minerals: calcium, copper, iron, magnesium, manganese, phosphorous, potassium, selenium, and zinc

Pork Vitamins: A, B1, B2, B3, B5, B6, B9, and B12. Minerals: calcium, copper, iron, magnesium, manganese, phosphorous, potassium, selenium, and zinc

Rabbit Vitamins: B1, B2, B3, B5, B6, B9, and B12. Minerals: calcium, iron, magnesium, manganese, phosphorous, potassium, selenium, and zinc

Turkey Vitamins: B1, B2, B3, B5, B6, B9, and B12. Minerals: calcium, copper, iron, magnesium, manganese, phosphorous, potassium, selenium, and zinc

Chapter 17: Supplements

The topic of supplements seems to come up whenever raw diets are discussed. I think it's common in this day and age to try and use supplements as Band-aids to fix things that are better addressed via diet (this isn't always the case, of course, but I've noticed a trend towards over-supplementing without getting the diet on track first). While a species-appropriate raw food diet doesn't exclude supplements, it's important, when you're considering supplementing, to ask yourself what substance or nutrient is deficient. Remember, a supplement is supposed to replace a nutritional gap in the diet you're feeding. If there's something missing from your dog's diet you feel you need to supplement, see if there's a way you can get it in whole food form first. If not, consider supplementing—but only after you make sure the diet is as correct, balanced, and complete as possible. Providing nutrients in whole food form is much more beneficial in most cases than providing them as a supplement, because they're more bioavailable to your pet.

No matter what you feed your dog, you've probably wondered if there are any supplements you should be giving to help them be as healthy as possible. It's a tough question, and probably one of the ones I hear most frequently. And it's no wonder—there's so much conflicting information out there...and even more than that, there's just so **much** information floating around! Some people swear by this supplement, others by that supplement. Some people say you shouldn't supplement at all, and others say every dog needs supplementation throughout their whole lives. It can be enough to make your head spin (it sure has mine!).

While it's next to impossible to put together a global supplement list that works for every dog in every situation, I did think it would be helpful to put together a list of some of the supplements I think are most valuable to dogs. Plus, I thought it would be a good idea to break down when and why I think these supplements are helpful for dogs, so you can decide for yourself if it's something you might want to give your pooch. To make things even easier for you, I'll also share which supplements I've had success with or heard positive things about.

Ready to demystify supplements? Let's get started!

Probiotics

If you're transitioning your dog from a processed food diet to a balanced, varied, raw diet; if your dog has been on antibiotics; or if they're showing signs of an imbalance (for example, excessively gooey or waxy ears, skin issues, UTIs, diarrhea or vomiting, rashes, and so on), supplementing their food with probiotics is a really good idea. Probiotics are beneficial bacteria that, along with other amazing benefits, promote and support health and the efficient functioning of the digestive system.

If you feed a species-appropriate raw food diet, particularly a well-balanced prey model or whole prey diet, your pet is already getting probiotics in their meals. They're found in liver, spleen, and other organs. Another great source of probiotics is green tripe (if it's organic and pasture-raised, like the tripe from www.greentripe.com—if it's not, you run the risk that it doesn't have many probiotics at all). I give my dogs green tripe once or twice a week (for all the benefits it contains, not just probiotics).

However, even if your pet gets probiotics through their raw meals, if you transitioned them to a raw diet within the last 6 months, or if you've given them antibiotics, or if they have an issue that would suggest an imbalance in their gut flora, you should supplement the probiotics they're getting in their food with an additional high-quality probiotic, preferably for at least 6-9 months (and, if possible, even longer—it takes a long time to build the gut flora back up!).

I personally like Pet Flora Vitality Science (for smaller dogs) and Prescript-Assist (marketed for humans, but fine for dogs, and more affordable than Pet Flora Vitality Science when it comes to large or giant-breed dogs). But these aren't the only options out there, so pick one that works for you. I would look for a supplement with a minimum of 10-12 strains of "good" bacteria and 20-40 million (or more!) beneficial bacteria per serving.

Enzymes

Enzymes are another vital supplement you might want to consider giving, particularly if your dog is coming off kibble or canned food. Enzymes are responsible for thousands of vital functions in the body, including detoxification, healing, digestion, and absorption of nutrients. If your pet's body doesn't have enough enzymes, they will die. In the wild, carnivores naturally get enzymes from the meat and bones of their prey. If your pet has been on a kibble-based diet, her enzyme levels are undoubtedly very low, because the process of cooking and processing the kibble kills all the live enzymes that were in the meat. With each raw meal your pet eats, they'll gain vital live digestive enzymes. If you want to kick up their enzyme level (which is a good idea, if you're transitioning from kibble), green tripe is a great option—it's packed with digestive enzymes and tons of other nutrients.

Turmeric paste

Turmeric is well-known for its anti-inflammatory properties. And, since cancer and other diseases start with inflammation[52], it's important we as pet parents do everything we can to decrease and prevent inflammation.

Turmeric paste (also called golden paste) is a great supplement to add to your dog's meals. To make turmeric paste, follow this easy recipe (widely available on the web, but I got this version from the great folks at Vibrant K9 (www.vibrantk9.com):

Turmeric paste recipe

Ingredients:

- ½ cup organic turmeric powder
- 1 cup water
- ⅓ cup raw (unrefined) organic cold pressed coconut oil
- 2 tsps. freshly ground organic black pepper
- Organic ginger powder (optional)
- Organic cinnamon powder (optional)

Bring the water and turmeric to a boil, then lower the heat and simmer 7-9 minutes (until you have a thick paste). If you need to add additional water to achieve the right consistency, do so.

When you have a thick paste, cool the paste until it's warm. Add the freshly ground pepper and oil (and the cinnamon and ginger, if using) and stir well. Let the mixture cool.

Note: Very rarely, pets that are fed this paste will start to smell like a litterbox.

The ginger and/or cinnamon may help this, so if your pet gets stinky, try adding them in. Otherwise, there's really no need to add the ginger or the cinnamon to your recipe.

Yield: ~2 cups

Store in glass mason jars (this recipe fills four ½-cup mason jars). You can freeze 3 of the filled mason jars and keep the 4th in the fridge. It will keep for about 2 weeks when refrigerated. Krista Powell of Vibrant K9 told me you can tell when the turmeric paste has lost its potency because it starts to smell metallic. She also said when turmeric is given in this paste form, it's about 2,000% more viable than when it's taken as a pill. Pretty cool, since people can consume this turmeric paste too!

You can give the paste with every meal. Start out with 1/8 tsp and gradually build up (to a heaping tablespoon). Giving too much too quickly can give your pet diarrhea, so take it slow. And be careful when you're cooking it—the paste will stain.

Fish oil

Our pets need omega-3 fatty acids: they support skin and coat health, joint health, help control inflammation, reduce allergies, and more. Essential fatty acids (which are fatty acids your pet can't produce himself) must be obtained through diet. If you're feeding a balanced, varied species-appropriate raw diet already, adding wild-caught whole raw sardines (frozen, thawed, or semi-thawed) every week is a great way to help your pet get their omega-3s. I often recommend whole raw sardines instead of supplementing with fish oil. We get our sardines at the local Asian market.

If your pet needs some additional supplementation beyond what the sardines provide, krill oil is a great choice (Dr. Mercola Krill Oil for Pets is one option). There are less pollutants and contaminants in krill than in fish (because they're at the bottom of the food chain), krill oil doesn't contain heavy metals (while fish oil must be tested to make sure mercury levels aren't too high), dogs tend to absorb it better than fish oil, and it has more of the omega-3 fatty acids that we're going for[53]. Krill oil is often more expensive than fish oil, though, so if you decide to go with fish oil (instead of the sardines or the krill oil), make sure it doesn't contain soy or other questionable ingredients. One option you might consider is Bonnie & Clyde Wild Omega-3 fish oil.

The 4 best supplements for your dog

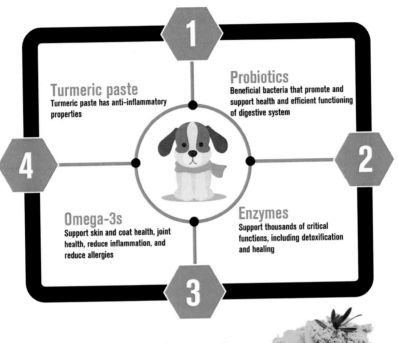

Turmeric paste
Turmeric paste has anti-inflammatory properties

Probiotics
Beneficial bacteria that promote and support health and efficient functioning of digestive system

Omega-3s
Support skin and coat health, joint health, reduce inflammation, and reduce allergies

Enzymes
Support thousands of critical functions, including detoxification and healing

1
2
3
4

Turmeric paste recipe

Ingredients:

- ½ cup organic turmeric powder
- 1 cup water
- 1/3 cup raw (unrefined) organic cold pressed coconut oil
- 2 tsps. freshly ground organic black pepper
- Organic ginger powder (optional)
- Organic cinnamon powder (optional)

1) Bring the water and turmeric to a boil, then lower the heat and simmer 7-9 minutes (until you have a thick paste). If you need to add additional water to achieve the right consistency, do so.
2) When you have a thick paste, cool the paste until it's warm.
3) Add the freshly ground pepper and oil (and the cinnamon and ginger, if using) and stir well.
4) Let the mixture cool.

WolfBear's Story

This story was written by Cheryl York Olmstead about her beautiful German Shepherd, WolfBear. Cheryl has studied animal naturopathy and carnivore nutrition, and I am grateful she has allowed us to tell her and WolfBear's story in this book.

I love animals and nature. Growing up, my grandmother called me the "Pied Piper," because I made friends with every furry or feathered creature I met. Like many kids, I loved dogs best, and my sister and I would occasionally set up camp in our backyard, snuggled in between our three dogs for an adventurous night under the stars.

During the times that I didn't share my life with a dog, I longed for one and would often check the rescue pages *just in case* a window would open, and fate would allow me to welcome a new best fur friend into my arms. Looking back, I've loved many dogs, each one exceptionally.

I'm a firm believer that our walk of faith allows us to go through many seasons (joy, sadness, tribulation, and even sickness) to prepare us for the journey ahead. We are refined by these experiences and they are the foundation as well as building blocks of our lives. If we ignore our foundation or a block is askew, our purpose and journey is weakened.

Dogs make up part of that journey; each one arriving at the perfect time, weaving their lives in and around ours. They bring us joy, healing, companionship, and when they leave us, inevitable heartache. Each dog is a unique gift, an individual in personality and temperament. But there is usually one dog in our lives that stands out from among the rest. Perhaps without the pets we've loved previously, we would not be able to love *that one special dog* in the way that we do.

The special one, sometimes referred to as a "heart dog" or "soul dog," is the dog with whom we connect with on a higher plane. There is a closer bond, a relationship, and a way of communicating with this best friend that cannot easily be put into words. Everyone who has experienced this relationship with their own *heart d*og knows exactly what I mean.

My heart dog is resting beside me as I type this; his name is WolfBear. He's my brave boy, friend, companion, playmate, and healer. I can't imagine life without him and I want to give him the best, healthiest, longest life possible. I want to stretch out every minute of it so that I can appreciate and enjoy him for as long as he's entrusted into my care.

He is a gem of a dog. Yet, I'm certain, without the love and loss of the dogs before him, our relationship would not be what it is today. By loving and caring for the dogs that came before him, I learned lessons on health and nutrition, which prepared me to learn how to meet his needs better.

On January 20, 2012, at twelve weeks, WolfBear arrived by airplane at the Dallas airport. A German Shepherd, he was already in the earliest beginnings of future protection sports training, yet his owner needed to rehome him. At the time, we had one long-coat German shepherd named Harley and had been looking for another female like her. WolfBear is a male with a standard coat. But one look at a picture of his adorable, needy little face and we knew it was meant to be!

After picking WolfBear up from the airport, we drove the three hours home while he slept like a log in his crate. I could not wait to get my hands on his adorable puppy self and introduce him to Harley. I dreamed of sweet puppy kisses, fuzzy puppy snuggles, and holding him close.

Once home, what I got when I opened his crate was a twenty-five-pound land shark that had been in training to increase his prey drive and encouraged to bite. He latched his razor-sharp teeth onto anything that moved with extraordinary intensity. Unfortunately, his first demonstration was on my husband's forearm.

He was not a vicious or mean dog. He was simply doing what he was trained to do from six to twelve weeks, and he did it very well. He was a wooly black and tan warrior who took his job seriously, and that part of his personality was not quite expected.

Hours after meeting him, I realized WolfBear didn't know how to relax. He had been working for his food, in training all day from a very young age, and his intensity level was off the charts. Dreams of kisses and cuddles quickly evaporated for fear he'd take a bite of my face. Harley took the brunt and although they played, her cheek quickly was chewed to a bloody pulp, which was unacceptable.

At this point I called in a very well-respected trainer experienced with sporting dogs to evaluate WolfBear. The trainer said he had never seen a puppy with that level of intensity yet assured me he was just doing what he learned to do and gave me tips on how to work with him.

If there was an upside, it was that WolfBear already knew his basic commands, was house trained, crate trained, and extremely smart. He loved his toys and quickly bonded to all of us. I began to hand feed him and engaged him in light training and lots of play. Sadly, he also suffered from severe allergies.

It was apparent that owning WolfBear would require an investment into his health and physical and mental wellbeing. We loved him enough to give him that and in no time, he realized he no longer needed to perform. I witnessed the exact moment of transformation when the mantel of intensity fell from his countenance, his eyes lit up, and he visibly relaxed for the first time. Joy!

Owning WolfBear is a privilege and a delightful challenge. He is extremely social, adores people, and is never far from his ball. He is generous with sweet doggy kisses, loving nibbles, and is the perfect 105-pound mischievous snuggle buddy.

He is also very high energy and could be the poster child for the need to adhere to the 8 Laws of Health (*Note: Cheryl is referring to the 8 naturopathic laws of health, which include nutrition, exercise, clean water, sunshine, proper supplementation, moderation, fresh air, rest, and trusting in the natural process.*). His immune system was very weak when we got him, and he requires fresh and natural food to keep him free from harmful medications and breaking out into itchy fits complete with red paws, yeasty ears, and anal gland misery.

Being my only dog, his minimal requirement of two hours of exercise a day forces me to enjoy the outdoors when I might be tempted to work too many hours. His freethinking, smart mind, and his ability to communicate, is engaging, and fosters a relationship of deep respect and emotional and spiritual connection.

My faith has grown in learning how to care for him naturally. I'm able to give him this gift and for that I am grateful. Through owning him and Harley, who suffered her own serious health challenges, the course of my life changed. I spent many years researching about dog health and wellness; as a professional website and content marketing copywriter, my specialty is now focused on enabling dogs to thrive. I'm about to unveil my new website, The Canine Life, and I'm also in the process of taking animal naturopathy courses. I'm passionate about wanting to spread the news that dogs can live happier and healthier lives that fulfill them physically, mentally, and spiritually when we provide them what they need to thrive.

WolfBear. Photo credit Cheryl York Olmstead

Chapter 18: Fasting Your Dog

Fasting reduces inflammation and is a form of healing. *If you decide to fast, just build a fast day into your meal plan by increasing the amount you feed the day before the fast.* Fasting, which is done by animals in the wild[54][55][56], gives the body a break from the duties of digestion. Our dogs, which have very elastic stomachs, evolved to eat large meals intermittently (gorge and fast), and it is that intermittent fasting that gives their digestive system a chance to rest and heal[57]. One analogy that illustrates the importance of fasting is to think about working for months at a time without any vacation or time off on the weekends. Eventually, anyone who does this gets burned out and irritable. Their productivity goes down, they can't focus as well, and they may start to get stressed or sick. When the digestive system—whether it is ours or our pets—is asked to work constantly without a break, the same thing happens. Fasting provides a "vacation" for the digestive system. When the body is digesting, it must use energy that could otherwise go towards healing (such as reducing inflammation)—it cannot heal and digest at the same time. Intermittent fasting also improves the immune system (which is vital in maintaining optimal health) by reducing free radical damage and reducing cancer cell formation[58]. In the wild, animals that are sick will fast, sometimes for days, to give their bodies a chance to come back into balance and reduce stress on their internal systems[59].

When it comes to how often you should fast your healthy, raw-fed dog, you have lots of options. You will have to experiment to find what is best for you and your pet, but I can share several different models for you as a starting point. If you currently feed your dog twice per day, start by reducing the amount to once per day (feed them the same amount in one meal instead of two). You may notice a healing response, or detox, when you do this. Your dog may vomit or experience some diarrhea. Let everything settle down and even out again before you change the feeding frequency again.

Once everything is back to normal, you may decide to feed your dog every other day (this is what I typically do with my own dogs). On some occasions, you may decide to fast your dog for two days in a row (I sometimes do this if I feed an extra-large meal). Or, you may decide to allow them to eat as much as they want at mealtime, and then fast them until their bellies are back to normal size. You may decide to fast them one day per week. Or, you may decide to feed them every day for a few months, and then fast them for a few days in a row (generally not more than 2 or 3 days at most in a row). There are lots of ways to fast, and as I said, you should experiment until you find something that works for you and your dog.

Dogs generally adapt quickly to fasting; it is, after all, a more natural way for them to eat. It only took a few days for my dogs to get used to it, and now they only get excited to eat when I start pulling the food out and they see mealtime is really going to happen. I know an agility trainer who fasts her raw-fed dogs intermittently, and she once told me that sometimes she briefly forgets to feed her dogs because they're so calm about meals. Her dogs (Border Collies) have lots of energy, but mealtime doesn't cause any stress in them, because they are used to fasting intermittently and because they eat at different times in the day.

If you decide to fast your dog, you may want to avoid exercising him or her intensely on their fast days, especially if they're detoxing or seem tired. You may find that a gentle walk on the fast day is perfect. Or, you may find your dog has more energy on fast days (mine do), and you may decide to let them run around and burn off energy. Keep an eye on your dog, and let him guide you in what he needs.

Chapter 19: Getting the Scoop on the Poop

Ask anyone who feeds their dog a species-appropriate diet what one of their favorite things about the diet is, and chances are high they'll mention their pet's, um, waste products. While it might not be dinner-party appropriate, the fact remains that your dog's stool is a subject worthy of discussion.

Is there really a noticeable difference between the droppings of a dog fed a raw diet vs. one on a processed-food diet? In short, yes, there's a huge difference. Processed-food diets—no matter how much the brand purports to be "high quality"—contain lots of material dogs simply can't use. Furthermore, because processed foods are cooked, the protein is denatured, which means the body can't use the amino acids in the protein and instead views it as something toxic.

Amino acids are the building blocks of proteins, so without them, none of the processes performed by proteins can be carried out. Our carnivores take in amino acids through the protein in their food. However, when that protein is cooked (and therefore denatured), the body can't use it. Remember our analogy of denatured protein being like smashed blocks? The body can't use those smashed amino acids to build proteins any more than you could use smashed blocks to build a wall. The body needs to eliminate all the stuff it can't use, including the unusable proteins, and we see this in part in the volume, consistency, and smell of our pets' feces.

I was at the Living Desert Zoo in Palm Desert, CA recently, and I was talking with one of the reptile handlers about how they feed the animals there. We realized both of us (the Living Desert and I) buy food for our animals from Layne Labs. When she found out we have dogs and feed them a raw diet, her first comment was, "Their poop must be amazing!". It made me laugh, but she was exactly right. By feeding a raw diet, our animals' bodies can use almost all the nutrients and amino acids in their food—they can take advantage of almost everything. When they defecate, their droppings are small, relatively speaking (there just isn't much waste material that they need to get rid of). The droppings are also fairly hard compared to kibble-fed dogs'. Their stool doesn't smell as bad as a dog eating kibble, and it doesn't attract as many flies. Animals fed a raw diet defecate much less frequently than their kibble-fed counterparts (again, they just don't have as much waste to get rid of), and it decomposes and goes away very quickly.

A dog fed a processed-food diet, however, has a significant amount of waste it must eliminate from each meal. Compared to a raw-fed dog, their droppings are usually immense, soft, and smelly.

Our dogs were designed to have to strain just a little bit when taking a bowel movement, which helps to keep their anal glands nice and clear. Nowadays, impacted anal glands are one of the top reasons people take their dogs to the vet[60], and cleaning out anal glands is an almost-routine service offered by many groomers and vets. But, when everything is working properly, the very act of going to the bathroom takes care of that for our dogs.

Like pretty much everything else relating to the health of your dog, feeding them the diet they were designed over millennia to eat has a profoundly positive effect on their health. Every single system, every single organ, every single process, and every single cell is impacted for the better. Even something as seemingly innocuous as poop is affected. And not only is it affected: The change that occurs, stool-wise, when a dog is fed a balanced, varied raw diet demonstrates the health of their digestive systems, and it demonstrates their bodies are using almost all the nutrients in their food. It's huge! Plus, you can't beat the side effect of not having to pick up oodles of poop, right?

Minotaur's Story

Minotaur's owner contacted me as a last resort to see if I could help her save his life. Minotaur suffered from seizures, and while only 2 years old, he was having a really difficult time maintaining a good quality of life. Spoiler alert: We worked together, and today, Minotaur, a beautiful German Short-Haired Pointer, has a zest for life like you wouldn't believe.

It wasn't always like that, though. In our first phone call, his owner told me she'd tried "everything." By "everything," she meant every conventional treatment the vets could come up with. Nothing was working, and they were advising her to euthanize him. I distinctly remember our first phone call: "I have nothing to lose by trying," she told me. "If it works, we can maybe save him. If not, at least I'll know I gave it my best shot."

We immediately got Minotaur switched over to a raw diet, and we made sure he was getting plenty of zinc (he was exhibiting some other signs of zinc deficiency, and zinc deficiency can cause seizures). You should know that when she first contacted me, he was having seizures at least once per day, and often several times in a 24-hour period. It was bad. She was understandably a little skeptical of what sort of effect switching to a raw diet would have (she fed a "premium" kibble), but she agreed to go along with it. I explained to her that, if he were my own dog, I would want to support his immune system and remove the excess toxins as soon as possible, and then once I'd done that, I'd want to explore natural modalities to help my dog even further.

About a week after switching him to raw, she called me and told me he'd only had one seizure (one!) that entire week. The next week, he had two, but they were shorter in duration than usual. And all she'd done, up to that point, was switch his diet. I want to say here that Minotaur's story is certainly not the norm, but it's not rare, either.

From there, she continued with the raw diet, but we also added in some supplements: herbs, homeopathy, and a zinc supplement specifically for dogs. He didn't have another seizure for the next two months, and then he had one. However, he didn't have another one after that, and the last time I talked with her, he'd been seizure-free for over 8 months.

This is not to say that, if your dog is suffering from seizures, switching them to a raw diet is a magical cure. However, for Minotaur, making this switch set the stage for a much stronger foundation, and the supplements helped support his body and address the imbalance causing the seizures in the first place.

Chapter 20: Detoxing Your Dog and What to Expect

Up to this point, we've been focusing on everything relating to diet. I did this deliberately, because diet is the foundation of your dog's health. A strong foundation = your dog thriving. A weak foundation, on the other hand? An unhealthy dog. And understanding that, and understanding how to correct an unhealthy (diet) foundation, is vital if you want to keep your best friend flourishing throughout their life. So now, let's add to your foundation: Let's talk about detoxing your dog (which is actually the start of achieving optimum health—after all, you have to get rid of the bad to make room for the good, right?), and then let's talk about addressing some specific, common chronic issues in a natural, holistic way.

When you move your dog to a raw diet, you may see them go through a detox phase (also called a healing response). This detox is a natural part of the healing process; in fact, it's the initial phase of healing[61]. Like ours, when an animal's body gets out of balance because it's taken in more toxins than the liver, kidneys, and lungs can filter out (toxins can come from diet, medicines, and more), the body starts to detox. Because of this detoxification, the body may display illness-like symptoms that can range in severity from mild to intense. This is because the body's systems are working to eliminate waste products and toxins in preparation for healing and regeneration[62]. In case you're wondering, the symptoms of detoxification[63] can include:

- Lethargy
- Joint pain and stiffness
- Bad breath
- Mucous discharge
- Hot spots
- Diarrhea

- Vomiting
- And more

If you're following a conventional approach and your dog begins to exhibit illness-like symptoms, it's a sign their body can't flush the toxins out faster than they come in. If no changes are made and the toxins continue to come in faster than the body can get rid of them, then the illness-like symptoms you're seeing (in other words, the acute conditions) will develop into chronic disease. However, if changes are made to reduce the amount of toxins coming in—for example, your dog stops eating kibble and starts eating a raw diet—the body can start to come back into balance. While this is occurring, you'll see the detox phase. It's important to keep in mind that, while the detox includes symptoms like those it displayed prior to the detox, the detox itself is not an indicator of disease or illness. Rather, it's an essential part of the healing process because it allows the body to rid itself of the toxins and morbid matter that were contributing to illness and, if left unchecked, would eventually turn into chronic disease.

The detox phase differs among all animals. It can occur immediately upon switching to a more natural approach, or it may take several months to appear. It can also last for different lengths of time. A general rule of thumb is the detox phase can last for one month for each year of the animal's life[64]. However, this varies greatly by individual and by how you approach the detoxification process. Viewing the detox positively can be incredibly beneficial—and it should be viewed in a positive light, because it's an indication your pet is starting to truly heal. If you lack trust in the natural healing process, you may tend to see this phase as an indicator of illness and return to conventional medicine to suppress the presenting symptoms. This is a mistake. By remembering the goal is true health, not just symptom suppression, you can step back and let the animal's body heal itself.

Part of our role in caring for our animals is to give their bodies what they need to support them through the healing process (which includes the detox phase). We also must keep in mind that treating our animals holistically involves addressing mind, body, and spirit. So, when we see detox occurring, the best approach is to get excited about it (I know, it sounds crazy, right? And yet, it makes a huge difference.). Think about it—you know your dog picks up on your emotions. So, if you feel sad about "what they're going through" in the detox—if you feel sorry for them as their body is detoxifying—they pick up on it. It drags them down, weakens their systems, and makes the whole process more miserable for everyone. On the other hand, if you can look at it as a cause for celebration—your dog is starting to achieve true health and wellness, which can only lead to a better quality, longer life—they'll pick up on that and move through their detox faster.

In some instances, the detox phase can become too intense for the body[65]. In these instances, you should seek the services of a holistic veterinarian or a certified animal naturopath. They can help your pet get through the detox safely. They may provide additional support in the form of herbs, essential oils, or some other natural therapy. They may also slow down the rate of detoxification to allow your animal's system more time to detox.

With trust, patience, and lots of love, your pet will move through the detox phase to achieve true vitality, not just a Band-Aid suppression of symptoms that will eventually blow into a full-scale, chronic disease.

Chapter 21: Dealing with Diseases Naturally

Many people who turn to raw diets do so because they've had a dog with a health challenge. So, I wanted to talk a bit about addressing health issues naturally. Remember, of course, the standard disclaimer applies, both to this section and throughout the book: *All information contained in this book is intended for educational purposes only. It is not provided to diagnose, prevent, or treat any disease, illness or injured condition of the body or pets, and the author, publisher, and contributors accept no responsibility for such use. Anyone or their pets suffering from any disease, illness, or injury should consult with their physician or veterinarian. The statements herein have not been evaluated by the Food and Drug Administration.* Alright... now that we've jumped through that hoop, let's get to it.

The immune system

70–80% of your dog's immune system is in their gut. The immune system is made up of bacteria and mucous membranes (the mucosal immune system). As you know, the immune system is vital to protecting the body, which it does by creating a barrier against bacteria and viruses. If they succeed in getting past that barrier, the healthy immune system detects that and destroys them before they start to reproduce. And, if they do end up reproducing, the immune system will keep fighting them until they're destroyed[66].

It's important to keep the immune system as strong and healthy as possible. If your dog has been fed a conventional diet, been given antibiotics, steroids, or many other conventional medications, or been exposed to toxins (including OTC flea and tick medications), their immune system has been compromised. To get them back to true vitality, you have to strengthen their immune system. There are several steps to doing this:

1. Feed a raw diet
2. Eliminate all cooked and processed diets and treats
3. Supplement with species-appropriate probiotics, enzymes, and other immune-boosting supplements
4. Exercise (moderately, consistently)
5. Allow for proper rest
6. Let animals be themselves (by this, I mean let your dog eat grass, roll in icky things, and in general, just "be a dog")
7. Take puppies to natural/public areas to be exposed to "germs" and "viruses"

Immune-boosting supplements

As you go through this list, keep in mind most dogs don't need any supplement/natural modality given routinely for a long period of time. If you aren't sure what supplements to give or how long to give them, work with a holistic veterinarian or certified animal naturopath.

Antioxidants. Antioxidants decrease various chemicals that cause cell damage. They include Vitamins C and E, among others. Vitamin C is most present and bioavailable to dogs in raw liver (and least present in muscle meats)

Glyconutrients/saccharides. One great supplement is NingXia Red Juice for Pets, which is high in antioxidants, glyconutrients, and saccharide contents.

Biological response modifiers (BRMs). One excellent BRM is bovine colostrum, which contains purine pyrimidine complexes, cytokines, and other protein compounds that act as BRMs. As an interesting side note, research supports the use of colostrum in the treatment of rheumatoid arthritis, osteoarthritis, and other autoimmune conditions.

Zinc. Zinc is a mineral that aids in the proper functioning of the immune systems, reduces pro-inflammatory cytokines, stimulates white blood cell activity, reduces stress levels, aids in energy metabolism, and increases healing rate of wounds. Review the section "Zinc deficiency" later in this chapter for more information about zinc, including what forms are most bioavailable to dogs, where to find whole-food forms of zinc, and important information about zinc toxicity.

The stronger your dog's immune system is, the quicker their body will heal. A strong immune system is the key to health and vitality. From a natural and holistic perspective, supporting the immune system is the best way to address chronic health issues.

What does it mean to fix?

I recently saw a Facebook post about a dog with hot spots. The person who wrote the post was bemoaning the fact her dog had hot spots again, but ended on what she undoubtedly thought was an optimistic note. "No need to worry!", she said. "We took her [the dog] back to the vet, and it's nothing that antibiotics and cream can't fix!" When I saw that, it made me pause for a minute. She was talking about her dog's hot spots, and then she said antibiotics and cream will fix them.

My dictionary gives the simple definition of "fix" as:

- to make (something) whole or able to work properly again: to re-pair (something)
- to deal with or correct (a problem)

But in this case, is that what the antibiotics and creams are doing? I want to explore this for a second, because I think that, as a society, we often see a problem in our dogs (or ourselves, but let's just stick with the dogs for this one) and we attempt to "fix" the problem by making the symptoms go away. Dog has hot spot. Vet prescribes antibiotics and cream. Hot spot disappears. Dog is fixed. Or is she?

So much of what we believe is based on our five senses—what we can touch, taste, see, smell, and hear. Our senses are based in the reptilian brain, and we rely on them to give us information about our environment and the world around us. We've evolved to understand our environment based on what we can see, or touch, or hear—so if we no longer see a hot spot, then our five senses (and our reptilian brain) tell us the problem is fixed. No symptom = no problem, and no problem = health.

There's a flaw in this logic, though, that becomes clear when we step back and look at the cycle so many of our pets undergo on a routine basis. Let's stay with the hot spot example. To fix the hot spot, the dog is given antibiotics and some sort of cream. The antibiotics that are prescribed are broad-spectrum, which means they kill all the bacteria indiscriminately. Unfortunately, this includes the "good" bacteria. However, bacteria don't come back into the system at equal rates, and in fact, the "bad" bacteria come back much more quickly than the good. This leads to an imbalance,

135

and the good ones often can't gain a foothold because they're outcompeted by the bad. So, now we have an imbalance. The cream is often palliative, which means it helps to suppress itching and the pain, but it doesn't get at the root of what was causing the hot spot.

Imbalances occur for a reason. Those reasons can be varied, but they aren't random. There is a cause and an effect. So, in the case of our dog with the hot spot (or diabetes, or poor oral health, or weight problems, or pancreatitis, or skin allergies, or cancer, or any of a myriad of other issues we see in our dogs every single day), there was a reason the dog got those hot spots—a cause. By giving the antibiotics, are we addressing that cause? Does wiping out all the bacteria truly address that root cause? Because if the cause of hot spots was normal bacteria, then every single dog would have hot spots, because every single dog has bacteria. No—what it boils down to is there is an imbalance somewhere. Perhaps there are too many "bad" bacteria. But in that case, does introducing antibiotics—which lead to imbalances because the "bad" bacteria come back faster than the "good" and edge the good out—address the root cause, or exacerbate it? If conventional treatments truly "fixed" the issue, then once a dog got hot spots and was given antibiotics and a cream, they would never experience another hot spot again. But that's usually not what happens. In our (real-life) example, the dog had hot spots "again," and she went back to the vet for them. She's been to the vet before, and she's been for this same reason. So clearly, when we compare the results against our dictionary definition of fix, we see the so-called fix provided by the cream and the antibiotic didn't repair the issue, correct the problem, or make the body able to work properly again. So how is it a fix?

Remember the skin is an eliminative organ, and hot spots are a sign the body is trying to eliminate toxins. The skin is erupting with toxins, and the conventional answer—the "fix"—is to throw the system out of balance even more by wiping out all the bacteria, including the beneficial bacteria, throughout the body.

When I first saw that post, I started thinking about what we now mean when we say a medication "fixed" our dog. For lots of people, it means the symptoms were, for the time being, suppressed. However, if you are seeking true and optimal wellness, a fix really means the root cause was addressed. When the root cause is dealt with, the symptoms go away because there's no longer anything causing them, and the body remains in a state of balance.

To truly address the hot spots, then, the body must be allowed to rid itself of the toxins without having more introduced. That means the diet must be cleaned up. It should be appropriate for a carnivore. The constant barrage of poisons, both internal and external, must stop. The body must be given a chance to move through the detox phase without additional conventional "treatments" throwing it more out of balance. And the good bacteria must be supported with probiotics so they can once again thrive and keep the "bad" bacteria balanced (which, not incidentally, means they no longer cause problems and are no longer "bad"). That is what it takes to truly "fix" the issue.

This overarching concept—that bringing the body into balance is vital for "fixing" health issues—is true for all the chronic diseases and conditions we see in our pets today. Sometimes it only takes a few small tweaks to help the body come back into balance and thereby remove the root cause of the issue. Sometimes it requires a complete overhaul. But no matter what, the true solution is not to suppress the symptoms. Just because the symptoms go away doesn't mean the issue is gone, and if the symptoms come back, or other issues crop up, this becomes very clear.

You know, all of this reminds me of something, so I'm going to share it with you here. My husband and I live in a part of Southern California with lots of rattlesnakes. A family friend of mine who has horses and rides all over the hills around here (and with whom I have ridden often) recently told me she's coming across lots of rattlesnakes that don't rattle. She didn't know exactly why this was, but her best guess was there are lots of people around here who kill rattlesnakes. When the snakes are quiet, people don't notice them as readily, and therefore they don't kill them. The problem, of course, is that even though the snake doesn't rattle, it's still there, and it's still dangerous, but unfortunately, now it doesn't give a warning. The same thing is true of the health issues we see in our pets. When the body gives a warning sign something is out of balance—like hot spots—and we suppress those symptoms, the issue isn't gone. It may have gone quiet, like the rattlesnakes my friend comes across these days, but it can still be deadly. I for one would much rather know when the body is out of balance while there's still time to fix it, rather than having a serious issue strike suddenly with no warning, like a rattlesnake that doesn't rattle before it lashes out. I'd prefer to assist the body in truly fixing the problem, and use symptoms as road maps for true and optimal vitality. Wouldn't you?

The new normal (and why it isn't)

Let's get real: in this day and age, we're used to dogs with a myriad of health issues: bad teeth, itchy skin, voluminous (and smelly!) poop, behavior issues (aggression and reactivity, for example), impacted anal glands, obesity, "doggy odor" (yep, that's a health issue), runny eyes, and auto-immune diseases. Indeed, these are so prevalent in our dogs that when you read this list, you might have thought some of them weren't actually health issues. In fact, most of us think of these issues as "normal." In reality, though, while these issues are common, they certainly aren't normal. Dogs, even those of advancing age, shouldn't have these issues. And when they do, it's a sign something is wrong.

In general, when dogs experience these issues, conventional veterinarians provide "treatment" that suppresses symptoms without getting at the root cause (remember the "fixes" we were just talking about?). Because the root cause isn't addressed, the issues keep coming back, often worse than before. Other times, dog parents ignore the issues, thinking they're due to an animal's age, or breed, or just bad luck.

I'm a naturopath, not a veterinarian, so I come at this from a different perspective. Far from believing these issues are normal, I view them as signs the immune system is out of balance.

The top 10 reasons people take their dogs to the vet

In this section, let's look at the top 10 reasons people take their dogs to the vet[67], and think about how you might address them from a natural (naturopathic) perspective. And, just because we can, let's include a few other chronic health issues and how you might address them. Before we get to all that, though, here's the list of the top 10 reasons dogs see the doctor:

1. Atopic or allergic dermatitis (skin allergies)
2. Ear infections
3. Benign skin neoplasia (non-cancerous tumors)
4. Pyoderma (hot spots)
5. Osteoarthritis
6. Periodontitis/tooth infections
7. Upset stomach
8. Intestinal inflammation/diarrhea
9. Cystitis or urinary tract disease
10. Anal gland sacculitis/expression

Our bonus list includes:

1. Chronic kidney disease
2. Coprophagia (eating feces)
3. Zinc deficiency

4. Seizures
5. Doggy odor

Skin allergies

Why do our pets suffer from allergies? And how can we help them overcome these issues? While this is a vast topic, let's look at some of the basic reasons for allergies and talk about some of the things you can do to help your dog find relief.

What causes skin allergies

When an animal's body is out of balance, it presents with different symptoms because of that imbalance. Diarrhea, hot spots, itchiness, and lethargy are all signs the body is out of balance. Skin allergies, and all the itching that goes along with them, are not, in and of themselves, a disease. They're a symptom of a body that is not in harmony. They're indicators your pet's body has built up too many toxins and is frantically trying to rid itself of them. Because the skin is the largest eliminative organ, when the liver and kidneys are overloaded with toxins and the immune system is desperately working to bring everything back into balance, many toxins are forced out of the body through the skin. This causes itching, hot spots, inflammation, and yeast infections, among other things. And as difficult as it is to see our beloved dogs in discomfort, it's important to view these symptoms (often labeled as "allergies") as clues that the body is out of balance. Trying to suppress them without addressing the cause of the symptoms ensures your dog will never find true and long-lasting relief.

Allergies—in humans and in animals—occur when the body's immune system overreacts to something in the body itself or in the environment. This is crucial to understand. The body's overreaction is causing the problem; the problem is not caused by whatever is in the body or environment. Let's take a little closer look at this, because understanding this imbalance is key to understanding what causes allergy symptoms.

The immune system includes Th1 cells and Th2 cells; these cells must be in balance or the whole system is thrown off. For example, if Th2 becomes too prevalent, it will overproduce antibodies that attack things not normally considered threats. Th2 is intended to trigger attacks on bacteria, viruses, and pathogens; when it's overabundant, it starts to trigger attacks on its own body and on normal species-appropriate foods. Th1 and Th2 get out of balance when toxins (which can be pesticides, household cleaning products, inappropriate foods, heavy metals, vaccines, and so on) build up in the body faster than the body can get rid of them. This imbalance weakens the immune system, and in this weakened state, it overreacts to what it perceives are foreign substances and releases histamines and antibodies normally used by the body to fight microbial invaders, triggering a whole host of symptoms: itching, upset stomach, hot spots, runny or red eyes, and more. Often, the triggers for this reaction (the foreign substances) are inappropriate foods (such as kibble), pollens, dust, mold spores, or grass (many of the same things that trigger our allergies!).

Conventional approaches to "treating" allergies

Many times, when you take your dog to a traditional veterinarian for allergy symptoms, they'll tell you the symptoms are caused by a food allergy, flea allergy, or some other environmental allergy. They will often advise you to switch to a different protein source (rarely do they advocate you switch to a raw diet, however). They treat the symptoms instead of addressing the root cause. Because the root cause isn't addressed, the symptoms come back over and over, and usually they get worse. This is because the body builds up a resistance to the treatments that were suppressing the symptoms, so you must increase the frequency and/or the dosage. And, to make matters worse, often the suggested remedies contribute to the problem. For example, think about steroid shots, which are given by many veterinarians to suppress itching. Your veterinarian may give a steroid shot, for example, of cortisone or prednisone. These are immunosuppressants, which means they suppress the immune system. The immune system is overactive, but when it's suppressed, it can no longer do its job and keep the body healthy. If the immune system is out of balance, your pet will never be able to achieve true health. In addition, steroids can cause multiple side effects, such as increased thirst and urination, increased hunger, panting, general loss of energy, development or worsening of infections, vomiting, or nausea[68].

Veterinarians may also recommend and/or prescribe antihistamines, such as Benadryl. Again, these act as a Band-Aid because they only address the symptom (itching, runny eyes, etc.) and not the actual cause of the problem. And, if the body remains out of balance, it will probably require higher and higher dosages to achieve relief. Think of the Band-Aid solutions as putting a patch on a torn shirt sleeve. The tear is still there, and eventually it will tear again, because the fabric is weak. The patch doesn't fix the shirt; it just provides a temporary solution. This is exactly what the steroids and antihistamines do.

Addressing allergies naturally

We've established traditional "cures" for allergies don't really fix the problem. So what, then, will help? Remember the body possesses the innate ability to heal itself—actually, it's only the body that can truly heal itself. What we must do is give it the proper support to achieve balance again. Balance is achieved when the toxins are eliminated, the body is nourished properly, and all the systems are working in harmony. There are several steps to this, and depending on the severity of your dog's symptoms, you may have to provide them with a little additional support as they get back into balance. Remember, we are not looking to suppress the symptoms, we are looking to achieve total health. Once that's achieved, the symptoms will no longer be present because the body won't be in a state of imbalance.

Our goal when faced with allergies is to remove the excess toxins as much as possible from our pet's environment (and by environment, I am referring to both their external environment and their internal environment). The first step is to make sure your dog is eating a raw diet. Switching your dog to a raw diet will go a long way towards ridding their internal environment of toxins and revitalizing and balancing their immune system to clear out the toxins they do encounter. You also need to make sure they're getting clean, fresh water (see the section "Not all water is created equal" in Chapter 22: "Moving Beyond the Feeding" for more information). This ensures they aren't adding to the toxin load every time they take a drink.

In addition to providing them with a raw diet and clean, fresh water, you should consider switching your household cleaners away from those that contain harsh chemicals, and consider stopping use of toxic pesticides (including OTC flea and tick medications) and herbicides.

Once you've switched your dog to a raw diet and eliminated ongoing sources of toxins (such as fluoride in the water and flea/tick preventives), it's time to start rebuilding their immune system. Remember, allergies are a reaction to the immune system being out of balance. The immune system needs to be rebuilt so it can respond appropriately to different foreign substances. To rebuild the immune system, provide whole, natural sources of probiotics, enzymes, immunomodulators, and essential fatty acids. Let's briefly look at each of these to see what it does and where you can find it.

Because conventional medications, processed food, and toxins wreak havoc on the "good" bacteria in your dog's gut, it is important when rebuilding the immune system to reintroduce the good bacteria. This is done through probiotics. A healthy supply of probiotics allows the body to absorb vitamins, minerals, and nutrients much more readily. It also maintains a healthy balance of bacteria so the "bad" bacteria don't gain a foothold in the body. You may need to supplement with probiotics, particularly if your dog has been on a processed-food diet. To do this, feed green tripe and/or provide a probiotic supplement (one example is Pet Flora from Vitality Science).

Enzymes are another vital supplement, particularly if your dog is coming off kibble. Enzymes are responsible for many critical functions in the body, including detoxification and healing. They also allow the body to digest and absorb nutrients from food. They regulate thousands of functions, including thinking. If the body doesn't have enough enzymes, it will die. In the wild, carnivores naturally get enzymes from the meat and bones of their prey. If your pet has been on a kibble-based diet, its enzyme levels are undoubtedly very low, because cooking and processing kills all the live enzymes that were in the meat. Green tripe is a great source of enzymes, as are other types of raw, hormone-free, antibiotic-free, pasture-raised, organic meat.

Immunomodulators can aid in regulating the immune system—essentially, strengthening a weak system or calming down an overactive system. This makes them especially helpful for animals that suffer from allergies, as those animals' immune systems tend to overreact to any foreign substance that comes along. One great immunomodulator is bovine colostrum. Supplementing with this will help the immune system become more balanced.

Essential fatty acids (meaning fatty acids they can't produce themselves and must get through their food), especially omega-3 fatty acids, are incredibly good for the immune system. You may know fatty acids are good for your dog's skin and coat, but they play vital roles in other areas as well, such as joint health, control of inflammation, and allergy reduction. You should focus on supplementing with omega-3 fatty acids and avoid omega-6 and omega-9 fatty acids. It is important to provide these to pets by feeding a raw diet, because cooking can destroy the essential fatty acids. Additionally, many commercial pet foods contain far greater amounts of omega-6 fatty acids than omega-3 fatty acids.

Fish, such as sardines, contain a high amount of fatty acids. Interestingly, beef fat contains a low percentage of fatty acids. This is one reason why feeding variety is so important. It ensures your dog gets all the nutrients she needs for optimal health. You can get whole, frozen sardines (wild caught) to feed to your dog (I give them as treats). I generally feed them a couple of sardines a week to keep their coats healthy and to help supplement their omega-3 fatty acid levels.

In addition to supplements, you may want to consider using essential oils to help your dog's allergies. Make sure any essential oil you get is pure, therapeutic grade. It shouldn't contain fillers or impure ingredients. I've successfully used lavender essential oil (from Young Living) to help my dog, Barkley, with his allergies. When his allergies are flaring (which does still happen from time to time), I rub a few drops of lavender essential oil in my hands and then pet him. This simple approach generally calms down his itching and biting. I repeat as necessary. You can experiment with different types of essential oils to find out what blend works best for your dog.

If your dog's allergies are severe, coconut oil may also help. You can apply it to the areas where he's itching (it's OK if he licks it off, although if you can keep him from licking it for a bit so it has time to work, that's best). You can also feed it so he gets it internally. Before Barkley's allergies were under control (when we were still flushing out the excess toxins introduced from following conventional practices and rebuilding his immune system), I would use coconut oil internally and externally for him, and it helped a lot.

Finally, remember to keep a positive attitude even though your pet is experiencing allergies. They pick up on our emotions, and when we feel sad or frustrated or disappointed, even if it's because we're sad they're in discomfort, it can depress their energy and their immune system and slow down their healing. Remember their symptoms are a clue something is out of balance, and greet the journey to true health with joy. As they become healthier, the symptoms will begin to subside, and real health will be achieved.

Ear infections

In what will become a common refrain (if it hasn't already), I'm going to tell you here that ear infections are a sign something's out of balance. Ear infections (the medical term for them is *otitis externa*) are the number 2 reason people take their dogs to the vet. And, just like skin allergies, when conventional approaches are used to "treat" them, they tend to come back over and over again. For example, many conventional vets recommend antibiotics for them. But antibiotics, which are broad-spectrum (meaning they kill everything, not just "bad" bacteria) can cause an imbalance in "good" vs. "bad" bacteria that can lead to more ear infections in the future.

If you're wondering if your dog has an ear infection, there are some symptoms to watch for:

- Tilting or shaking the head
- Brown or reddish discharge inside the ear

- Ear odor
- Redness or swelling in the ear
- Scabs or crusty areas in the ear

Note: If you notice symptoms like unusual eye movements, walking in circles, or having trouble with balance, it's important to get your dog to a holistic veterinarian to be checked for a more serious infection.

Ear infections can be caused by bacterial imbalances, yeast, allergies, or hormone imbalances. In all of these cases, they're a sign something is out of balance; once it's brought back into balance (in other words, once you address the root cause), the ear infections will stop.

If you're noticing chronic ear infections, there are a few things you can do to help break the cycle:

1. **Address the diet.** Switch your dog to a balanced, varied, raw diet.
2. **Eliminate toxins.** This includes antibiotics (remember, they destroy "good" bacteria and cause imbalances that can lead to more ear infections), steroids (which suppress the immune system), and OTC flea and tick treatments (they're poisons).

If your dog has an ear infection, there are some non-toxic things you can do to give him relief quickly, while you change his diet and lifestyle to stop the chronic ear infections. These include:

1. **Apple cider vinegar.** One caveat to this one: if your dog's ears are inflamed, don't use apple cider vinegar, as it will be very painful to them. However, if they aren't red and inflamed, mix apple cider vinegar with equal parts distilled water. Soak a cotton ball in the solution, then use it to gently clean your dog's ear flap. Don't push it deeply into the ear canal, or use a Q-tip in the canal. At best, you'll push dirt and bacteria deeper into the ear. At worst, you'll rupture your dog's eardrum.
2. **Calendula.** Calendula is an amazing herb that can be used for lots of things, including ear problems. You can get a pre-made infusion, soak a cotton ball with it, and gently apply it to your dog's ear flap.
3. **Coconut oil.** Ah, coconut oil. Antibacterial, anti-fungal, and all-around amazing. With this one, try simmering 2 tablespoons in a saucepan (on low heat). You can add in two fresh garlic cloves (they're also anti-bacterial). Once the oil is liquid, let it cool

enough so it won't burn your dog's ears but not so much it's no longer liquid, then dip a cotton ball in the mixture and gently apply to your dog's ear.

4. **Essential oils**. Dilute your chosen oil with equal part olive oil or fractionated coconut oil. Dip a cotton swab in the mixture and gently apply it to your dog's ear flap. Some good oils to try are Myrrh, Thyme, Wintergreen, Helichrysum, Mountain Savory, Basil, ImmuPower, Melrose, Thieves, Purification, and Exodus II. Note I only use Young Living oils for my dogs, myself, and my family.

It's best to apply any of the above ideas 2 or 3 times per day for about a week. If you don't see any improvement, see a holistic veterinarian or a certified animal naturopath.

Benign skin neoplasia (non-cancerous tumors)

Non-cancerous tumors can include a wide variety of things, including pimples, skin tags, cysts, and more[69]. If you notice the tumor is rapidly growing, bleeding, or is causing your dog pain, you should get it checked out right away.

I have to tell you an anecdotal story about non-cancerous tumors. Our dog Cleo started getting some benign tumors when she was older. She had a few small ones on her muzzle, a couple on her back, and a larger one on her back leg. While they weren't cancerous and weren't causing her obvious discomfort, we wanted to see if there was anything we could do about them that would be non-invasive but would help reduce or eliminate them. We started dropping Frankincense essential oil (from Young Living) on them daily, and within about a month, the small ones on her muzzle and back were about 95% gone! The larger one on her back leg started shrinking as well. We kept applying the Frankincense until the ones on her muzzle and back were completely gone and the one on her leg was significantly reduced in size.

Frankincense has been shown to be antitumoral, as well as an immunostimulant, an antidepressant, and a muscle relaxant[70]. So, it's no surprise to me it had such a profound impact on Cleo. While I'm not saying it will be able to eliminate your dog's non-cancerous tumors, it may be something you'll want to look into further (along with getting the diet on track and eliminating toxins as much as possible, of course).

Hot spots

According to the website petinsurance.com, hot spots are one of the most common reasons people take their dogs to the vet. In fact, hot spots rank fourth in the top 10 reasons dogs go to the vet! And it's no wonder—hot spots are irritated, infected, hot, red, moist lesions that are both painful and itchy to your dog. They often grow rapidly, and in many dogs are chronic and cause a lot of discomfort to the dog and stress (and money, in terms of vet bills and treatments) to the owner.

According to conventional wisdom, hot spots can occur whenever something irritates a dog's skin and leads to scratching or biting of the irritated area. Most people believe hot spots are the result of allergies, getting wet, insect bites, lack of grooming, ear or skin infections, or excessive licking and chewing[71]. However, like so many things relating to pet care, this doesn't truly get at the heart of what causes hot spots, and certainly doesn't lend to being able to address them effectively (hence why, in so many instances, they become a seemingly chronic condition).

For most people, if their dog starts to lick or chew excessively, or if there is any indication of a hot spot, they take the dog to the vet. Common conventional approaches to dealing with the hot spot usually include shaving the area around the hot spot, prescribing antibiotics and painkillers, applying or administering medication to kill fleas, ticks, and other parasites, adding a dietary supplement to increase essential fatty acids, prescribing steroids or antihistamines to relive itching, and recommending a hypoallergenic food (which is still processed kibble) to address any potential food allergies. Often, people are also advised to get their dog groomed regularly and get them shaved, especially in the summer, and they're told to maintain a regular flea and tick prevention program using over-the-counter flea and tick medications. They are also advised to make sure their dog gets plenty of exercise and isn't subjected to lots of stress[72].

However, what most people find—because the hot spots keep coming back—is these measures don't effectively address the issue. That's because conventional treatments don't get at the root cause of the hot spots. At best, they suppress the symptoms, and at worst, they exacerbate the problem—and so the hot spots keep coming back.

To understand why this is, let's first look at the root cause of hot spots. Because when you think about it logically, saying hot spots are caused by itching or scratching, exposure to rain or swimming, or the dog not being clipped in the summer doesn't make sense. Dogs itch and scratch, and if they are doing so excessively, it means something is out of balance, and that imbalance is directly related to the hot spot eruption—it's not the itching and scratching that caused the hot spot, it's the imbalance. Similarly, the belief that dogs that are exposed to rain or water will develop hot spots doesn't make sense. Many dogs spend a great deal of time in the water and never have a problem. Many dogs that don't spend time in the water do have problems. While getting wet may seem to trigger an eruption, a healthy, balanced dog should be able to swim and get wet without any problem. Dogs in moist environments may be more prone to hot spot eruptions, but again, because not every dog in a moist environment suffers from hot spots, this can't be the root cause of the eruption. And many dogs with long coats that aren't shaved in the summer never have a problem with hot spots. Plus, keeping a dog's fur shaved in the summer removes their protection from the sun and UV rays and eliminates the insulation that their fur provides. Remember, dogs don't cool themselves by sweating like we do; they pant. In fact, dogs can only release sweat through their foot pads, through what are called merocrine glands. While they do have sweat glands (called apocrine glands) all over their body (found with the hair follicles), these glands don't release sweat, they release pheromones, which aid them in communicating with other dogs[73].

So, what's going on when a dog presents with hot spots? Essentially, when you see hot spots erupting on your dog, it means your dog's body is being overwhelmed by toxins that are coming in at a faster rate than the liver and kidneys can handle. The skin is the largest eliminative organ, and so the toxins start to "erupt" out of the skin as part of the body's frantic effort to rid itself of them. And when you add antibiotics and steroids and flea/tick preventives on top of it, the toxic overload increases while at the same time the body's ability to stay balanced and handle the toxins decreases.

Like us, our dogs are designed to detox every single moment of every day. Interestingly, as I was reading the book *The Reboot with Joe Juice Diet* (remember, I just embarked on a juice fast!), I realized he conveyed this perfectly. Yes, he was talking about people, but in this instance, the same holds true for our dogs: "[Your dog's] liver, kidneys, bowels, lymphatic system, and skin all aid in the elimination of toxins and waste"[74]. Furthermore, just like with us, their systems can get "clogged, inflamed, rusty, and slow because we put too much pressure on them and don't give them the pure fuel they need. What that means is that [their] natural detoxification processes have a much harder time of it because of [their] lifestyle. Chemicals [...] in the environment—herbicides, pesticides, fungicides, petrochemicals, paints, cleaning products—all contribute to taxing [their] natural detox systems, not to mention all the prescription drugs [they are given]"[75].

Both antibiotics and steroids throw the body into a state of imbalance. Antibiotics wipe out all the bacteria and gut flora, which severely inhibits the ability of the immune system to do its job, while at the same time leading to future problems because the "bad" bacteria tend to grow back more quickly than the "good" bacteria. This can lead to further imbalance, which often presents as ear infections, yeast infections, and other issues (which, not surprisingly, do lead to dogs itching and scratching excessively...and that excessive, out-of-balance scratching and itching can cause a flare-up of hot spots in a dog with an excess of toxins. And so, the roller coaster continues...). And steroids suppress the immune system, so the dog's body is less able to stay healthy, ward off pathogens and viruses, and keep the dog in tip-top shape. Administering these when the system is already completely out-of-whack just makes it worse.

Furthermore, applying products topically or administering them internally to control parasites also cause a flood of toxins into the dog's body. These products contain poison intended to kill the parasites. But what that means is your dog's body is exposed to poison—often directly on the skin—at the very same time the skin is trying to shed out toxins! It's a lose-lose situation for your dog's immune system, and therefore, a lose-lose situation for your dog.

So, if the conventional treatments don't help—and any of you with pets that suffer from hot spots know exactly how difficult and frustrating this can be—what can be done? It's relatively simple, although not necessarily easy or quick, especially if you've been following conventional treatments for a long time. The first step is to make sure your dog is on a raw diet so they receive all the nutrients they need in a highly bioavailable form while eliminating all the stuff they don't need. A raw diet supports their entire body, including their immune system, digestive system, organs, and body processes.

When you feed a species-appropriate raw food diet, you lessen the work the liver and kidneys have to do, because they don't have to remove waste at a rate that exceeds what they're designed for. You reduce the workload of the pancreas, bring the stomach pH to an appropriate level, and flood your dog with the nutrients he or she needs to keep their body systems in good working order.

But, to address the toxin issue, you need to go beyond diet. Flea and tick preventives, such as Frontline and K9 Advantix, are poison, and when you apply them to your dog, the poison goes through their skin; their body must then work to eliminate that poison (see Appendix C for more about the dangers of conventional flea and tick preventives, and some safer alternatives). So, another vital step in helping your dog come back to optimal balance and reducing the load on the immune system is to stop flooding your dog's body, internally and externally, with poisons. These are toxins the body must get rid of, and if the kidneys and liver are already overloaded, the skin may have to help remove the toxins, and hot spots may result.

In addition to the things you put directly and deliberately onto your dog, you also have to consider the effects of things like herbicides and pesticides, as well as toxic cleaning products. Our dogs run around outside on the grass and in our yards with no protection between their feet and the ground. They brush up against foliage and sniff everything. This means they're exposed to everything you put in your yard, including chemical fertilizers, weed killers, and other herbicides. If your yard or house is sprayed for bugs, they encounter residual pesticides. And because they're closer to the ground and in direct contact with the floors of the house (if you let them inside), they're also exposed to whatever is in what you use to clean your house and floors.

So, take a good look at what you are putting down in your house and yard. If you want to use better cleaners, there are lots of recipes for non-toxic cleaners of every sort on the internet. You can also go to the Environmental Working Group's (EWG) website at www.ewg.org, and look at their ratings for various cleaning products (go to http://www.ewg.org/guides/cleaners/content/top_products). The goal is to reduce or remove toxins in the environment as much as possible, so your dog's kidneys and liver don't have to deal with them and get overwhelmed.

You may also want to support your dog with natural modalities when they're going through a hot spot episode. Various essential oils, such as lavender[76], feel soothing to the skin and are good at helping the body and especially the skin to rebalance (and remember, hot spots are caused by an imbalance, which the skin is trying to assist in relieving). Additionally, colloidal silver may help support your dog's immune system while providing antibacterial, antiseptic, and anti-inflammatory benefits in a safe and natural way[77].

Keep in mind it may take some time for the body to flush out all the toxins, and you may see the hot spots get worse for a while as the body detoxes. It's important to be patient as the body seeks to heal itself. It took a long time for the imbalance to get to the point where hot spots are seen, and it will take time for everything to rebalance. If you go back to conventional treatments, which suppress the issue without really addressing the root cause, you may make it more difficult for the body to come back into balance, and you will probably have to start over, with an even more intense case. It can be very difficult, but the natural modalities may provide some relief.

Hot spots can be a frustrating, distressing issue for you and your dog. However, as with most things, when you get to the root cause of the problem, you'll find you can help support your dog so they can overcome their chronic hot spots in a natural way. By removing toxins and helping to rebalance and strengthen their immune system, you enable their organs and body systems to function properly, and their bodies will begin to flush out toxins effectively. Because there will be significantly less toxins going in, their skin won't "erupt" in an effort to rid the body of excess toxic material. Your dog will return to a state of balance by healing and rebalancing him or herself, just as nature intended.

Osteoarthritis

You're starting to see the signs: your best buddy doesn't bounce up to greet you quite as quickly as she used to. She doesn't run quite as much as she once did, and when she does, she sometimes has a little hitch in her stride. She's getting older, and she sometimes moves stiffly, slowly, when she wakes up in the morning. She's less inclined to jump on the bed and snuggle next to you on the couch. And you know, in your heart of hearts, that these signs add up to one thing: your dog is suffering from arthritis.

What is arthritis?

The type of pain and stiffness I describe above (commonly referred to as arthritis) is osteoarthritis, and it affects 25-30% of dogs (according to some estimates, that number is on the rise). It's a chronic condition that arises when the cartilage surrounding a joint deteriorates, often because of chronic inflammation. Because cartilage covers the ends of bones and acts as a kind of barrier/shock absorber to keep them from scraping against each other, as the cartilage wears down, the bones it surrounds can rub against each other, which is uncomfortable at best and painful at worst.

Natural and easy ways to address arthritis

Make sure your dog is the proper weight

One of the simplest but most overlooked ways to address arthritis is to make sure your dog is the proper weight. One of my friends once said to a dog that was on the plump side, "You aren't fat, doggy! You're just big-furred!" (He's a nice guy, and he didn't want the dog to feel bad for being heavy.) However, if your dog has arthritis, they shouldn't be "big-furred."

150

You should be able to easily feel your dog's ribs when you press on their sides. When you look at them from the side, you should be able to see a nice waist tuck, and when you press on their chest, you shouldn't be able to feel a big layer of fat. Here in America, we've gotten used to seeing dogs that are too heavy, so sometimes a dog that's the ideal weight looks too thin to us, at least at first. Remember, especially when you're dealing with arthritis, that it's better for your dog to be slightly thin than slightly heavy. It will make a huge difference to your dog's comfort and longevity.

Exercise is key

Ok, stay with me on this one: If your dog is experiencing the joint pain and discomfort that comes with arthritis, then it's especially important to make sure she's getting appropriate and adequate exercise. It may seem counterintuitive...if it's painful for her to move around, then you might feel like the last thing you want to do is make her move around. But when our dogs don't get exercise (especially if they're overweight on top of it), not only do their joints have excessive strain, they also don't get continually strengthened and stretched. It's a recipe for disaster.

Of course, you want to be smart about what you ask your dog to do. Particularly if your dog is already showing signs of arthritis, you can (and should!) start them out with gentle walks so you don't stress their muscles out. If your dog is in a lot of discomfort, a slow, short (10 or 15 minutes) walk twice a day is a great place to start. As they start to build up endurance, you can increase the distance and the speed. Let your dog guide you...you want them to be comfortable, but you also want to make sure their joints and muscles get used on a frequent, consistent basis.

Diet

For a long time, most people believed "wear and tear" was the root cause of arthritis. However, we now know chronic inflammation is behind joint disease and damage[78]. One of the biggest contributors to chronic inflammation is a processed-food diet. The carbohydrates, fillers, and toxic chemicals in most kibble, along with the methods used to make kibble, can all trigger inflammation[79]. And because your dog's body is hit with these inflammation triggers every single meal, your dog exists in a sort of low-grade, chronically inflamed state. Eventually, arthritis and other diseases of chronic inflammation (including cancer) occur[80].

Even if your dog has been eating kibble for years, changing them to a raw, balanced, varied species-appropriate diet can have a profound impact on their joint health. Case in point: We switched our senior dog, Cleo, to raw when she was about 15 years old. At the time, she was suffering terribly from arthritis: the pain was affecting every aspect of her life, and it was also causing her to be reactive towards other dogs (understandably—chronic pain can make anyone grumpy!). Within a relatively short time of changing her diet, she was feeling much better—enough that she could join us and our other dogs on the hikes she loved so much. She lived to be 19 years old, and she had a high-quality, pain-free life up to the very end.

Supplements

While keeping your dog at the appropriate weight, feeding her a species-appropriate diet, and making sure she gets adequate and appropriate exercise can go a long way towards relieving arthritis, sometimes your dog may need a little extra help. If you've tried the first three tips and you feel like your buddy still doesn't have all her zest back, there are a few more things you can try.

Omega-3s

Two of the best anti-inflammatories are the omega-3 essential fatty acids EPA and DHA (essential fatty acids refer to fatty acids that your dog can't make herself, but instead must get through food). If your dog has arthritis, you might want to try increasing the omega-3s she's getting. While many people feed fish oil, I prefer to give my dogs supplementation in whole food form wherever possible. I feed my dogs whole raw frozen (or semi-thawed) sardines from our local Asian market. The sardines are packed with omega-3s, the dogs love them, they're cheap, and they're convenient. Make sure you get wild-caught sardines. You can also feed herring, mackerel, and other oily fish (if you feed wild-caught salmon, avoid salmon from the Pacific Ocean and from streams in the Pacific Northwest. It can contain bacteria that can be fatal to dogs[81]).

If you can't find sardines or other whole raw fish, consider supplementing with krill oil. I find krill oil to be a better choice than fish oil because krill have less contaminants and are lower in mercury than fish (because they're at the bottom of the food chain). Plus, krill oil has more omega-3s than fish oil[82]. One option to try is Dr. Mercola Krill Oil for Pets.

MSM

MSM (Methylsulfonylmethane) is one of the best supplements available for dogs with arthritis. MSM occurs naturally in every cell in the body; it's a sulfur compound that helps maintain flexible membranes and strong connective tissue. MSM is great at reducing inflammation (remember, chronic inflammation is what causes arthritis), and it also aids with reducing the swelling that comes along with arthritis. I used MSM from Wolf Creek Ranch (www.wolfcreekranch.net) for Cleo, and I was consistently very happy with it.

Turmeric

Turmeric paste is an amazing anti-inflammatory. Check out the chapter about supplements for a great turmeric paste recipe and more info about turmeric.

Glucosamine and Chondroitin Sulfate

Glucosamine[83] and chondroitin sulfate are two powerful supplements to use when your dog has chronic arthritis. Glucosamine has been shown to help with arthritis pain, and it may also help rebuild and strengthen cartilage that's been damaged by chronic inflammation. Whole raw chicken feet are a great source of glucosamine/chondroitin sulfate (like I said, I prefer to provide nutrients in whole food form wherever possible, because they tend to be more bioavailable and better absorbed). Green-lipped mussel also contains high amounts of glucosamine. If needed, you can also give your dog a high-quality canine glucosamine/chondroitin sulfate supplement.

Alternative therapies

Sometimes when our senior girl, Cleo, overdid it a bit—especially when she was 17 or 18—she needed a little extra help to get back to her best. And one of my favorite ways to help ease her joints and help her bounce back fast was with essential oils. I found Young Living's Frankincense oil to be especially powerful for her. I would either put some in my hands and massage her with it, or I would drop it down her back (6-8 drops spread out down the length of her spine). The results were always amazing! I remember one evening when she was having some trouble getting up from her bed to go for a walk. I dropped the Frankincense down her spine, and within 30 seconds, she jumped up and ran to the door; when I opened it for her so we could go on our evening walk, she proceeded to jog (with no indication of stiffness or pain) down the street. She didn't stop jogging (sometimes breaking into a full-out run) until we got back to the house. My husband was there and was shocked at what a difference it made. Powerful stuff, I'm telling you.

Massage therapy and TTouch are also great for giving relief to dogs with arthritis. The good news is you can learn both massage and TTouch techniques yourself (YouTube videos and books are both great resources). Once you learn them, you can do them anytime your dog is in discomfort. Both are gentle ways to help your dog feel better, and I can tell you from experience (I've used them for Cleo and other dogs that were in pain) that both are highly effective.

Conclusion

So, there you have it: how to ease your dog's arthritis easily, using natural methods that get to the root cause of the problem instead of just masking the symptoms. The more of these ideas you put into practice, the better off your dog will be. So, give them a try. Speaking from personal experience, I know how good it feels to see your senior dog full of energy, full of life, and free from pain and discomfort.

Periodontal and tooth problems

Many pet owners notice their pet's teeth have lots of tartar and plaque, and their gums are red and inflamed. They also notice their dogs have bad breath. Some people brush their pet's teeth, some people get their teeth professionally cleaned (which also generally means they have to be put under, which can be dangerous and expensive), some buy them dental chews, and some just ignore the issue until it gets so bad the dog needs serious dental attention. While poor oral health is not always because of a poor diet, oftentimes it is. Contrary to popular belief, processed pet food tends to contribute to plaque and tartar because it gets stuck on the teeth or in the gum line. A species-appropriate raw diet, however, scrapes the teeth clean, and it doesn't leave any nasty residue on the teeth. Many dogs that are fed a species-appropriate raw diet have sparkling white teeth, healthy gums, good breath, and healthy jaws. Unfortunately, poor oral health is another example of what we now consider normal because it is so common, but the good news is that typically it can be easily addressed by fixing the diet.

154

If you make the switch to raw (three cheers for you, if you do!), chances are high everything will go smoothly. But sometimes, dog parents find they face a nasty little problem: diarrhea. It's hard to stay enthusiastic about the whole process if your dog is experiencing this (and let's face it: lots of dogs do). But have no fear: I'm here to help. So, take heart, my fellow raw feeder: there is hope. You can soon have your dog on the right nutritional track, without this icky side effect.

The good(?) part of diarrhea

You might be asking yourself how I can possibly say anything about diarrhea is good. And my answer is that diarrhea is a common detox symptom that occurs when we switch our dogs to a species-appropriate raw diet. If you've been feeding kibble, your dog has probably built up a bunch of toxins in their body, and when you stop putting in the toxins and start supporting them nutritionally, their body starts to get rid of those toxins. In many dogs (although not all of them), this shows up as diarrhea. So, in the sense that diarrhea can be a sign your dog's body is purifying, it can be a good thing. However, knowing that intellectually doesn't mean it's really something you want to deal with for more than a day or two.

That brings us to the other good news: there are things you can do to help reduce both the duration and amount of diarrhea your dog has, especially if you've moved through the detox phase. And in case you're wondering, you can tell your dog is in the detox phase because, even though they may be experiencing things like diarrhea or itchy skin, they otherwise act like normal. They won't seem listless, lethargic, and "off." Instead, their energy levels will be normal, they'll be excited to see you, and they'll be happy to eat, play, and run around (or snooze on the couch, if that's their normal state).

The 80/10/10 rule

Most people who have started feeding a raw diet have heard about the 80/10/10 rule. That's the rule that says you should aim to feed your dog about 80% muscle meat, 10% bone, and 10% organ (5% liver and 5% non-liver) over the course of a week. It's based on the composition (for lack of a better word) of a deer, which most raw feeders consider to be the perfect natural prey for a wild canid.

Here's the thing: some dogs need more than 10% bone. Give them just 10% bone, and the results aren't pretty.

Wild canids eat a variety of different animals, and each of those animals have a different percentage of meat, bones, and organs. Sometimes they get more bone, sometimes they get less. And remember, wild canids generally don't have damage done to their immune systems or digestive systems like our domestic dogs do. So, their guts are healthier, and they don't get exactly 10% of bone each week. If your dog has diarrhea from a raw diet, be OK with upping the bone percentage a bit. You can always back off down the road (once you've gotten their stool to a good place) and see if everything maintains. But if it doesn't, it's fine. Feed your dog according to their requirements, not according to a general guideline.

The effect of certain proteins

One of the tenets of raw feeding is variety. It's important to feed different proteins to your dog to maintain a robust and complete nutrient profile. It's also important to feed a variety to keep them excited about mealtime! For some dogs, though, certain proteins might cause diarrhea.

If you've been feeding raw long enough to get through the healing response/detox stage and your dog is still having diarrhea issues, consider trying different proteins. Some dogs have diarrhea when fed pork, for example, or when fed beef organs (as opposed to other types of organs). Be willing to experiment, and then avoid the proteins that cause problems for your pet.

Natural remedies to try

If adding more bone and switching proteins doesn't help relieve the situation, there are some natural things you can try. They don't "cure" diarrhea, per se, but they will support your dog's body so it can re-balance and overcome the root cause of the diarrhea.

Probiotics

Remember a lot of diarrhea involves an imbalance in the gut flora. Giving probiotics consistently can, over time, make a big difference for your dog's digestive health and quality of stools. Two good options are Pet Flora Vitality Science (for smaller dogs) and Prescript-Assist (for large or giant breed dogs).

Herbs

Some people say the Chinese herb *Po Chai* works very well for diarrhea. It generally comes in sets of ten or twelve small vials filled with tiny pellets. For a large dog, I've seen it recommended to give one vial three times a day; small dogs should get ½ vial three times of day. If you're unsure, check with someone familiar with giving herbs to dogs. Keep giving this herb until the diarrhea has fully cleared up.

Homeopathic remedies

In general, you want to get a pellet or two in your dog's mouth (right next to its inner cheek) with each "treatment." Let it dissolve there. If your dog spits it out, try dissolving it in water and then using a syringe to get it into your dog's mouth so it comes into contact with the inside cheek. Many people recommend giving 1–2 pellets every 4 hours for a total of three treatments. Don't give any food for 10 minutes before or after. If your dog isn't noticeably better after 24 hours, try another remedy.

Podophyllum 30C: For typical diarrhea with a forceful, gushing stool, especially if it smells unusually bad[84].

Mercurius corrosivus 30C: For frequent bloody stools with much straining, usually after eating toxic substances or from a viral infection[85].

Arsenicum album 30C: For diarrhea from eating spoiled meat. Usually there are small, frequent bowel movements, and your dog may be weak, thirsty, and cold[86].

Pulsatilla 30C: For dogs that have overeaten or had food that is too rich or fatty. They may become subdued and timid, and may not be thirsty (which is unusual during diarrhea)[87].

You should be able to get any of these remedies from Amazon.

Cystitis or urinary tract issues

So now we come to urinary tract disease, #9 on our list of the most common reasons people take their dogs to the vet.

Something to keep in mind is many bladder issues are rooted in inflammation, not bacteria, so antibiotics don't do anything for them[88] (plus, as we've discussed, giving antibiotics can set your dog up for recurring issues down the road).

If you've ever had urinary tract problems (if you have, I'm sorry—they're the worst!), you'll probably be familiar with some of the signs[89]:

- Frequent urge to urinate
- The urine may or may not have blood in it. If it does, it can be obvious (blood clots) or barely noticeable (just a trace amount at the very end)
- General restlessness
- Immediately after urinating, your dog may squat and/or strain to go again
- Waking up multiple times in the night to try and go to the bathroom

Your dog may also lick herself (often intensely) before and/or after urinating.

Since antibiotics aren't the way to go, what can you do to get your dog back on track in a safe, natural way if they're suffering from a UTI?

Like everything else in here, make sure they're on a raw diet. That will help reduce inflammation. Also, reduce or eliminate anything that will destroy "good" bacteria: keeping a strong population of good bacteria can help keep your dog's body in balance and working properly. There are also some natural remedies you can use to help support your dog's body in reducing the inflammation/infection.

Homeopathic remedies

- *Nux vomica*: Particularly if the dog was given an OTC flea/tick preventive or a heartworm pill shortly before presenting with UTI symptoms. It's also a good choice if your dog strains when urinating or is constipated.
- *Mercurius* (either *Mercurius vivus* or *Mercurius solubilis*): Particularly if your dog has blood in the urine, is urinating frequently at night, is especially restless at night, and/or is straining (either for peeing or diarrhea).

Giving the remedies:

You can use the pellet form of the homeopathic remedy (the 30C potency is a good option). As Dana Scott from *Dogs Naturally* magazine describes, a good way to prepare the remedies is the following[90]:

1. Take 3 pellets (it doesn't matter what size your dog is) and crush them to powder.

2. Add the crushed pellets to ½ cup of purified water.
3. Stir for about 30 seconds.
4. Dribble a bit of your pellet/water solution into your dog's mouth. Your goal is to wet the mucous membranes.
5. If the symptoms are severe, give 3 doses total, 15 minutes apart. If the symptoms are milder, give 3 doses total, 30–60 minutes apart.
6. Watch your dog for an hour or so. You're looking for a lessening or cessation of the symptoms.
7. Store the remaining mixture covered at room temperature. If you notice your dog's symptoms return, repeat the process (if the issue doesn't clear up, talk to a holistic veterinarian or a homeopath).

Essential oils

If you decide to use essential oils, you can apply them a few different ways. Dilute the oils (equal parts essential oil and olive oil or fractionated coconut oil), then apply a few drops on the skin covering the bladder 3–6 times per day[91], or dilute 2–4 drops of the essential oil and use the blend in a warm compress over the affected area 1 or 2 times daily[92]. Some essential oils to try include Myrrh, Spikenard, Melaleuca Alternifolia, Juniper, Oregano, Lemon, Mountain Savory, Thyme, Cistus, Rosemary, Clove, Inspiration, Thieves, Melrose, DiGize, R.C., or Purification[93]. Remember, I only use Young Living essential oils for my dogs (and my family).

Impacted anal glands

Take something as seemingly ordinary as feces; we're used to seeing large amounts of smelly poop from our pets. Often, it's also relatively soft, which of course makes it harder to clean up. Contrast this with the feces of a raw-fed animal. Their fecal matter is much smaller, both in size of individual stools and the overall quantity of stool. It has much less of an odor, it's harder, and it decomposes more quickly. This is because raw diets have way more bioavailable nutrients than processed pet food, so your dog can use more of their food. Processed pet food has a lot of filler and junk that your pet can't use; this filler gets shed out in the feces, which leads to the vast amount of poop we see from dogs fed a conventional, processed-pet-food diet.

When your dog eats a raw diet, he gets the appropriate amount of calcium and phosphorous in his diet. His stool tends to be much harder (because of the calcium), which means he must strain a little bit to push it out. This straining keeps the anal glands clean, clear, and in good working order. So many dogs regularly need to get their anal glands cleaned out by the vet or a groomer—in fact, this is so common most groomers include this as a standard part of their grooming! However, when dogs are fed a species-appropriate raw diet, they typically don't have anal gland issues.

Chronic kidney disease

Before we really dive into the discussion, I should point out kidney failure in dogs can take one of two forms: acute kidney (or renal) failure and chronic kidney failure. Acute kidney failure is often triggered by something like a severe bacterial infection or a urinary obstruction. It may also come about because of the dog ingesting a toxic substance, such as antifreeze or a poisonous plant. Dogs that are severely dehydrated can also develop acute kidney failure.

Acute kidney failure

If your dog develops acute kidney failure, he or she will probably exhibit severe vomiting, be very lethargic, and show no interest in food at all. Less frequently, your dog may also appear disoriented, stumble and/or show a lack of coordination, and/or strain to urinate. If you suspect your dog is experiencing acute kidney failure, you should seek veterinary help immediately.

Chronic kidney failure

Unlike acute kidney failure, chronic kidney failure in dogs often takes months or years to develop. In general, dogs don't even begin to show symptoms of chronic kidney failure until 70-75% of kidney function has been lost. While not every dog will show the same symptoms, common symptoms of chronic kidney failure include[94]:

- Vomiting
- Diarrhea
- Constipation
- Depression
- Lethargy
- Increased thirst
- Lack of appetite
- Acute blindness
- Seizures

- Bloody urine
- Weight loss
- Increased urination (both in frequency and amount)

These symptoms will often come on slowly over a period of time. If you suspect your dog has chronic kidney failure, your vet can do a blood test and urinalysis. Once it's been diagnosed, though, what should you do?

While there isn't a cure for chronic kidney disease, there are things you can do to help support your dog's body so he or she can live as optimal a life as possible. To help you understand what your options are, it's important to understand a little bit about the kidneys themselves.

Understanding the kidneys

The kidneys are part of the body's filtration system. They help sift out waste products (such as glucose, salts, urea, and uric acid) and extra water from the blood. The waste products and extra water become urine, which then goes to the bladder for elimination. While the kidneys can filter an extraordinary amount of waste, if there's a build-up of toxins in the body, they may not be able to filter it out quickly enough; if this happens, the kidneys may become clogged. Over time, this can compromise kidney function and lead to them being extremely over-worked or even damaged. In these instances, chronic kidney failure often results. When the kidneys are supported and aren't subjected to more toxins than they can handle, they are much less likely to become clogged or damaged.

Addressing kidney failure

So, what do you do if your dog has chronic kidney failure? The answer often depends on how far gone the kidneys are, but no matter what, it's important to aim to reduce the toxin load on the kidneys.

Dietary considerations

While most treatments for chronic kidney disease include dietary changes, conventional practice advises feeding dogs with kidney failure a low-protein diet. However, this belief appears to be a result of research that was done on kidney disease in rats. Unlike dogs, rats are omnivores; they aren't equipped to handle high amounts of protein[95]. Our dogs, on the other hand, are carnivores, and they—from their dentition to their digestive systems—are designed to handle a raw diet. The key is to feed them high quality, raw protein that is antibiotic- and hormone-free; this ensures their bodies can assimilate the nutrients with a minimum of effort, and (as I've said before) it ensures they don't take in toxins every time they eat. Studies are being done that support the fact that restricting protein intake in dogs with chronic kidney failure doesn't actually aid in renal function; based on these studies, even some conventional vets are beginning to understand restricting protein isn't helpful[96].

Many people recommend diets low in sodium for dogs with kidney failure. While a species-appropriate raw food diet doesn't have an excessive amount of sodium, many processed dog foods do. Again, high quality, raw, fresh meat, bones, and glands will be easily and readily assimilated by the body; in other words, your pet's kidneys won't be further taxed when your dog eats this way, because more toxins aren't being introduced.

If your dog has chronic kidney failure, you will need to pay attention to how much phosphorous they're getting. Bone does have a high amount of phosphorous, but it shouldn't be removed completely. You may need to adjust somewhat if the disease has become severe—for example, you may want to focus on feeding meatier bones such as poultry breasts or thighs, and avoiding bones with less meat, such as poultry backs and wings. You may want to avoid beef and pork ribs as well. You may decide to feed egg-shells instead of feeding bone at all. Make sure, though, you continue to feed bone or eggshell, as these contain calcium and other nutrients that are vital for keeping the system functioning as smoothly as possible[97].

Calcium is important in part because it binds to phosphorous and helps to remove excess amounts of phosphorous from your dog's body. Fattier meats can also help to reduce phosphorous levels, but remember they should be fed raw to avoid overtaxing the other organs (especially the pancreas) and to help ensure the proteins and nutrients are bioavailable to your dog.

Many dogs with kidney failure show signs of depression, dizziness, and muscle weakness. Magnesium can help the body return to balance and overcome these issues, and can be found in a wide variety of whole food sources, including rabbit, chicken, turkey, pork, goat, ostrich, eggs, beef, salmon, sardines, and bison. See Chapter 16, "Vitamins, Minerals, and Where to Find Them," for more details.

Omega-3s are an essential fatty acid (meaning they're vital to the proper functioning of your dog's system, but your dog can't produce them itself) that, among other things, help support the kidneys. Fish and fish oil are a good source of omega-3s for dogs, as is krill oil. Flaxseed oil, on the other hand, is very difficult for our dogs to break down and assimilate.

You may also consider giving probiotics and digestive enzymes to your pet. If you choose to give these as a supplement, look for ones specifically formulated for dogs. Raw green tripe is loaded with probiotics and digestive enzymes, and allows dogs to get these things from a whole food source.

While a balanced species-appropriate raw food diet is vital for supporting a dog with chronic kidney disease, there are a few other things that are also important.

Exercise

Exercise is vital for keeping the systems functioning as normally and optimally as possible. If your dog is very weak, you can try a short gentle walk, or even try holding your dog while gently bouncing on a trampoline. This can be very helpful in flushing out the circulatory system.

Water

It is important to give pure, filtered water—remember, we want to avoid introducing more toxins into your dog's system. Most tap water contains high levels of toxins, such as chlorine, fluoride, and other chemicals, along with trace amounts of aluminum, nitrates, insecticides, herbicides, and even prescription medications (for more information, see the section "Not all water is created equal" in Chapter 22: "Moving Beyond the Feeding"). So, give your pet filtered water, especially if their kidneys are already overloaded with toxins.

CoQ10 supplementation

Research has been done that shows one milligram of CoQ10 per pound of body weight daily can help reduce creatinine levels[98]. Creatinine, the waste product of creatine, is normally filtered out of the blood by the kidneys. However, when the kidneys stop functioning properly, they can't filter out the creatinine effectively. Creatinine levels in the blood is one of the ways to determine whether a dog is in kidney failure, and if so, how advanced it is.

Conclusion

Unfortunately, in general, damage done to the kidneys is not reversible. However, there are many things you can do to help support the kidneys and ensure they function as optimally as possible. If your dog is diagnosed with kidney disease, talk to a holistic veterinarian as well.

Coprophagia (eating feces)

One of the most common questions dog owners ask me is how to get their dogs to stop eating poop. It's rare (in fact, I've never heard of a single instance) for cats to engage this behavior (known as coprophagia), but for dogs, it seems to be a common problem. Before you can figure out how to stop it, though, it's important to understand why it happens.

The most common reason a dog engages in coprophagia is because they aren't getting enough of some nutrient or mineral, or because there's an imbalance in their digestive system. They may, for example, have too much "bad" bacteria and not enough "good" bacteria (perhaps because of being given antibiotics), or they may not be getting enough live digestive enzymes or vitamins in their food. They may also eat poop because they've seen other dogs do it and learned it from them, or because they're stressed. I've also heard of puppy mill dogs (who live in incredibly stressful conditions, both physically and psychologically) that eat poop, probably because of stress and an imbalanced diet.

Dogs need digestive enzymes to live and thrive. These enzymes are incredibly delicate, and when kibble or canned food is processed, it destroys these enzymes. Your dog's body, unfortunately, doesn't produce enough digestive enzymes to make up for the lack of them in the processed food, and over time, they go into an enzyme-deficit. In many cases, dogs that are fed kibble and/or canned food experience this enzyme-deficit, and they are driven to find those enzymes elsewhere, such as in the feces of other animals.

It's not just enzymes dogs are searching for when they eat feces. They're also after the microbes they need to regenerate the "good" bacteria in their gut. Feces often has very high levels of these microbes, so dogs eat the poop to try and correct that imbalance as well.

It's important to understand this, so when you see your dog eating poop, you'll know he isn't trying to be disgusting, or defiant, or bad, or gross…he's trying to correct an issue or imbalance he's dealing with.

I can speak from personal experience about this, because I used to experience this issue with my dogs regularly. Before we knew differently, we used to feed our dogs kibble. And guess what? Our dogs ate poop—their own, the other dogs', the poop in the litter box…it was rampant. It wasn't always that way, of course, but over time, it seemed like they were eating more and more poop. I didn't have an effective solution for it, and I didn't even really understand why they were doing it. All I knew was they **were** doing it, I thought it was gross, and I wanted them to stop. Fast forward to when they had all been on a raw diet for a while, and the poop eating was pretty much nonexistent.

And that brings us nicely to how you might be able to address the issue, if you're experiencing it with your own dogs. Depending on why your dog is engaging in this behavior, there are different things you can do to address it; read on for some ideas for dealing with this issue.

First and foremost, you should make sure your dog is eating a balanced, varied, raw species-appropriate diet. By feeding your dog this way, you help to replenish the digestive enzymes and maintain a healthy gut. You also make sure your dog is getting all the nutrients he needs for optimal vitality. This one simple switch was all it really took for our dogs to stop eating poop. *Side note: Green tripe is loaded with digestive enzymes and probiotics and is a great food to include in any dog's diet, especially if they are showing signs of an imbalance (such as eating their poop or the poop of another animal).*

Clean up after your dog after he goes to the bathroom. Same goes for any other animals you have. Bottom line—if you clean up the poop, they won't be able to eat it.

Because eating poop can be a response to stress, anxiety, or boredom, make sure your dog is getting adequate exercise and their minds are kept busy throughout the day. If you notice your dog frequently paces, doesn't settle down, and rarely stays still throughout the day, you need to increase his exercise. Your dog should want to lay down and rest after an exercise session. Depending on your dog, you may need to give them focused exercise sessions several times throughout the day. The more tired they are, and the more enrichment they have, the less stressed they are. The less stressed they are, the less likely they are to engage in behaviors you don't like.

If you decide to use over-the-counter deterrents (which have only been found to be effective up to 2% of the time), make sure you use ones that are non-toxic and don't contain monosodium glutamate (MSG). If you've tried everything and nothing else works, you may also want to consider microbiome restorative therapy[99].

While this is one habit that is certainly less-than-charming to us, it can give you clues about the state of your dog's digestive health. And, like so many other things, once you address the root cause of the issue—be it an imbalance, a deficit, or something else—there's a high likelihood the behavior—the symptom, if you will—will go away.

Doggy odor

Another common issue many dog owners report is a "doggy" smell. While common, though, this issue isn't normal. When you think about it, it doesn't make sense a carnivore and predator would have a distinct and strong odor. Having a strong odor would make it much more difficult to sneak up on their highly sensitive prey. Wild wolves and other wild canines don't have a doggy odor, and dogs fed a raw diet don't have a strong odor either. Dogs fed a processed food diet tend to smell, which most owners address by giving them baths, but once those same dogs are switched to a raw diet, the odor disappears. Again, while doggy odor has become very common, it's not normal. In fact, it's an indicator the body isn't functioning at an optimal level.

Zinc Deficiency

There's an issue facing dogs that, while not very well known, can be fatal. And this issue, my fellow dog parents, is zinc deficiency. Zinc deficiency mostly affects Huskies and Malamutes, but it's recognized as impacting other breeds too, most notably giant breeds (especially Great Danes and St. Bernards) and large breeds, such as German Shepherds and Dobermans. And unfortunately, even if your dog isn't one of these breeds, zinc deficiency can still affect her. Given that the issue isn't familiar to most people but impacts lots of dogs, I wanted to share some information about it with you, especially how to recognize it and what to do about it.

Before we dive in, I'd like to encourage you to do as much research as possible about this issue if you suspect your dog has a zinc deficiency. There's some really good information available online, and you can also talk to a veterinarian or a certified animal naturopath (in either case, make sure you find someone who's familiar with zinc deficiency in dogs). This is especially true when it comes to supplementing to help with zinc deficiency: you can harm your dog if you supplement inappropriately, and too much zinc can be fatal to dogs.

That being said, let's look at how zinc, and conversely, a zinc deficiency, affect the health of your dog.

Zinc and dogs

Zinc is the second most commonly used mineral in your dog's body. If it's not present in adequate amounts, it can lead to a wide range of issues, and it can eventually result in death.

Malabsorption and mal-digestion

Some dogs can't effectively use the nutrients that come into their body. There are a lot of reasons for this, but usually it's because their body doesn't properly absorb vitamins, minerals, and other nutrients present in the food (malabsorption) or their digestion is impaired (mal-digestion). Interestingly, both malabsorption and mal-digestion are often related to the dog's diet.

I get that zinc is important. But what exactly does it do?

After iron, zinc is the most plentiful essential trace mineral in your dog's body. It's a powerful antioxidant and aids in various metabolic processes in the body. Zinc works by itself and with other nutrients, such as copper, B-complex vitamins, vitamin A, calcium, and phosphorous, to support the body and aid in different essential bodily functions.

Here's the kicker: even though zinc is one of the most important trace minerals, the body has no way to store zinc. That means the body needs a regular, adequate supply of zinc; if it doesn't get this, it becomes deficient in zinc.

Studies have shown only 15–40% of ingested zinc from the mammalian diet is well absorbed, and if a dog has malabsorption or mal-digestion issues, this percentage is even lower[100]. Furthermore, certain foods can make it more difficult for your dog to absorb zinc properly, which only adds to the deficiency problem.

One issue, multiple symptoms

Frequently, when a dog is zinc deficient, she'll present with a variety of symptoms. In many cases, the symptoms change over time, with different symptoms appearing as the deficiency continues. Because the symptoms often appear unrelated to each other, conventional treatment may try to address the symptoms individually. However, if the underlying issue (zinc deficiency) isn't addressed, the symptoms will continue and get progressively worse. The good news? With the right approach, you can help ensure your dog doesn't become zinc deficient (and you can help them overcome it if they do have a zinc deficiency). Since zinc deficiency is related to diet, providing the right diet goes a long way towards keeping your dog balanced and thriving. But more about that later.

Your dog's body uses zinc for many processes. There's an order in which these processes occur; if there isn't enough zinc, not all the processes can be completed. Over time, if this happens consistently, your dog's health will begin to suffer in various ways. In general, the signs of zinc deficiency[101] present in the following order:

1. *Chronic digestive issues* (owners sometimes assume these are food allergies). These often include diarrhea and a lack of appetite (the lack of appetite is sometimes attributed to being a "picky eater").

2. *Crusty, raised patches of dermatitis.* These most often occur around the eyes, on the muzzle, on the paws, or on the groin. Sometimes mistakenly diagnosed as hot spots or skin allergies.

3. *An under-functioning or overreactive immune system* (in other words, the immune system is unable to handle infections, or it responds to everything as though it's a threat). In general, during this stage, your dog may present with various seemingly unrelated illnesses, but in reality, they're all immune-system related. At this point, cancer may develop.

4. *A malfunctioning thyroid gland,* leading to weight gain or weight loss, increased or decreased appetite, skin and coat problems, and secondary infections. Your dog may also have a persistent cough. The body's hormone levels are generally out of balance at this point.

5. *Major organ failure* (including kidney failure, liver failure, and/or heart failure).

6. *Seizures.* These occur because, if there is insufficient zinc, taurine in the brain can't function effectively as a neurotransmitter smoother, and erratic neurotransmitter firings (in other words, seizures) can result.

It's important to note here that while this is generally the symptomatic order zinc deficiency follows, some dogs don't follow this list. They may skip a few symptoms, or they might skip the initial symptoms and jump right to the end (or close to the end) of the list. Being proactive in making sure your dog is getting and absorbing the right amount of zinc (instead of waiting until your dog is exhibiting symptoms) is the best policy when it comes to making sure your dog never has to deal with this.

Zinc and diet

As you know, I'm a huge proponent of giving dogs nutrients in whole food form. Feeding your dog a balanced, varied, species-appropriate raw diet can help increase zinc levels naturally. Plus, because the nutrients in raw diets are so bioavailable, your dog's body can absorb them relatively well (and that includes zinc).

If you feed your dog a processed kibble, be aware many dog food manufacturers add zinc to the food, but they add a cheap source of zinc in the form of zinc oxide or zinc sulphate. Your dog's body can't easily absorb or use these forms of zinc, and often, zinc deficiency will result.

For more info, check out my chart of which raw, species-appropriate foods have various vitamins and minerals, including zinc, in Chapter 16: "Vitamins, Minerals, and Where to Find Them".

Supplementing zinc

If you're feeding a balanced, varied raw diet but your dog isn't showing any improvement, you may have to supplement. One commercial supplement is Zinpro, which is an organic supplement of zinc methionine. Your dog's body can absorb this type of zinc easily into their bloodstream.

There are other zinc mineral supplements available, but before you start supplementing this way, there are some things to keep in mind[102]:

- The body doesn't have a way to store zinc, so it must get it regularly in adequate amounts
- Research suggests dogs need a lot more zinc than humans do (up to 100 mgs daily, while humans generally need less than 15 mgs daily)
- In general, you can only tell your dog is zinc deficient if they develop one of the signs I discussed earlier
- Not all forms of zinc work equally well for dogs
- Zinc supplements work best when given four hours after your dog has eaten (giving it four hours after, instead of with the meal, reduces the chance that calcium will interfere with the body absorbing the zinc)
- Zinc interacts with copper, iron, calcium, and vitamin A, so supplementing incorrectly can cause imbalances in other nutrients that can lead to adverse reactions in your dog

Most usable to least usable forms of zinc:

- Zinc citrate, picolinate, and gluconate are highly absorbable and easily used by your dog's body
- Chelated zinc is slightly less absorbable than zinc picolinate and zinc gluconate, but it generally doesn't cause as much stomach upset as some other forms of zinc
- Zinc methionine is relatively bioavailable and well-digested by most dogs
- Zinc sulphate is hard on the stomach, so in general, it is

recommended you crush it and add it in the food. However, this makes it less absorbable

- Zinc oxide is very difficult for your dog to absorb. However, it's cheap, which makes it the zinc of choice for many dog food manufacturers when adding zinc to their dog food

Zinc toxicity

Zinc can cause problems when given in large amounts. Single doses of 225–450 mgs can cause a dog to vomit, and lethal doses of zinc start around 900 mgs. Zinc toxicity presents in dogs in a variety of ways: excessive panting, vomiting, lethargy, diarrhea, rapid breathing with an erratic or fast heartrate, and even jaundice. If your dog experiences zinc poisoning, get them to a veterinarian immediately.

Determining how much zinc to give

The general rule of thumb is 25 mgs of zinc per 50 pounds of your dog's weight. If you don't see an improvement in your dog after six weeks at this level, you may want to increase the daily dosage to 50 mgs[103]. Always, if you aren't sure, consult with an expert who is familiar with zinc deficiency in dogs.

Conclusion

Zinc deficiency, while dangerous, doesn't have to be a long, drawn-out death sentence. Being proactive—feeding a balanced, varied raw diet—will go a long way towards making sure your dog never faces this issue. And by being aware of the signs, you can act to address it through supplementation if needed.

Seizures

Like everything else in this chapter, if your dog has seizures, it means something is fundamentally out of balance. Below are some things you can try that may help your dog if they are experiencing this heart-wrenching condition.

Switch to a raw diet

Good news for you—this book shows you how to do that! Make sure you feed them food that is antibiotic- and hormone-free, and organic/

pasture-raised/grass-fed as much as possible. Hormones and antibiotics can have an adverse impact on the brain and lead to further problems.

Stop vaccinating as much as possible

One side effect of vaccines can be seizures, and there is a large body of information available that shows a dog that has seizures shouldn't be vaccinated.

Stop using toxins

Stop using pesticides, whether they're conventional flea/tick (and other parasite) preventatives, pesticides and herbicides on your lawn and garden, or pesticides (sprays, etc.) in your house. These generally contain neurotoxins that can further damage the brain.

Rule out thyroid problems

If you haven't already, you may want to rule out a possible thyroid issue. Jean Dodds, DVM, can do thyroid testing. Your veterinarian will need to send the bloodwork off for you. Dr. Dodds' website is at www.hemopet.org (go to the "Hemolife Diagnostics" section of the website).

Provide supplements for dogs with seizures

The supplements listed here are items you may want to try. Remember, the goal is to bring your dog's immune system back into balance. You don't need to give all of these, and in fact, it's usually best to try one thing at a time so you know what's working and how your dog responds to it. Bear in mind, too, these supplements will not, in and of themselves, "heal" your dog and eliminate the root cause of the seizures, but they may assist with palliation and/or helping your dog move into a state of vitality by supporting and helping to rebalance his body. Do your research to determine the appropriate amounts to give, and to ensure there are no contraindications.

- Mountain Rose Herbs Tranquility Blend: https://www.mountainroseherbs.com/products/animal-extract-tranquility-blend/profile
- Pet Alive EaseSure-S: http://www.nativeremedies.com/petalive/products/easesure-soothes-nervous-system-cats-dogs.html

- Bright Wings, Inc. Balance Me: http://floweressencesforanimals. com/product/balance-me-2/
- Bach Rescue Remedy for Pets: http://www.bachflower.com/ rescue-remedy-pet/
- Ice packs (applied during a seizure): http://dawgbusiness.blogspot. com/2012/08/veterinary-highlights-arresting-canine.html

Natural modalities that may help:

In some cases, animal chiropractic has been shown to have a positive effect on dogs with epilepsy. You can find an animal chiropractic doctor at http://www.avcadoctors.com/.

Acupuncture has also been shown to be helpful to some dogs with epilepsy. Go to http://www.aava.org/ to find a veterinary acupuncturist.

Acupressure and massage may also be helpful. You can find a practitioner by going to http://www.nbcaam.org/member-listing.

Noel Socks' Story

The following story is shared by Alison Peloquin about her sweet Boxer, Noel Socks. Socks came to Alison overweight, unhealthy, and in need of major physical and emotional support. Alison wholeheartedly embraced Socks, switching her to a raw diet and learning how to implement natural healing modalities to help her thrive. As time went on and Alison started to share her and Socks' journey on Facebook, she touched the lives of hundreds of other pet parents. Alison and her husband are now the proud "parents" of a beautiful white boxer named Caolainn. I am so grateful to Alison for letting me share her and Socks' story in this book.

It's funny how we as humans look for "that one" role model who can inspire, educate, love, and even comfort us, yet many times we pass them right by because they walk on four legs instead of two. These values were taught most recently to me by a humble little fawn-coloured European Boxer named Noel Socks who was "that one." Although I have a very long list of two-legged "ones," this mighty little hero took me on a personal journey of discovery that has changed the way I not only look at my pets but also the world around me.

Noel Socks belonged to close family friends who were struggling with her sudden behavioural changes. Although very loving and friendly around family friends, Socks would not be the same around strangers. This was very difficult for our friends, as they were the owners of a hunting/fishing lodge. So when the discussion came up that they were going to have to re-home their dog, we offered to care for Socks.

Thus in October 2011 what was to become an incredible journey began with a dog who taught us countless lessons, five of which I look upon as amazing roads we walked together. The first most important road was that of unconditional love and trust. Socks had to be reassured that not all people were out to hurt those she loved, and although it took time for her to not be afraid of men wearing black or people in uniform, she never wavered in looking to us for guidance. Together we learned that when I was nervous and fearful of what her reaction would be she automatically would be nervous and fearful because she was aware of my uncertainty. If she was barking at the doorbell and I'd raise my voice to quiet her she would only respond even louder, because to her if I was yelling then she needed to yell too. I also became aware that part of Socks' fears came from her personal space being crossed. As humans we all have experienced the feeling of meeting someone new who towers over us and gets right up in our faces. We don't allow this to happen to ourselves or our children, yet daily we do this to our dogs. So, I began the habit of stopping and squatting down beside Socks, and together we met each fearful encounter as equals. Admittedly our walk times took much longer as we had to do this with every dog or scary item we passed, but with time Socks learned to trust again and also brought me to the realization that we do not own or dominate our pets. We choose to cohabitate with them, and they need to be treated with the same dignity and respect we give our spouses and children. As humans we fully understand and respect behavioural issues in our loved ones. We may even seek out help for them to learn how to cope in the big wide world, but as pet owners we try to "break" our pet's issues. We need to remember that they are sentient beings with feelings and personalities just like us. By coming to that realization, we can help any dog function in the world in which they live.

By learning to understand our dog's behavioural needs we also find, that just like our human family members, diet and health affect our pets. This second road was the most eye-opening journey Noel Socks took me on. As a wife and mother, I have always looked at what I feed my family, yet as a pet owner I never did, because I trusted that what I was told by our vet, the retail world, and also what all my friends did was right. I sit here writing this shaking my head at how naïve I was. Here I am, the daughter of a retired registered nurse, who was raised with the knowledge of how diet affects our health. I have always strived to maintain a proper balance by reading ingredient labels and buying fresh non-processed foods for my family, but I never once thought to do the same not only for Noel Socks but also for our cat Beauregard. It was not until we sat in our vet's office one day just after Socks had turned 5 years old that I started to wonder about these things. Our visit to the vet was to seek advice on her stiffness in her left hind end, the urine infection she seemed to have, the large black furless spots that had developed, and our concern for the sudden rapid weight gain. Our vet checked Socks over and said that all these concerns where typical for a "senior" boxer and to just get used to it. I left that visit feeling overwhelmed and concerned, as to me a "senior" dog should be one that is double-digit age. As we struggled with Socks' health issues, we were fortunate to meet an amazing dog breeder/groomer who took one look at Socks and confirmed that yes, there was a major problem with her health. Long story short, our little boxer bum was the product of the tainted kibble era and suffering from thyroid issues that would have eventually killed her. Raina Addy, the owner of Best Friends and Raina's Grooming, took the time to educate us on just what the benefits of raw feed were. To this day, her quote of, "Would you feed your child a bowl full of Cheerios 3 times a day?" has stuck in my brain. Soon the whole concept of raw feeding made sense to me, and as you can see in the picture, Noel Socks benefitted from this change. Unfortunately, because of damages done due to many years of cheap processed foods, over-vaccination, and the many chemicals used to treat flea, ticks, and heartworm, Socks' immune system suffered irreparable damage, and this brought us to seek out the holistic approach to care for these issues. I soon came to understand that the old saying of "keep it simple stupid" is in fact very sound advice, and that just as I treated our family health issues naturally, I also needed to treat Socks the same. When Socks was diagnosed with a Mast cell tumour and the vet wanted to do surgery, we looked to an ancient treatment method using turmeric, raw honey, and bromeline. The results, just like those of her raw feeding, were stunning, and became a learning curve for us and even our vet. I often get asked if I support raw feeding/holistic care for our pets, and my answer is always the same. Yes I do, because my dog became a walking, barking textbook of proof that this form of care brings out only the best in our pets.

While grappling with Socks' behavioural and health issues, I began to walk a third road, thanks to the challenge of being asked to see the world through the eyes of my dog. This challenge brought me to a whole new world of discovery of what beauty and wonder there is around me, and how I had become complacent with my surroundings. We live in the heart of the Niagara Region, only 20 minutes away from one of the world's greatest wonders—Niagara Falls. By starting to actually look at what Socks was looking at when walking with her, I was overwhelmed to rediscover the beauty of the area I live in. I began to make sure that everywhere Socks and I went my camera went too. Socks became a great sport in our adventures of early morning trips down to the Falls to photograph the sun coming up, me resting my camera on her head to take pictures from her perspective, and the greatest discovery, the simple joy of watching a sunset together. My laptop is full of photos of people, pets, and even wildlife we have met while on these adventures. Little did I realize that each one of these memories would help to heal the hurt that would come from walking the fourth road with my Socksie.

The Friday of one Labour Day weekend, as Socks and I sat on the mound at Elite Equine Centre watching my daughter's horse grazing in the paddock, the geese wandering the fields, and the sun setting, little did I know that my world as a dog parent to this remarkable being was coming to an end. The next day Socks stopped eating, and by the Sunday night we knew that our time with this amazing creature was going to be shorter than we wanted. Labour Day Monday our hearts were broken as we witnessed Socks have multiple heart seizures, one after another. Although not willing to eat, Socks was still drinking and was active enough that I felt we might make it over this new health issue and still get to celebrate her 9th birthday in October. Unfortunately, that would not be the case, and on Wednesday September 9th we took that one last car ride together to have the vet confirm what we already knew within our hearts. Our precious little baby girl's body had given all it could give, and it was time to let Socks know that she had taught us everything she could and that she need not suffer any more. As my little Socks-a-saursa lay in my arms taking her last breath, I realized just how much she had changed my life. I also realized that grief is a natural event in our lives, and whether it be the death of a loved one or our pets we need to mourn the loss, otherwise we dishonour the memory of that person or pet. It is perfectly fine to cry and be sad at the loss of a pet. Just days after Noel Socks' death, I was asked what song best described each of my pets, and the first thing I thought of for Socks were the first two verses of the hymn How Great Thou Art. My walk down these four roads with Socks had brought me to see the power of unconditional love, the wonder and beauty of my surroundings, the heartbreak of loss, but also the preparation of the fifth and final road.

When we first began our raw feeding journey, I had actually used modern media to create a Facebook page that Socks' original owners could use to see all that we were doing with their dog while in our care. As we began to research and learn more about the raw/holistic care of Socks, what was just a personal page became a group page where people from all corners of the world came to share in this journey. The legacy that my boxer bum prepared is overwhelming to me, as through her I have met so many other amazing pet owners who have shared their experiences, knowledge, and support as we all continue to learn more about natural, healthy ways to care for our pets. They have also, in this time of sadness, given me purpose to continue to learn and grow in my knowledge and have inspired me to continue to reach out and help others. This legacy that Socks has left has changed me forever and I find myself in awe of how one of God's little creatures could have given so much in such a short time with us.

My advice to each of you is to get out there and experience the world through the unconditional love and wonder that our pets bring into our lives. Celebrate and share these moments, not only with your family members but also with friends and even strangers. For by doing this I know I have become a better wife, mother, and person who is more aware of how my actions and reactions affect others. Where this final road takes me I'm not totally sure, but I do know that my desire to learn and educate others on how to enjoy their time with their four-legged "ones" will not fade away. I also know that somewhere around one of the bends in this road there is another wiggle butt who will come into my life and take me even further than where I am right now. But until that time comes, I am celebrating the wonder and joy of just how much this precious little Boxer taught me.

Benefits of Raw Feeding

Noel Socks August 2012   **Noel Socks September 2014**

amp photos

Noel Socks, before eating a raw diet and after. Photo credits Alison Peloquin

Chapter 22: Moving Beyond the Feeding

So, we've talked about why you shouldn't feed kibble, and what you should feed instead. We've talked about how to get started feeding raw. We've looked at dealing with some chronic health issues naturally, so you really get to the root of the problem. Now, if you'll indulge me a little longer, I want to share a few more things I think you should know to keep your dog flourishing.

Not all water is created equal

The tap water in most places in America contains chlorine, fluoride, and various dissolved minerals, among them chlorides, sulfates, and bicarbonates. Much of the water supply also contains trace amounts of aluminum, nitrates, insecticides, herbicides, and prescription medications (including antibiotics, anti-convulsants, mood stabilizers, and sex hormones). There is no required testing for drugs in our water supplies, so it is difficult to know exactly what is present in our water and in what amounts, but researchers regularly find the above-listed minerals and chemicals in our water[104].

Chlorine bleach (in the form of chlorine dioxide) is added to almost all of America's public water supply as a disinfectant. This practice began in the early 1900s, when the dangers and long-term effects of chlorine weren't known, but the practice has continued because it's cheap. While cheap, however, it's not safe. One of the things chlorine does is neutralize oxygen. In essence, this means once it's inside the body—whether it's our pet's body or ours—it depletes the body's oxygen, which in turn makes the body's pH levels more acidic. This disrupts the immune system, which as you know can throw the whole system out of balance, cause allergy symptoms, and lead to various illnesses and diseases. It's interesting to note water that occurs in nature contains small amounts of hydrogen peroxide, which moves the body's pH to more basic levels. Natural water was intended to help support the correct oxygen levels and pH balance in our dogs' bodies, as well as ours, and therefore support the immune system.

The ill-effects of chlorine don't end there. When chlorine products encounter organic proteins, they produce byproducts called trihalomethanes (THMs). One example of a THM is chloroform, which is a carcinogen. In fact, studies have shown an association between THMs and cancers of the liver, kidneys; THMs have also been shown to be contributing factors in colon and bladder cancers, diabetes, and kidney stones. Chlorine also damages enzymes, which means that when it is ingested (through the water), it causes further havoc to the immune system. It can also decrease absorption of calcium while increasing calcium and phosphorous excretion[105].

Fluoride is also added to the water supply across America, under the guise that it's good for dental health. However, there's a lot of evidence showing fluoride is a bioaccumulative poison when ingested. The EPA, OSHA, and others classify fluoride as a toxic substance[106][107]. Fluoride is used in pesticides, insecticides, and fungicides, as well as being the main ingredient in many rat poisons. It's worth remembering that fluoride is cumulative in its effect upon the body, so each time you or your pet drink fluoridated water, its effects increase. That means, while the amount of fluoride in the water might not be enough to cause adverse effects, over time, it can pose a problem. Some of the most common known effects of fluoride ingestion include cancer, brittle teeth, heart disease, and arthritis.

There is much more in our public water supply than just chlorine and fluoride. Check out this list (in alphabetical order) of the top 100 most common toxins found in the US public water supply[108]:

Top 100 Common U.S. Water Toxins

1) 1,1,1,2-Tetrachloroethane
2) 1,1,2-Trichloroethane
3) 1,1-Dichloroethane
4) 1,1-Dichloropropene
5) 1,2 Dibromo-3-chloropropane
(DBCP)
6) 1,2,3-Trichloropropane
7) 1,2,4-Trichlorobenzene
8) 1,2-Dibromoethylene
9) 1,2-Dichloroethane
10) 1,3,5-Trimethylbenzene
11) 1,3-Dichloropropane
12) 1,4-Dioxane
13) 2,2-Dichloropropane
14) 2,4,5-T
15) 2,4,5-TP (Silvex)
16) 2,4-D
17) 2-Hexanone
18) 2-Nitropropane
19) Acetochlor
20) Aldicarb
21) Aldicarb sulfone
22) Aldicarb sulfoxide
23) Alpha-Lindane
24) Aluminum
25) Ammonia
26) Aniline
27) Anthracene
28) Antimony
29) Arsenic
30) Atrazine
31) Barium
32) Benzene
33) Benzo[a]pyrene
34) Beryllium

35) Bromate
36) Bromide
37) Bromobenzene
38) Bromodichloromethane
39) Bromoform
40) Bromomethane
41) Cadmium (total)
42) Carbaryl
43) Carbon tetrachloride
44) Chloroethane
45) Chloroform
46) Chloromethane
47) Chromium
48) cis-1,2-Dichloroethylene
49) Cyanide
50) Dalapon
51) Di(2-Ethylhexyl) adipate
52) Di(2-ethylhexyl) phthalate
53) Dibromochloromethane
54) Dibromomethane
55) Dicamba
56) Dichlorodifluoromethane
57) Dichloromethane (methylene chloride)
58) Dieldrin
59) Dinoseb
60) Endrin
61) Ethylbenzene
62) Ethylene dibromide (EDB)
63) Heptachlor
64) Heptachlor epoxide
65) Hexachloro-cyclopentadiene
66) Isopropylbenzene
67) Lindane
68) m-Dichlorobenzene

69) Manganese
70) Mercury
71) Metolachlor
72) Monochlorobenzene
(Chlorobenzene)
73) n-Butylbenzene
74) n-Propylbenzene
75) Naphthalene
76) Nitrate
77) Nitrates & nitrites
78) o-Chlorotoluene
79) o-Dichlorobenzene
80) Oxamyl (Vydate)
81) p-Chlorotoluene
82) p-Dichlorobenzene
83) p-Isopropyltoluene
84) Pentachlorophenol
85) Picloram
86) Radium-226 & Radium-228
87) sec-Butylbenzene
88) Simazine
89) Styrene
90) Sulfates
91) tert-Butylbenzene
92) Tetrachloroethylene
93) Thallium
94) Toluene
95) Total haloacetic acids
96) Total trihalomethanes
(THMs)
97) Toxaphene
98) Trichloroethylene
99) Trichlorofluoromethane
100) Vinyl chloride

So how do you make sure you're providing your pets with clean, pure water? The best way to do this is to provide them with filtered water. Unfortunately, not all filters are created equal, nor are all bottled waters truly pure. Many bottled waters are just tap water that's been bottled, and some of them contain fluoride and various minerals. Check the label to see if chlorine or fluoride has been added back to the water. Also, note that Brita water filters often do not completely remove chlorine and fluoride. Reverse osmosis filtration systems and the Berkey water filter (with the optional fluoride filters) are more expensive, but if you can get them, they're a good option. We use the AquaLiv water filtration system in our house; in addition to knowing we're drinking water that's good for us, it also tastes amazing, and it's more hydrating than any other water I've had. Obviously, we give that water to our dogs and our cat, and even use it to water our house plants. If you don't want to get a water filtration system, you can also get bottled spring water in safe plastic bottles; well water is another great option if you have access to a well.

One other bit of information: it's worthwhile to invest in a stainless-steel bowl for your pets to drink from. Just like with their food dishes, plastic bowls can harbor bacteria and leach chemicals out (into the water). Make sure you clean the water dish and refill it daily, or whenever it gets low.

It's vitally important to provide your pets with clean, pure water. Doing so helps keep all their systems, including their immune system, healthy. It supports their bodies in maintaining balance and health, and may even encourage them to drink more because the water is more natural and may taste better. Giving them clean water is part of the total approach to helping your dog achieve and maintain true, lasting health, so they can thrive throughout all your years together.

Exercise

Exercise is one of the most neglected aspects of health in Western society today. Our dogs are frequently obese or overweight. While much of this is due to diet, lack of exercise also plays a key role. Exercise has a myriad of benefits, both physically, mentally, and emotionally. And ultimately, remember true health is achieved when the body, mind, and spirit are appropriately balanced. It's our job to support our pets in achieving and maintaining balance. This requires a holistic approach—balance by its very nature means more than one factor is involved, and all the factors must be in harmony. Exercise is one of these factors.

Let's start with the role exercise plays in the immune system. Like us, our dogs have lymph fluid, which moves throughout the body (through lymph vessels) picking up bacteria, waste products, toxins, and even tumor cells. The lymph fluid carries this toxic waste matter back to the lymph nodes, which are located throughout the body. The lymph nodes then break down this waste matter and dispose of it. Our dogs have twice as many lymph vessels as blood vessels, but unlike blood (which is pumped through blood vessels by the heart), the lymph fluid only moves as a result of exercise or physical stimulation, such as deep tissue massage. This difference is vital; the lymph fluid must have exercise to move[109]. If the lymph doesn't move, the waste matter will build up, which causes inflammation. Chronic inflammation can cause various diseases, including cancer, to appear.

Being hunters, our dogs are designed to move around in search of prey and then expend vigorous effort bringing the prey down. And although our pet dogs may not have to hunt for their meals anymore, their bodies are still adapted to need this kind of exercise to achieve optimum wellness. Exercise strengthens and tones your pet's lungs, heart, and overall muscle tone. It aids them in staying at an appropriate weight. Obesity, of course, throws the body out of balance, and even animals on a raw diet can become overweight or obese if they're fed too much or aren't exercised enough. Exercise also helps lower blood glucose levels, and the increased blood flow aids in insulin absorption.

In addition to all the physical benefits to exercise, it has lots of mental and emotional benefits as well. Remember the old adage "A tired dog is a good dog"? That's because exercise helps maintain brain health, drain excess energy, promote better sleep, and release endorphins in the brain that contribute to overall happiness and wellness.

It's vitally important to make sure your pet gets regular, daily exercise. The amount and intensity of the exercise will vary based on several factors. No matter what, though, they should move around and exercise every single day. The only exception to this may come if your pet is injured or if you are fasting your dog; when fasting, if your dog seems tired, you can let them rest.

When you're considering how much exercise is the right amount, you can start with general guidelines. For example, if you have an active 2-year-old border collie, it will require quite a bit of intense exercise. A 13-year-old Pug will require much less. A good rule of thumb to determine the right amount of exercise is to watch your dog when the exercise is over; if he or she lies down and rests or falls asleep afterwards, it was an appropriate amount. If your pet is still running around or still seems hyper, then it wasn't enough. And if your pet drags around and still seems lethargic the next day, then it was too much. You should also pay attention to trends over time: if your dog is awake for much of the day, then they aren't getting enough exercise. Animals that get an appropriate amount of exercise tend to sleep for much of the day. This follows the natural cycle of carnivores in the wild, who engage in moderate exercise while searching for prey (think of a wolf pack trotting for several miles to find a deer they can bring down) and then a shorter burst of intense exercise when chasing and bringing down their prey. Once they have made their kill, they eat (gorge) and then sleep most of the rest of the day. Because they have drained their energy in the process of the hunt, they don't have nervous energy left over preventing them from settling down and relaxing.

Dogs have a certain amount of energy that builds up in their system each day. This is cumulative over time, so if the energy isn't drained one day, the next day it doesn't reset to zero. Whatever amount of energy they had from the day before gets added to the energy of the new day. This will keep going until the energy is drained by exercise. Think of it as an empty cup that gets a certain amount of liquid added to it each day. For example, let's say that the cup holds 3 cups of liquid, and each day ½ cup of liquid gets added. If you don't drain the liquid, on the second day the cup will have a full cup of liquid in it, then 1 ½ cups of liquid on the third day, and so on. Eventually, it overflows, and then you have a mess. Your pet's energy is like this too. Draining the energy is crucial.

Since dogs both tend to move around in search of prey and then expend lots of energy in the actual chase, just taking your dog on a moderately-paced, 20-30-minute walk once a day often isn't enough. Also, dogs tend not to move around much when they are left to their own devices, especially as they get older. Therefore, just having a big yard or a big house doesn't help much with exercise if your pet is left on its own. So, what are some ways you can make sure your dog getting enough exercise?

Many people take their dogs for walks; this is fine, but it is important to make sure the walk is long enough to burn off some energy and move the lymph around. Use the rule of thumb I mentioned above—if you get back from your walk and your dog is still active, then go for a longer duration and try to walk more quickly. If walking isn't doing it, you might try taking your dog out with you for a run or for a bike ride. There's a great tool called the WalkyDog PLUS that makes bike riding safe for you and your dog. It prevents the dog from getting tangled up in your bicycle, and if they lunge at something (a cat or a squirrel, for example), it absorbs the shock so you don't get pulled over. I've used the WalkyDog PLUS on dogs of all shapes, sizes, temperaments, and energy levels, and it's worked with all of them, even if they've never seen a bike before. It's important to make sure you keep the bike at a speed where they can comfortably trot alongside (rather than having to run full-out), especially when first starting out. Let their paws toughen up a little bit if they aren't used to running on the pavement, and opt for shorter sessions more frequently. If they start to drag or they seem tired, slow down and let them rest. And of course, use common sense. If it's hot outside, your dog isn't in good shape, or they just aren't keeping up, don't force the issue. Pay attention to them and let them dictate how far or fast you go, particularly with a run or a bike ride.

Many dogs really like going for runs. Taking your dog on a run with you can make the run a lot more fun. If you don't like running but have a friend that does, see if they'd be willing to take your dog with them when they go. Or, look for a reputable dog walker or talk to a local running club and see if they would be willing to take your dog for a run. While it's important to exercise good judgement in deciding who you trust to take your dog out, if you find a responsible runner who loves dogs and is familiar with them, it can be a wonderful way to make sure your pet gets some good exercise.

If your dog likes to play with toys, you can play fetch with them. Using a Chuckit!® or something similar will help you throw the ball farther than you could without one; that means your dog has to run farther to get the ball and bring it back to you. You can also play Frisbee with your dog. If you have access to a swimming pool and your dog likes the water, you can let them swim. Of course, teach them where the steps are and monitor them when they are in the pool! You can also opt to try an organized sport like agility, Flyball, or sheepherding with your dog; this can greatly increase your bond with them and burn energy at the same time.

Whatever you end up doing, remember your dog was built to move around. Help him flourish by supporting that need, and give his body the exercise it needs to thrive.

Chapter 23: Parting Thoughts

Congratulations! You made it! So now, all that remains is to put it into action. Of course, I know that's usually the hardest part. Things that seem easy when we're thinking of them theoretically can be much harder when we're thinking about them in reality. But really, switching your dog to a raw diet and getting them back on the path to true vitality isn't hard. Just to recap, here's what you're gonna do:

1. Transition your dog from kibble to raw. Either go slowly or do it cold turkey, whichever works best for you. If you aren't sure how to do it, review the section about transitioning again. It covers both methods and the pros and cons of each.
2. Decide if you're going to feed a commercial raw, prey model, whole prey, or some combination thereof.
   a. If you're feeding commercial raw, find a supplier (and maybe even two) and rotate between their formulas.
   b) If you're feeding prey model, feed a wide variety of proteins, organs, boneless, and bone-in pieces.
3. If you're feeding whole prey, feed as wide of a variety as you can get, and consider supplementing with prey model for even more variety.
4. Ignore the fear-mongering and misinformation out there. You know your dog best, and feeding variety and achieving balance over time is what you're aiming for. Every meal does not have to be balanced in and of itself.
5. Tune in to your dog to make sure their nutritional needs are being met. Stool too soft? Increase the bone percentage. Dog not able to settle down and relax? Give them more exercise. Can't feel their ribs? Feed a little bit less.
6. Last step (but probably most important, even though many raw feeders might disagree with me): relax and have fun! We're learning

new things all the time, so there's always going to be new information out there. Don't worry if it doesn't seem like you're doing things exactly the way someone else is doing them. You're going to do just fine, and so will your dog! Remember: balance over time and variety is where it's at. And if you aren't sure whether you're doing it "right," seek out a certified animal naturopath or a holistic veterinarian to help you.

I'm really proud of you for deciding to take back your dog's health. By choosing to feed them a raw diet, you're empowering yourself and doing what's best for your best friend. Raw feeding isn't the status quo (yet!), and I know it can be hard to go against status quo. But by picking up this book and implementing what I'm telling you, you're taking a huge step towards supporting your dog on the path towards optimal vitality and wellness. So yeah—from one pet parent to another, I really couldn't be prouder of you. You've got this!

Appendix A: A List of Good (in My Opinion) Meat Suppliers

Wondering what meat suppliers you can use to get started? If so, you're in luck! Here are some suppliers I think have especially high-quality products. Of course, it's always important to do your research, particularly when it comes to sourcing (and in the case of the commercial raw companies, formulations). Manufacturers and suppliers do change both sourcing and recipes, so investigate before you purchase. If a company isn't listed on here, it doesn't mean it's bad, it just means it didn't make my "top 5" list (either I felt it had too much fruit/vegetable/starch compared to meat, bones, and organs; or I couldn't identify where the products were sourced from; or the formulas weren't, in my opinion, as strong as another company's). To select companies, I looked at (current) sourcing, species-appropriate recipes, and customer service.

Top 5 Commercial raw suppliers (in alphabetical order):

- Gentle Harvest Meat Me Pet Food
- Small Batch
- Vibrant K9
- Vital Essentials Freeze Dried
- Vital Essentials Frozen

Top 5 prey model/whole prey suppliers (in alphabetical order):

- Hare Today, Gone Tomorrow
- My Pet Carnivore
- Rabbits4U
- Raw Feeding Miami
- Simply Rawesome US

Specialty prey model/whole prey suppliers (in alphabetical order):

- Layne Labs
- Greentripe.com

Appendix B: Performing the Heimlich Maneuver on a Dog

It's scary but true: dogs can choke on things. If your dog starts to choke, it's important you know how to respond. When you know what to do, you can stay calm and help your best friend get through the emergency safely. Just so you know, I've had to use the below steps myself. Our dog Motley was having trouble breathing: he could still get some air, but he was wheezing and coughing and in distress. I couldn't see anything when I looked in his mouth, so I went ahead and performed the Heimlich using the steps outlined below. After 5 or 6 rapid squeezes, he coughed out a feather he'd been playing with. A few seconds later, he was back outside playing with Elle, none the worse for wear.

If you think your dog is choking, or they seem like they're having difficulty breathing, take the following steps (I learned these from Dr. Jeannie Thomason):

1. Holding your dog securely, open its mouth and look at the back of its throat. If you can see what's causing your dog to choke or obstructing your dog's breathing, open it. If possible, have someone help you by holding your dog's mouth open while you remove the object (this will help you see the object better, so you don't accidentally push it farther down your dog's throat).
2. If you can't see the object, plant your dog's forelegs on the ground, holding his hind legs in the air with his head hanging down. If you have a small dog, pick him up and hold him by his hips with his head pointing down. Sometimes, this is enough to get the object to fall out. If it doesn't, move on to the next step.
3. With your dog standing on all 4 feet, elevate his hind legs slightly and hold them between your knees.
4. Put one hand below the last rib and another hand on your dog's

back. Press the stomach in one fluid motion. Squeeze rapidly 4–5 times (or until the object is coughed out).

5. Check to see if the object is completely dislodged. If part of it's still jammed in your dog's throat, strike between your dog's shoulder blades sharply with an open palm, then repeat step 2.

Dr. Thomason also told me if your dog is small enough, you can pick him up and hold his back against your stomach with his head up and his feet hanging down. Put your fist under his ribcage, feeling for the little hollow area just under the ribs. Cover your fist with your other hand and push up and in using a strong thrusting motion. Do this 3–5 times, then check your dog's mouth for the object.

If the object doesn't come up and your dog is no longer breathing, perform artificial respiration while someone drives you and your dog to a vet. In this instance, you need to seek veterinary help immediately.

Performing the

HEIMLICH MANEUVER

on Your Dog

Open your dog's mouth and check if you can see what's causing them to choke/obstructing their breathing.

If you can't see the object, plant your dog's forelegs on the ground, holding his hind legs in the air with his head hanging down. If you have a small dog, pick him up and hold him by his hips with his head pointing down. Note sometimes this is enough to get the object to fall out. If not, move on to the next step.

With your dog standing on all 4 feet, elevate his hind legs slightly and hold them between your knees.

Put one hand below the last rib and another hand on your dog's back. Press the stomach in one fluid motion. Squeeze rapidly 4–5 times (or until the object is coughed out).

If the object isn't dislodged, strike between your dog's shoulder blades with your open palm, then repeat step 2. (On the next paragraph): If the object doesn't come up and your dog isn't breathing, perform artificial respiration while someone drives you and the dog to the vet IMMEDIATELY.

Appendix C: Controlling Fleas and Ticks Naturally

We use over-the-counter (OTC) products to control parasites like fleas and ticks almost without thinking. However, as you consider the safety of OTC preventives, keep the following information from the National Resources Defense Council in mind:

"Many and perhaps most Americans believe that commercially available pesticides, such as those found in pet products, are tightly regulated by the government. In fact, they are not. Not until the passage of a 1996 law focused on pesticides in food did the Environmental Protection Agency (EPA) begin examining the risks from pesticides in pet products in earnest. To this day, the EPA allows the manufacture and sale of pet products containing hazardous insecticides with little or no demonstration that a child's exposure to these ingredients would be safe. Just because these products are on store shelves does not mean they have been tested or can be presumed safe. So just use natural nutrients and additives and stop using pesticides.

Of course, as bad as these products may be for pet owners and caregivers, they often are worse for the pets themselves. Based on the very limited data available, it appears that hundreds and probably thousands of pets have been injured or killed through exposure to pet products containing pesticides. As with small children, pets cannot report when they're being poisoned at low doses[110]."

It's not just the National Resources Defense Council that cautions against these types of products. The Environmental Protection Agency also said, "products intended to treat cats and dogs for fleas and ticks kill hundreds of pets each year and injure tens of thousands[111]." Furthermore, the EPA received "44,263 reports of harmful reactions associated with topical flea and tick products in 2008, up from 28,895 in 2007. The reactions reported ranged from skin irritations to vomiting to seizures to, in about 600 cases, death of an animal[112]."

Two of the most common flea and tick preventatives (via topical application) are Frontline® Plus and K9 Advantix®. Let's look at the active ingredients in Frontline® Plus first, and then look at K9 Advantix®.

192

Frontline® Plus

The active ingredients in Frontline® Plus are Fipronil and (S)-methoprene. Fipronil is used to kill adult fleas and ticks by disrupting their central nervous systems. However, Fipronil is also very dangerous, both to pets and people. For example, studies have shown Fipronil mutates proteins and kills human liver cells at very low concentrations[113]. Additionally, another study found that, after one day of applying Frontline® to an adult dog, petting it for just five minutes while wearing gloves resulted in exposures much higher than the small doses found to mutate and destroy cells[114]. Furthermore, any surface the animal touched was affected, and dander and shed hair were also found to be toxic for a period of time. Fipronil has been found to break down very slowly in the environment: it can last for 7-12 months on vegetation, and it also breaks down quite slowly in soil.

Although the manufacturer, Merial, denies there's any relation between Frontline® Plus and reported side effects, numerous pet owners have reported seizures and even death after applying Frontline® Plus to their pets. Additionally, it should be noted this chemical is cumulative, so even if your pet doesn't experience adverse reactions when you first apply it, it can lead to severe issues down the road.

A study that was conducted using mice showed that Fipronil led to nerve cell damage, impaired spinal cord development, developmental delays, smaller brains, reduced cognition, hearing impairment, hair loss, thyroid cancer, adverse reproductive effects, and disruptions in endocrine activity[115].

(S)-methoprene, the other active ingredient in Frontline® Plus, is used to kill flea eggs and larvae. Like Fipronil, it's a pesticide, and studies have shown (S)-methoprene can cause vomiting in dogs, along with behavior changes, breathing changes, and "body movements[116]" (which, I believe, means tremors and seizures). It also has been found to have negative effects on reproductive health.

K9 Advantix®

K9 Advantix® contains the active ingredients Imidacloprid and Permethrin. Permethrin is not just used in flea and tick preventatives; it's also used to kills pests on crops and in yards. Like Frontline® Plus, K9 Advantix is a pesticide—a poison—we're asked to apply directly to our pet's skin. Side effects noted in K9 Advantix® are rashes, vomiting, diarrhea, seizures, and nerve pain/damage. Small dogs are reported to be more susceptible than large dogs, although both can be affected[117].

According to the Material Safety Data Sheet for Imidacloprid, the product can be fatal if swallowed and harmful if inhaled. It also, as all the Material Safety Data Sheets for the chemicals in these products do, cautions you to avoid contact with skin, eyes, and clothing. It advises you to remove and wash contaminated clothing, and even advises safety goggles as protective clothing when working with or around the chemical[118]. The Material Safety Data Sheet is a "detailed information bulletin prepared by the manufacturer or importer of a chemical that describes the physical and chemical properties, physical and health hazards, routes of exposure, precautions for safe handling and use, emergency and first-aid procedures, and control procedures[119]." When the Material Safety Data Sheet (also called the MSDS) advises against contact with skin, I think it's a red flag that should make us stop and think about why the instructions are then advising us to apply that same product to the skin of our pets. And, as I mentioned, it's not just Imidacloprid that advises you to avoid skin contact; the MSDSs for the other active ingredients in flea and tick preventives do too.

Flea and tick products in general

Frontline® Plus and K9 Advantix® are not the only flea and tick preventatives available, and almost all of them are dangerous to your pet. Although the companies do not admit their products cause adverse reactions, the Environmental Protection Agency, the National Resources Defense Council, many scientific studies, and numerous pet owners have found these products cause adverse, sometimes severe reactions in pets, up to and including death. And, since the toxicity is cumulative, continued use of these products can lead to more and severe issues.

In light of this rather sobering information, let's look at some ways you can handle fleas and ticks naturally.

Diet

When you feed your dog a raw diet, their bodies can come into harmony. Their internal terrain—especially their immune system—is supported, and it becomes balanced and strong. And, as anyone who has been feeding a species-appropriate raw diet for any length of time can tell you, the dog no longer attracts fleas and ticks the way a conventionally fed animal does. People who don't feed raw have a hard time believing this, but it's the case: I've seen it first-hand with my own pack, heard about it from numerous other raw feeders, and had multiple clients witness the change in their own dogs as well.

Before I started feeding my dogs raw, we regularly had flea and tick infestations. The only way we knew to control them was through regular applications of Frontline® Plus, and when we decided to stop applying that because of the dangers it contained, the flea and tick population on our dogs exploded. Everyone, especially Elle, was miserable. Constantly itching, it seemed our dogs were at the mercy of every flea for miles, and we would come back from walks and hikes to find ticks all over them. However, once they were on raw and had moved through the detox phase, the infestations stopped. There were no more. We didn't use Frontline® Plus, or even any "natural" commercial product, to control the parasites. We simply built up their immune systems, and the fleas and ticks no longer seemed interested. They didn't infest our dogs or cause any more problems.

Does this mean our dogs never pick up a single tick? Of course not. We take them lots of places with ticks, and every once in a great while I find a solitary tick crawling on them, and in even rarer instances, one may latch on. And, while I haven't seen a flea on any of them since we switched their diet, I wouldn't be surprised to learn they might have had one or two hitch a ride for a brief time. However, we haven't had an issue with them. When we find a tick, we simply remove it and move on. We trust our dogs' own internal defenses to keep them parasite-free.

Balance in all things

It's important to remember we want to help our pets achieve balance, not stagnation. Nature is ever-changing, and a strong immune system is one that can adapt to those changes and, in the adaptation, become stronger. Fleas and ticks play an important role in this. They're part of the ecosystem, and so the goal of a natural health program should not be to eradicate them altogether using conventional preventatives. Without some adversity, the immune system cannot stay nimble, and the occasional flea and tick can be understood to be part of this adversity.

I know this notion is foreign to how most of us grew up. We seek to eradicate everything that seems the least bit unpleasant. Just look at all the anti-bacterial hand soaps, disinfectants, and harsh toxic cleaners that are touted to destroy, eradicate, and kill all (or at least 99% or more) germs. Similarly, conventional flea and tick preventatives aim to eradicate all fleas and ticks from your pet. But I suggest nature, and therefore a natural health program, focuses on the relationships and balance between all things. As Maneka Gandhi once said, "Shift your perception to tolerance. Instead of seeing every interaction as a trespass that requires a retaliation of toxic force, why not embrace these encounters as an opportunity?"

You don't have to go it alone. Ants, spiders, and birds are natural predators of ticks. Ants also eat fleas and flea larvae. Beneficial nematodes eat fleas, grubs, beetles, termites, and more. Praying mantises eat a wide range of other insects, including grasshoppers, flies, mosquitoes, caterpillars, and beetles. Crab spiders help control fleas, flies, aphids, and leafhoppers. Ladybugs can help control aphids, spider mites, and weevils. Green Lacewings will voraciously consume aphids, caterpillars, beetles, and white flies. The Flower fly is very effective against aphids, and Minute Potato Bugs consume spider mites and insect eggs. Nature provides natural parasite control in a way that maintains a healthy balance. Unfortunately, when we spray pesticides and other poisons, we kill the very things that can provide safe, effective parasite control. We disturb the balance of things.

Natural flea and tick repellents

If you've just made the switch to raw, your pet may not have had enough time to balance their immune system and may need some additional help in repelling fleas and ticks. If that's the case for you, there are a few options for natural flea and tick repellents.

Therapeutic-grade essential oils (I only use ones from Young Living) are very effective at repelling fleas and ticks. However, they should be applied whenever you take your pet into an area where they will be exposed to fleas and ticks, rather than once per month like conventional treatments.

There are lots of essential oils that are great as natural flea and tick repellents, including Tea Tree, Lemongrass, Pine, Cedarwood, Lemon, Lavender, Sage, Thyme, Citronella, and Purification essential oils. One caveat: Certain essential oils can be toxic to cats, so please do your research before you use any essential oils around them.

To make a homemade flea repellent, I often put ½ cup of distilled water, 8-12 drops of the essential oil of my choice (my most frequent go-tos are Citronella and Purification, but I do use the others listed above), and a drop of Thieves hand soap (made by Young Living) or Castile soap (to help the oil and water blend) into a dark glass bottle, shake it vigorously, and then spray it directly on my pet (avoiding their eyes, inside their ears, and their little noses, of course). You can also use organic witch hazel (available through Amazon) in place of the water; if you go this route, you don't need to add the soap, because the oils will blend with the witch hazel. Sometimes I combine several different oils, such as Lavender, Lemongrass, and Peppermint, to be more effective against several pests at once (this blend, for example, would be helpful at keeping fleas, ticks, and mosquitoes away).

When using a natural flea and tick repellent like this, remember to spray it on your pet as needed. A few spritzes go a long way, too—you don't need to douse them. Spray it on yourself as well—after all, you don't want to get attacked either!

As you can see, fleas and ticks are part of the natural order of things. While none of us wants to see them infesting our pets, their presence (or lack thereof) can be a valuable indicator on the overall health of our dog. There are lots of natural alternatives to conventional preventatives available, and once you begin to really support your pet's immune system along with the environment in which they live in a natural way, you should find your flea and tick problem basically takes care of itself.

Endnotes

1   Amelia Josephson, "America's Pets by the Numbers: How Much We Spend on Our Animal Friends," Learnvest, last modified February 5, 2016. https://www.learnvest.com/2016/02/americas-pets-by-the-numbers-how-much-we-spend-on-our-animal-friends.

2   Dr. Karen Becker, "Why are These Popular Dogs Dying so Much Younger Than They Used to?," *Healthy Pets with Dr. Karen Becker,* last modified July 13, 2016. https://healthypets.mercola.com/sites/healthypets/archive/2016/07/13/pedigree-dog-lifespan.aspx.

3   Dr. Jeannie Thomason, "Cooked vs Raw," *The Whole Dog,* accessed December 9, 2017. https://www.thewholedog.org/artcookedfood.html.

4   Susan Thixton, "The Cooking of Pet Food," *Dogs Naturally,* accessed December 9, 2017. http://www.dogsnaturallymagazine.com/the-cooking-of-pet-food/.

5   Dr. Peter Dobias, "Synthetic Supplements for Dogs can Cause Serious Problems," *Dr. Dobias Natural Healing,* last modified August 23, 2014. https://peterdobias.com/blogs/blog/15188693-synthetic-supplements-for-dogs-can-cause-serious-problems.

6   Dana Scott, "Think You Can Avoid Pet Foods Made in China? Think Again!" *Dogs Naturally,* accessed December 12, 2017. https://www.dogsnaturallymagazine.com/think-you-can-avoid-pet-foods-made-in-china/.

7   Mary Roach, "The Chemistry of Kibble," *Popular Science,* last modified March 25, 2013. https://www.popsci.com/science/article/2013-03/chemistry-kibble.

8   "Pet Industry Market Size & Ownership Statistics," *American Pet Products Association (APPA),* accessed January 4, 2018. http://www.americanpetproducts.org/press_industrytrends.asp.

9   "Natural," *Association of American Feed Control Officials*, accessed December 14, 2017. http://talkspetfood.aafco.org/natural.

10   Thor, "What does 'Holistic' Mean?" *The Pet Pantry*, last modified April 7, 2012. http://www.feedyourpets.com/what-does-holistic-mean/.

11   "Organic," *Association of American Feed Control Officials*, accessed December 14, 2017. http://petfood.aafco.org/Organic.

12   "Organic," *Association of American Feed Control Officials*, accessed December 14, 2017. http://petfood.aafco.org/Organic.

13   "Human Grade," *Association of American Feed Control Officials*, accessed December 14, 2017. http://talkspetfood.aafco.org/humangrade.

14   "The Shocking Truth About Commercial Dog Food," *DogFoodAdvisor*, accessed December 11, 2017. https://www.dogfoodadvisor.com/dog-food-industry-exposed/shocking-truth-about-dog-food/.

15   "CPG Sec. 690.500 Uncooked Meat for Animal Food," *U.S. Food & Drug Administration*, accessed December 7, 2017. https://www.fda.gov/ICECI/ComplianceManuals/CompliancePolicyGuidanceManual/ucm074712.htm.

16   "Preservatives to Avoid in Dog (Cat) Food and Treats – Unsafe, Toxic, Carcinogenic…," *Ottawa Valley Dog Whisperer*, accessed November 8, 2017. http://ottawavalleydogwhisperer.blogspot.ca/2013/04/preservatives-to-avoid-in-dog-cat-food.html.

17   "Material Safety Data Sheet BHA MSDS," *ScienceLab.com*, accessed November 8, 2017. http://www.sciencelab.com/msds.php?msdsId=9923083.

18   "BHA—A Time Bomb in Your Dog's Food?" *DogFoodAdvisor*, accessed December 1, 2017. https://www.dogfoodadvisor.com/red-flag-ingredients/bha-in-dog-food/.

19   "CPG Sec. 690.500 Uncooked Meat for Animal Food," *U.S. Food & Drug Administration*, accessed December 7, 2017. https://www.fda.gov/ICECI/ComplianceManuals/CompliancePolicyGuidanceManual/ucm074712.htm.

20   "CPG Sec. 690.500 Uncooked Meat for Animal Food," *U.S. Food & Drug Administration*, accessed December 7, 2017. https://www.fda.gov/ICECI/ComplianceManuals/CompliancePolicyGuidanceManual/ucm074712.htm.

21   "What is BHT & Why You Should Avoid It," *The Good Human*, accessed December 4, 2017. https://thegoodhuman.com/what-is-bht-butylated-hydroxytoluene-and-why-you-should-avoid-it/.

22   "Material Safety Data Sheet Ethoxyquin MSDS," *ScienceLab.com,* accessed November 8, 2017. http://www.sciencelab.com/msds. php?msdsId=9923952.

23   Sarah Olson, "The Dangers of Propyl Gallate," *Stop Killing My Kids,* last modified July 29, 2010. http://www.stopkillingmykids.com/the-dangers-of-propyl-gallate/.

24   "Material Safety Data Sheet Sodium metabisulfite MSDS," *ScienceLab.com,* accessed November 8, 2017. http://www.sciencelab.com/msds.php?msdsId=9927597.

25   Robin Wasserman, "Dangers of Sodium Metabisulfite," *Livestrong. com,* last modified October 3, 2017. https://www.livestrong.com/article/208572-dangers-of-sodium-metabisulfite/.

26   "What is TBHQ…and is it Safe for Your Dog?" *DogFoodAdvisor,* accessed December 1, 2017. https://www.dogfoodadvisor.com/red-flag-ingredients/tbhq-dangeorus-dog-food-preservative/.

27   Shona Botes, "TBHQ – Why This Preservative Should be Avoided," *Natural News,* last modified February 14, 2011. https://www.naturalnews.com/031318_TBHQ_food_preservatives.html#ixzz4Kw6wvkwa.

28   Luke Pasco, *Heather Jean: The Working Sheep Dog* (Illinois: The Sheep Breeder, Inc., 1937), 31

29   Luke Pasco, *Heather Jean: The Working Sheep Dog* (Illinois: The Sheep Breeder, Inc, 1937), 32-33

30   "Pet Industry Market Size & Ownership Statistics," *American Pet Products Association (APPA),* accessed January 4, 2018. http://www.americanpetproducts.org/press_industrytrends.asp.

31   Dr. Jeannie Thomason, "Kibble is Kibble is Still Kibble," *Vibrant K9,* last modified November 18, 2016. http://vibrantk9.com/2016/11/18/kibble-is-kibble-is-still-kibble-written-by-dr-jeannie-thomason-the-whole-dog/.

32   http://www.fda.gov/ICECI/ComplianceManuals/CompliancePolicyGuidanceManual/ucm074712.htm

33   Dr. Jeannie Thomason, "Kibble is Kibble is Still Kibble," *Vibrant K9,* last modified November 18, 2016. http://vibrantk9.com/2016/11/18/kibble-is-kibble-is-still-kibble-written-by-dr-jeannie-thomason-the-whole-dog/.

34   "Do They Really Use Dead Dogs and Cats to Make Pet Food?" *DogFoodAdvisor,* accessed November 12, 2017. http://www.dogfoodadvisor.com/dog-food-industry-exposed/euthanized-pets-dog-food/.

35   "The Shocking Truth About Commercial Dog Food,"

DogFoodAdvisor, accessed December 11, 2017. https://
www.dogfoodadvisor.com/dog-food-industry-exposed/
shocking-truth-about-dog-food/.

36   Dr. Jeannie Thomason, "Kibble is Kibble is Still Kibble,"
Vibrant K9, last modified November 18, 2016. http://vibrantk9.
com/2016/11/18/kibble-is-kibble-is-still-kibble-written-by-dr-jean-
nie-thomason-the-whole-dog/.

37   "Common Cuts: A Guide to Raw Meaty Bones,"
PreyModelRaw.com, last modified September 10, 2013.
http://preymodelraw.com/page/articles.html/_/raw-chat/
common-cuts-a-guide-to-raw-meaty-bones-r15.

38   "Green Tripe Analysis," *Greentripe.com,* accessed December 1,
2017. http://greentripe.com/analysis.html.

39   Dana Scott, "Mixing Kibble with Raw? Here's the Problem,"
accessed December 1, 2017. http://www.dogsnaturallymagazine.
com/can-you-mix-raw-dog-food-with-kibble/.

40   Dr. Peter Dobias, "Is it OK to Mix a Raw Diet and Kibble?" last
modified April 7, 2017. https://peterdobias.com/blogs/blog/
is-it-ok-to-mix-a-raw-diet-and-kibble.

41   Marion Nestle, "Why Calories Count: The Problem with Dietary-
intake Studies," *The Atlantic,* last modified March 28, 2012. https://
www.theatlantic.com/health/archive/2012/03/why-calories-count-
the-problem-with-dietary-intake-studies/254886/.

42   "Red Meat," *Wikipedia,* accessed November 3, 2017. https://en.wiki-
pedia.org/wiki/Red_meat.

43   David Hu, MS, "How Red Meat can 'Beef up' Your Nutrition," *Food
Insight,* last modified October 22, 2015. http://www.foodinsight.
org/facts-beef-red_meat-healthy.

44   Hemmi N. Bhagavan, Ph.D., F.A.C.N., "Alpha Lipoic Acide: Its
Role in Human Health," *Phyto Therapy,* accessed December
3, 2017. http://www.phytotherapyusa.com/health-news/
alpha-lipoic-acid-its-role-in-human-health.

45   Dr. Judy Morgan, "Kick Kibble to the Curb – Dental Myths,"
Naturally Healthy Pets, last modified September 30, 2016. http://
www.drjudymorgan.com/kick-kibble-to-the-curb-dental-myths/.

46   "A successful 18th ESVCN congress at Utrecht University,"
Wageningen University & Research, last modified November 21,
2014. https://www.wur.nl/en/newsarticle/A-successful-18th-ES-
VCN-congress-at-Utrecht-University.htm.

47   "Carnassial teeth," *Encylopedia.com,* accessed
October 14, 2017. http://www.encyclopedia.com/

science/dictionaries-thesauruses-pictures-and-press-releases/
carnassial-teeth.

48   "Do Wolves/Dogs Eat the Vegetable Contents of Herbivores' Stomachs?" *Raw Meaty Bones for Healthy Pets,* last modified June 6, 2010. http://rmb4healthypets.blogspot.com/2010/06/do-wolves-dogs-eat-vegetablecontents-of.html.

49   Jeannie Thomason, VND, *Breeding and Raising Dogs the Way Nature Intended* (Arizona: Earth & Sky Universal Publishing LLC, 2015), 140.

50   Jeannie Thomason, VND, *Breeding and Raising Dogs the Way Nature Intended* (Arizona: Earth & Sky Universal Publishing LLC, 2015), 141.

51   Associated Press, "Why are Golden Retrievers More Likely to Die of Cancer than any Other Breed?" *DailyMail.com,* last modified May 7, 2015. http://www.dailymail.co.uk/news/article-3070422/Study-aims-uncover-cancer-plagues-golden-retrievers.html.

52   Philip Hunter, "The Inflammation Theory of Disease," *PMC,* last modified October 9, 2012. https://www.ncbi.nlm.nih.gov/pmc/articles/PMC3492709/.

53   "Could This be the Missing Ingredient for Your Pet's Optimal Health?" *Dr. Mercola,* accessed November 29, 2017. http://products.mercola.com/healthypets/krill-oil-for-pets/.

54   Dan Stahler et al. "Foraging and feeding ecology of the gray wolf (Canis lupus): lessons from Yellowstone National Park, Wyoming, USA," *PubMed.gov,* accessed December 4, 2017. https://www.ncbi.nlm.nih.gov/pubmed/16772460.

55   Dr. Karen Becker, "Therapeutic Fasting – This Dietary Habit of Wolves Might be Right for Your Dog too but Never for a Cat," *Healthy Pets with Dr. Karen Becker,* last modified October 6, 2011. https://healthypets.mercola.com/sites/healthypets/archive/2011/10/06/dietary-habit-for-overweight-pets.aspx.

56   Abel James, "How to Lose Weight Like a Lion: Fasting and Feasting for Fat Loss," *Fat-Burning Man,* last modified January 24, 2014. http://fatburningman.com/how-to-lose-weight-like-a-lion-fasting-and-feasting-for-fat-loss/.

57   Cindy Engel, *Wild Health: Lessons in Natural Wellness from the Animal Kingdom* (New York: Houghton Mifflin Company, 2002), 82.

58   "Fasting Can Help You Live Longer," *Peak Fitness,* last modified March 25, 2016. https://fitness.mercola.com/sites/fitness/archive/2016/03/25/health-benefits-fasting.aspx.

59   Cindy Engel, *Wild Health: Lessons in Natural Wellness from the*

Animal Kingdom (New York: Houghton Mifflin Company, 2002), 82.

60   "Top 10 Reasons Pets Visit Vets," *PetHealthZone,* accessed December 4, 2017. https://phz8.petinsurance.com/healthzone/pet-health/health-conditions/top-10-reasons-pets-visit-vets.

61   "A Healing Crisis: A Friend or a Foe?" *Dog~Nutrition~Naturally.com,* accessed December 8, 2017. https://www.dog-nutrition-naturally.com/healing-crisis.html.

62   "A Healing Crisis: A Friend or a Foe?" *Dog~Nutrition~Naturally.com,* accessed December 8, 2017. https://www.dog-nutrition-naturally.com/healing-crisis.html.

63   "A Healing Crisis: A Friend or a Foe?" *Dog~Nutrition~Naturally.com,* accessed December 8, 2017. https://www.dog-nutrition-naturally.com/healing-crisis.html.

64   Dr. Jeannie Thomason, "The Canine Healing Crisis…It's a Good Thing!" *The Whole Dog,* accessed November 29, 2017. https://thewholedog.com/the-canine-healing-crisis-its-a-good-thing/.

65   Dr. Jeannie Thomason, "The Canine Healing Crisis…It's a Good Thing!" *The Whole Dog,* accessed November 29, 2017. https://thewholedog.com/the-canine-healing-crisis-its-a-good-thing/.

66   Dr. Jeannie Thomason, "The Importance of a Strong Immune System in Our Dogs," *The Whole Dog,* accessed November 29, 2017. https://thewholedog.com/importance-of-strong-immune-system-dogs/.

67   "Top 10 Reasons Pets Visit Vets," *PetHealthZone,* accessed December 4, 2017. https://phz8.petinsurance.com/healthzone/pet-health/health-conditions/top-10-reasons-pets-visit-vets.

68   Ernest Ward, DVM, "Steroid Treatment – Long-term Effects in Dogs," *VCA,* accessed December 1, 2017. http://www.vcahospitals.com/main/pet-health-information/article/animal-health/steroid-treatment-long-term-effects-in-dogs/951.

69   "Skin Tumors in Dogs (Benign & Malignant)," *PetWave,* last modified August 15, 2016. http://www.petwave.com/Dogs/Health/Skin-Tumors.aspx.

70   *Essential Oils Desk Reference, 6th edition* (USA: Life Science Publishing, 2014), 101.

71   "What are Hot Spots in Dogs?" *WebMD,* accessed December 1, 2017. http://pets.webmd.com/dogs/what-hot-spots-dogs.

72   "What are Hot Spots in Dogs?" *WebMD,* accessed December 1, 2017. http://pets.webmd.com/dogs/what-hot-spots-dogs.

73   "Dog Odor," *Wikipedia,* accessed December 3, 2017. https://en.wiki-pedia.org/wiki/Dog_odor.

74   Joe Cross, *The Reboot with Joe Juice Diet* (Texas: Greenleaf Book Group Press, 2014), 15.

75   Joe Cross, *The Reboot with Joe Juice Diet* (Texas: Greenleaf Book Group Press, 2014), 15–16.

76   *Essential Oils Desk Reference, 6th edition* (USA: Life Science Publishing, 2014), 120.

77   "8 Proven Colloidal Silver Benefits, Uses & Side Effects," *Dr. Axe,* accessed December 11, 2017. https://draxe.com/colloidal-silver-benefits/.

78   Qian Wang et al, "Identification of a central role for complement in osteoarthritis," *PMC,* last modified June 1, 2012. https://www.ncbi.nlm.nih.gov/pmc/articles/PMC3257059/.

79   "The Kibble Situation," *Meridian Veterinary Care,* last modified February 8, 2014. https://meridianvetcare.com/pet-kibble-situation/.

80   "The Kibble Situation," *Meridian Veterinary Care,* last modified February 8, 2014. https://meridianvetcare.com/pet-kibble-situation/.

81   Jennifer Lee, *The Inner Carnivore* self-pub., 2014), 71.

82   "Why this Common Food May Not Be Your Best Bet for Essential Omega-3s...," *Dr. Mercola Premium Products,* accessed November 19, 2017. http://krilloil.mercola.com/krill-oil.html.

83   Lorie Long, "Using Glucosamine to Prevent Canine Osteoarthritis," *Whole Dog Journal,* last modified September 27, 2017. https://www.whole-dog-journal.com/issues/7_8/features/Canine-Osteoarthritis_15644-1.html.

84   J.T. Kent, *Repertory of the Homeopathic Materia Medica* (New Delhi: B. Jain Publishers (P) Ltd., 2002), 637.

85   J.T. Kent, *Repertory of the Homeopathic Materia Medica* (New Delhi: B. Jain Publishers (P) Ltd., 2002), 636.

86   J.T. Kent, *Repertory of the Homeopathic Materia Medica* (New Delhi: B. Jain Publishers (P) Ltd., 2002), 637.

87   J.T. Kent, *Repertory of the Homeopathic Materia Medica* (New Delhi: B. Jain Publishers (P) Ltd., 2002), 637.

88   http://www.dogsnaturallymagazine.com/top-remedies-for-uti-in-dogs/

89   http://www.vetstreet.com/dr-marty-becker/does-your-dog-have-a-urinary-tract-infection-learn-the-symptoms

90   http://www.dogsnaturallymagazine.com/
      top-remedies-for-uti-in-dogs/

91   *Essential Oils Desk Reference, 6th edition* (USA: Life Science
      Publishing, 2014), 538.

92   *Essential Oils Desk Reference, 6th edition* (USA: Life Science
      Publishing, 2014), 538.

93   *Essential Oils Desk Reference, 6th edition* (USA: Life Science
      Publishing, 2014), 538.

94   Dana Scott, "Top Remedies for UTI in Dogs," *Dogs Naturally*,
      accessed December 15, 2017. https://www.petmd.com/dog/
      conditions/urinary/c_multi_renal_failure_chronic.

95   Dr. Jeannie Thomason, "Kidney Disease in Dogs," *The Whole Dog*,
      accessed December 19, 2017. https://www.thewholedog.org/artkid-
      neyfailure.html.

96   Dr. Jeannie Thomason, "Kidney Disease in Dogs," *The Whole Dog*,
      accessed December 19, 2017. https://www.thewholedog.org/artkid-
      neyfailure.html.

97   Dr. Jeannie Thomason, "Kidney Disease in Dogs," *The Whole Dog*,
      accessed December 19, 2017. https://www.thewholedog.org/artkid-
      neyfailure.html.

98   Dr. Jeannie Thomason, "Kidney Disease in Dogs," *The Whole Dog*,
      accessed December 19, 2017. https://www.thewholedog.org/artkid-
      neyfailure.html.

99   Dr. Karen Becker, "Fecal Transplant: An Amazing Cure You've
      Probably Never Heard Of," *Healthy Pets with Dr. Karen Becker*,
      last modified December 13, 2015. https://healthypets.mercola.com/
      sites/healthypets/archive/2015/12/13/fecal-transplants.aspx.

100   "Zinc Deficiency: the Hidden Cause of Sickness in Huskies,"
      Snowdogguru, last modified July 21, 2014. https://www.snowdog.
      guru/zinc-deficiency-the-hidden-cause-of-sickness-in-huskies/.

101   "Zinc Deficiency: the Hidden Cause of Sickness in Huskies,"
      Snowdogguru, last modified July 21, 2014. https://www.snowdog.
      guru/zinc-deficiency-the-hidden-cause-of-sickness-in-huskies/.

102   "Correcting Zinc Deficiency in Huskies," *Snowdogguru*,
      last modified July 24, 2014. https://www.snowdog.guru/
      correcting-zinc-deficiency-in-huskies/.

103   "Correcting Zinc Deficiency in Huskies," *Snowdogguru*,
      last modified July 24, 2014. https://www.snowdog.guru/
      correcting-zinc-deficiency-in-huskies/.

104   Thomas Corriher, "The Dangers of Tap Water," *The Health*

Wyze Report, accessed August 3, 2017. https://healthwyze.org/reports/69-the-dangers-of-tap-water.

105   Thomas Corriher, "The Dangers of Tap Water," *The Health Wyze Report,* accessed August 3, 2017. https://healthwyze.org/reports/69-the-dangers-of-tap-water.

106   "Hazardous Substance Fact Sheet: Sodium Fluoride," *New Jersey Department of Health,* accessed December 8, 2017. http://nj.gov/health/eoh/rtkweb/documents/fs/1699.pdf.

107   Deirdre Imus, "EPA Reverses Itself on Fluoride," *Fox News Health,* last modified February 22, 2011. http://www.foxnews.com/health/2011/02/22/epa-reverses-fluoride.html.

108   Thomas Corriher, "The Dangers of Tap Water," *The Health Wyze Report,* accessed August 3, 2017. https://healthwyze.org/reports/69-the-dangers-of-tap-water.

109   Marilee Nelson, "16 Ways to Activate Your Lymphatic System," *Branch Basics,* last modified September 22, 2015. https://branchbasics.com/blog/2015/09/16-ways-to-activate-your-lymphatic-system/.

110   Karen Smith-Janssen, "Nontoxic Ways to Protect Your Pet," *NRDC,* last modified January 22, 2016. https://www.nrdc.org/stories/nontoxic-ways-protect-your-pet.

111   Associated Press, "Pet Deaths Prompt Warnings on Flea Meds," *Pet health on NBCNews.com,* last modified March 17, 2010. http://rss.msnbc.msn.com/id/35914331/ns/health-pet_health/?ns=health-pet_health#.WjMQ8t-nGUm.

112   Associated Press, "Pet Deaths Prompt Warnings on Flea Meds," *Pet health on NBCNews.com,* last modified March 17, 2010. http://rss.msnbc.msn.com/id/35914331/ns/health-pet_health/?ns=health-pet_health#.WjMQ8t-nGUm.

113   "Fipronil," *sailhome,* accessed October 3, 2017. http://www.sailhome.org/Concerns/BodyBurden/Sources3/Fipronil.html.

114   KA Jennings et al, "Human Exposure to Fipronil from Dogs Treated with Frontline," *PubMed.gov,* accessed October 3, 2017. https://www.ncbi.nlm.nih.gov/pubmed?cmd=retrieve&list_uids=12361121.

115   QM Qiu et al, "An Experimental Study on Acute Poisoning by Fipronil in Mice and Its Pharmaceutical Therapy," *PubMed.gov,* accessed October 3, 2017. https://www.ncbi.nlm.nih.gov/pubmed?cmd=retrieve&list_uids=16836887.

116   "Methoprene," *National Pesticide Information Center,* accessed November 20, 2017. http://npic.orst.edu/factsheets/methogen.html.

117   Marla Cone, "Small Dogs Prove Susceptible to Flea Poison,"

Scientific American, last modified March 18, 2010. https://www.scientificamerican.com/article/small-dogs-susceptible-flea-poison/.

118   "Material Safety Data Sheet: Imidacloprid Technical Insecticide," *Etigra, LLC,* accessed December 1, 2017. http://fleascience.com/wp-content/uploads/2015/12/MSDS-for-Imidacloprid.pdf.

119   "OSHA 3084," *United States Department of Labor,* accessed November 20, 2017. https://www.osha.gov/Publications/osha3084.html.

Index

Butylated hydroxyanisole. *See* BHA
Butyl hydroxytoluene. *See* BHT

C

Calcium 159, 162, 167
  and chlorine 179
Calendula 144
Cancer 5, 23, 102, 117, 136, 151, 168
  and THMs 179
Canned food. *See* Processed pet food
Carnassial teeth 59
Carnivores 22, 39, 41, 43, 101. *See*
  also Dogs
Cellulase 60
Chicken feet 153
Choking 189, 190
Chondroitin sulfate 29, 153
Chronic kidney disease. *See* Kidney
  disease
Coconut oil 143, 144
Colloidal silver 149
Commercial raw 29, 30, 56, 61, 87,
  105. *See* also Raw diet
  and 4D meat 57
  as an ongoing option 57
  as a transition option 56, 57
  bone 57
  convenience 57
  expense 57, 58
  feeding 56
  finding suppliers 96, 187
  fruits, veggies, and dairy in 57
  monitoring manufacturers of 58
  percentage of fruit and veggies 58
  selecting the best option 57
  transitioning to 38. *See* also Transi-
    tioning to raw diet
Constipation 25, 86, 107, 160
Co-ops 90, 98
Coprophogia 138
CoQ10 163
Corticosteroids. *See* Steroids
Cortisone 140
Creatine 163

Creatinine 163
Cystitis 138, 157. *See* also Urinary
  tract disease

D

Dehydrated food 61
Dermatitis
  and zinc deficiency 168
Detox 85, 86, 130, 131, 137, 147, 149,
  155, 156
  and fasting 124, 125
  and the healing process 131
  duration 131
  intensity 132
  onset 131
  symptoms 130, 131
DHA 152. *See* also Essential fatty
  acids
Diabetes 102, 136
Diarrhea 25, 38, 41, 86, 107, 130, 138,
  139, 155, 156, 160
  and herbs 156
  and homeopathic remedies 157
  and probiotics 156
  and the 80/10/10 rule 155
  and zinc deficiency 168
  as a detox symptom 155
Diets
  spectrum of quality 61
Doggy odor 69, 138, 139, 165
  and processed pet food 166
  and raw diet 166
Dogs 103
  amylase 60
  and aggression 85
  and constipation. *See* Constipation
  and diarrhea. *See* Diarrhea
  as carnivores 101, 126
  bad breath 154
  carnassial teeth 59
  carnivores 22, 58, 59
  cellulase 60
  choking 189, 190
  determining healthy weight 39, 150,

Immunomodulators 141, 142
Immunosuppressants 140
Inflammation 117, 124, 139, 151, 153, 158
  and arthritis 151, 153
  and bladder issues 157
  and glucosamine 153
  and processed pet food 151

K

K9 Advantix 193
Kibble. *See* Processed pet food
Kidney disease 23, 85, 138, 160
  acute 160
  and exercise 163
  and phosphorous 162
  and water 163
  causes of acute kidney disease 160
  causes of chronic kidney disease 161
  CoQ10 163
  low-protein diet 161
  magnesium 162
  raw diet 162
  symptoms 160
Kidney failure. *See* Kidney disease
Kidneys 41, 42
  purpose 161
Krill oil 152, 162. *See* also Supplements
  and omega-3s 118

L

Lethargy 139, 160
Liver 41
  introducing 41
Liver disease 23
Lungs 42
Lymph 181, 183
  and exercise 182

M

Magnesium 162
  sources 162
Massage 154

and seizures 172
Meal plans 105
Meat
  red vs white 49
Meat processors 93
Meat suppliers 187
  commercial raw 187
  prey model 187
  specialty suppliers 188
  whole prey 187
Mercurius corrosivus 157
Mercurius solubilis 158
Mercurius vivus 158
Merocrine glands 147
Methylsulfonylmethane. *See* MSM
Microbiome restorative therapy 165
Minerals 112
  functions 112
  in raw diet 29
  sources 112
MSM 152, 153
  anti-inflammation 153
Myoglobin 51

N

Natural
  legal definition 16, 17
Nux vomica 158

O

Obesity 23, 181, 182
Offal 40
Omega-3s 71, 118, 142, 152, 162
  and krill oil 118
  sardines 142
Oral health 154
Organic
  legal definition 17
Organs 38, 40, 41, 97, 98, 105, 156
  brain 42
  classifying 42
  heart 42
  introducing liver 41
  kidneys 41, 42

liver 41
lungs 42
pancreas 42
spleen 41
stomach 42
sweetbreads 42
thymus 42
Osteoarthritis. *See* Arthritis
Otitis externa. *See* Ear infections

P

Palatants 6
Pancreas 42
Pancreatitis 23, 85, 136
Periodontitis 138, 154
Permethrin 193
Pesticides 141, 149, 171, 193
Pet food industry 3, 4, 16, 21
  definition of holistic 17
  definition of human grade 17
  definition of human quality 17
  definition of natural 16, 17
  definition of organic 17
Pet food recalls 4
Pet Fooled documentary 4, 16
Phosphorous 159, 162, 167
  and chlorine 179
  and kidney disease 162
Picky eater 54, 168
  dealing with 54, 55, 56
  fasting 54
  transitioning to raw 54
Plant matter 60
Po Chai 157
Podophyllum 157
Poop. *See* Stool
Prednisone 140
Preservatives 7, 17
  safe 18
Prey model 29, 30, 52, 56, 61, 105. *See*
  also Raw diet
  finding suppliers 96
  meat suppliers 187
  specialty meat suppliers 188

transitioning to 38. *See* also Transitioning to raw diet
Probiotics 29, 43, 116, 137, 141, 156,
  162, 165
  when to give 116
Processed pet food 3, 5, 23, 25, 29, 30,
  57, 61, 70, 102, 103, 126, 131,
  155
  4D meat 18, 22
  and immune system 133
  and inflammation 151
  and oral health 154
  and zinc deficiency 168
  denatured protein 6
  doggy odor 166
  ingredients 21
  making 22
  mixing with raw 43, 44
  palatants 6
  premium 5
  preservatives in 7, 17
  safe preservatives 18
  spoiled meat and rancid fats 18
  synthetic vitamins 6
  transitioning to raw 87, 185
Propyl Gallate 19
Protein 126
  cooked 6, 22, 44
  denatured 6, 22, 44, 103, 126
  denatured by HPP 58
Pulsatilla 157
Puppies
  calcium 73
  fasting 73
  feeding frequency 77
  feeding raw 73
  how much to feed 39, 73
  immune system 134
  maintaining a healthy weight 74
  phosphorous 73
  raw feeding 77
  transitioning from processed food to
    raw 79
Pyoderma. *See* Hot spots

R

Raw diet 29, 30, 102, 131, 133
  80/10/10 29, 30, 39, 56, 78, 107, 155
  and aggression 85
  and allergies 141
  and arthritis 151
  and bacteria. *See* Bacteria
  and bone shards 87
  and constipation. *See* Constipation
  and detox. *See* Detox
  and diarrhea. *See* Diarrhea
  and disease 85
  and ear infections 144
  and fleas/ticks 194
  and hot spots 148
  and immune system 134
  and oral health 154
  and puppies 73, 77. *See* also Puppies
  and seizures 170
  and urinary tract disease 158
  and zinc deficiency 168
  balancing over time 38, 39, 86, 87,
     105, 109, 111, 185, 186
  benefits 69
  bloody gums 55
  bowls 48
  butchers 98
  calculating how much to feed 40
  commercial raw 29. *See* also Com-
     mercial raw
  complete and balanced 44
  co-ops 98
  denatured protein 126
  dental health 55
  doggy odor 166
  essential fatty acids 142. *See* also
     Essential fatty acids
  expense 44, 85, 90
  farmers 98
  farmer's markets 98
  fasting. *See* Fasting
  fears about 82
  feces. *See* Stool
  feeding affordably 90, 91, 93, 94, 95
  feeding as a vegetarian. *See* Vege-
     tarian
  feeding fur and feathers 96, 105
  feeding red meat exclusively 50
  fiber 105
  finding suppliers 96
  frankenprey 30, 57
  freeze-dried 29
  freezer 45
  gorge and fast 124
  how much to feed 39
  how much to feed puppies 39
  introducing new organs 38
  introducing new proteins 38, 86
  kidney disease 162
  kitchen scale 46
  logistics of feeding 45
  maintaining a healthy weight 96
  meat cleaver 46
  minerals 29
  mixing with kibble 43, 44
  movement 61
  online suppliers 97, 98
  organs 38, 40. *See* also Organs
  picky eater 54. *See* also Picky eater
  poultry shears 46
  preparation 49
  prey model 29, 52. *See* also Prey
     model
  proteins you can feed 35, 51, 52
  puppies 77
  raw food journal 47
  red meat. *See* Red meat
  red meat vs white meat 49
  refusing to eat 56
  rubber mallet 46, 47
  safely feeding bones 82. *See* also
     Bones
  sample meal plans. *See* Meal plans
  stool 38, 126, 127. *See* also Stool
  the process of feeding 47, 48
  tools 45, 46
  transitioning puppies from pro-
     cessed food to raw 79. *See* also
     Puppies

About the author

Kristin Clark is certified by the American Council of Animal Naturopathy as a Carnivore Nutrition Consultant and Small Animal Naturopath. She is the founder and Editor-in-Chief of Raw Pet Digest, an international online magazine devoted to natural feeding and health care for dogs and cats. She is also the author of *Let Food Be Their Medicine: Using Nature's Principles to Help Your Dog Thrive*. Through her company Raw Pets Thrive, Kristin offers species-appropriate food products, natural modalities, and consulting services to dog owners, to help support them in promoting and maintaining the health of their dogs. Kristin also speaks regularly on topics related to natural pet health promotion.

Visit her websites at www.rawpetsthrive.com and www.rawpetdigest.com to learn more.

Made in the USA
San Bernardino, CA
29 April 2018